Navigating
THE LAND OF IF

UNDERSTANDING INFERTILITY
AND EXPLORING YOUR OPTIONS

MELISSA FORD

NAVIGATING THE LAND OF IF
Understanding Infertility and Exploring Your Options

Copyright © 2009 by Melissa Ford

Published by
Seal Press
A Member of the Perseus Books Group
1700 Fourth Street
Berkeley, California

Library of Congress Cataloging-in-Publication Data

Ford, Melissa.
Navigating the land of If: understanding infertility and exploring your options / Melissa Ford.
p. cm.
ISBN-13: 978-1-58005-262-7
ISBN-10: 1-58005-262-2
1. Infertility—Popular works. 2. Fertility, Human—Popular works. 3. Human reproductive technology—Popular works. I. Title.
RC889.F58 2009
616.6'92—dc22
        2008039409

Cover and Interior design by Domini Dragoone
Printed in the United States of America by Edwards Brothers
Distributed by Publishers Group West

Dedication

TO JOSH, who always knows the right words, position one, and position two

TO THE CHICKIENOB AND WOLVOG, who are my heart, for your warm keppies and the double shnuzzles

Itinerary

INTRODUCTION

WELCOME TO THE LAND OF IF.

I know, those are probably six words you never particularly wanted to hear. You don't want to be here on this strange island. And if you've just disembarked, you're probably a tad confused. Even if you've long known you were destined to show up here, you probably are surprised by the atmosphere. It's not really a little-umbrella-in-your-drink sort of island. It smells of rubbing alcohol. It's littered with garbage cans packed to the brim with sanitary napkins. And it's populated with tense-looking men and anxious-looking women. It's hard to ignore one of the worst parts about this island: It's situated so close to the mainland—you can see it over the horizon on a clear day. But even though there are daily departures, and even though it's easy enough to end up here, it takes plenty of effort to get out.

The Land of If got its name not only because IF is the abbreviation for "infertility" in the online world but also because there are so many *if*s inherent in being here. There are *what if*s and *if only*s and *if this, then that*s. If (there's that word again!) you are accustomed to having a pretty tight rein on your life—accustomed to working hard and seeing the desired outcome, or being able to predict what comes next—the Land of If is going to be a particularly difficult stopover for you. Being here is all about living in uncertainty and doubt and wonder and hope: *If only I had gone to the doctor earlier. What if I hadn't bought my husband that package of tight briefs from Costco? What if my wife hadn't laid out our adoption profile to look like a scrapbooking-store explosion? If I go past the baby aisle at Target, then I will have a nervous breakdown between the onesies and binkies.*

I, for one, was shocked—shocked!—when I ended up here. Why was I shocked? I have no idea: My mother experienced eleven years of infertility while building her family. But, strangely, I believed that I would be fertile, and for much of my life, I knew next to nothing about infertility and pregnancy loss. I had absolutely no understanding of assisted reproductive technology (ART), either. In fact, the first time I met a child born through IVF (in vitro fertilization), I pitied him for what he had to go through as a fetus, pressing his tiny face up against the glass of his test tube, just to get the attention of the man in the white lab coat.

When my husband, Josh, and I decided, in the merry month of June, to conceive, I was so giddy that I started right away with plans for a February baby. But instead, February brought my husband and me the first diagnostic piece of our infertility puzzle: My progesterone was low. So we started treating that (with progesterone suppositories), but then other problems cropped up, until we had a final, but vague, diagnosis: "female-factor infertility."

Vague though it may sound, we're some of the lucky ones, because we actually have an understanding of what brought us to this island. There are plenty of inhabitants—maybe even you—who will never know what brought them to the Land of If. And that is just another one of the frustrating aspects of this place (along with the fact that there are no drinks with umbrellas): the lack of answers, or how the answers can lead to more questions.

With so many unknowns, your stay in the Land of If will probably be rife with uneasiness, but you can rest assured about one thing: For better or worse, your tour guide (that is, me) knows this territory very, very well. I've done my time here. I have experienced early loss, treatments, pregnancy, and preterm childbirth.

That said . . . one or two experiences cannot possibly be enough to get you through all of the nooks and crannies of this island. There are plenty of aspects of infertility and loss that I *haven't* experienced firsthand. But the inhabitants of the Land of If are a helpful bunch, and, like a giant pot of stone soup, this book came together based on the experiences of numerous men and women. They gave me the kind of invaluable information this book is packed with—the kind of information that comes from tons and tons of personal experience.

Sure, the medical professionals I dealt with were all very helpful in giving me a basic understanding of my medications and the procedures I would eventually undergo. But it was information posted by others like me, on bulletin boards and blogs, that *really* provided me with a higher education in infertility. Sure, it was a nurse who taught me how to give myself an injection. But it was a fellow Iffer who taught me how to make that injection less painful. Sure, my reproductive endocrinologist (RE) made decisions based on my test results, but it was a fellow stirrup queen who gave me a list of what kind of questions to ask, and which tests to request.

Now, don't get me wrong: Doctors have those initials after their name for a reason. They know their stuff, and before you act on any advice (including the advice found here), you should always check with your doctor. In fact, all medical information in this book was reviewed by a doctor.

THERE ARE PLENTY of guides out there that focus on treading the four paths leading out of the Land of If—books on adoption, treatments, third-party reproduction, and choosing to live child-free. And although this book definitely covers those four paths, its focus is not on how to leave this island, but on how to live on it . . . at least for now.

In addition to providing you with tons of insider information, *Navigating the Land of If* will give you the words to explain your crazy, complex emotions to people who've never been here before. It will give you the practical tools and confidence you need to be your own advocate and make decisions that work for you.

And in between those tough choices is the waiting: waiting to cycle, waiting to see the reproductive endocrinologist, waiting to see if you're pregnant, waiting to be chosen, waiting for a referral. All of that waiting could drive you insane, or at least could make you obsessive, spending hours Googling early pregnancy symptoms. Lucky for you, there's this book to coax you back into living life while waiting in limbo.

It will give you great excuses—both fake and real—for dodging other people's baby showers or leaving work for a 10:00 AM insemination. It will help you respond to pregnancy announcements with feigned or real happiness. It will help you gauge how much of your infertility news to spread, and to whom. Mercifully, it will give you plenty of great advice on staving off unsolicited or bad advice, and tons of tips on how to nip rude remarks in the bud. It will help you keep track of your own hormone levels, introduce you to the online and offline hangouts of other Iffers, and teach you the ins and outs of Iffish—that strange language composed of multisyllabic, impossible-to-pronounce medical terms and mysterious abbreviations.

But I can see that you're getting overwhelmed. That happens to people when they first get here—hell, it happens even if you've lived here for five years. Let's grab our backpacks and get started on moving around the island in a methodical manner. I'll take you around each neighborhood until you start figuring out the roads on your own. My hope is that you never get *too* familiar with this land, that your stay here is as brief and painless as possible. But while you're here, you should know that you have a friend, in book form, to turn to in the middle of the night, when the sea monsters offshore start howling and you just wish you were home.

Chapter 1

I REMEMBER WHEN my friend Alex and I traveled to Siena, Italy, in the heart of Tuscany. Tired but excited, we exited the bus terminal and dragged our wobbling suitcases over the cobblestone roads. We were relatively confident about our surroundings: On the plane, we'd read several guidebooks and had practically memorized a map of the town center. We got our bags to our room and went out to wander the streets. And after a couple of hours, we found a great little place for dinner. Our waiter came to our table and, seeing we were foreigners, asked us where we were staying. We told him.

"That place?" he scoffed, slamming my gnocchi on the table. "That neighborhood is *merda!* You should be staying *here! We* won the Palio two years ago!"

Even though we thought we'd done our homework, we didn't realize that although the people living in the city's seventeen neighborhoods enjoyed a collective sense of being Sienese, they also were engaged in a distinct kind of rivalry.

Unfortunately, that's sort of like the rivalry you'll probably encounter between the many neighborhoods of infertility: primary vs. secondary, biological vs. situational, and infertility vs. recurrent loss. Some of that divisiveness comes from the inhabitants of If themselves, but a good deal of it is due to hospitals, clinics, insurance companies, and adoption agencies, which tend to impose their rules on the Land of If as if they were some sort of colonial government. These establishments are sometimes so out of touch with the reality of living in the Land of If, and are oftentimes so focused on making money from the colonists, that they make life on the island even more difficult.

For example, fertility treatments are rarely covered by insurance companies, and currently, only twelve states have mandated coverage (an additional three have mandate-to-offer established).[1] The insurance companies' biggest argument against covering treatments is that they are not medically necessary. Granted, most reproductive endocrinologists and fertility doctors disagree with this outlook . . . but they're not paying your bills, are they?

And that's only the beginning (see the sidebar "Access: Denied," in this chapter).

As if the bureaucracy weren't enough, there are self-created internal tensions as well. Those experiencing primary infertility might think they have it worse than those experiencing secondary infertility; those with female factor may think their problems trump those with male factor. And you'll hear more about this kind of thing in the following sections.

That said, the level of support and community that I have found in the infertile world exceeds anything I have ever found in other aspects of life. People here are willing to share personal information, hold out a Kleenex, and pass along cheap dinnerware to throw against the wall. On our worst days, our community is on its best behavior: Divisiveness goes out the window, and the various neighborhoods come together in unity to offer support.

I wish it were that way every day, so allow your tour guide this little rant while we pause and consider the scenery:

People of all kinds end up in the Land of If. And whatever your actual reasons for being here, in the larger scope of things, it doesn't matter. Over here, we're all Iffers. Now, perhaps you agree with that concept in theory, but secretly, you still harbor some resentment toward certain islanders who—as far as you're concerned—don't have it "quite so bad" as you do.

Let me be very clear on this point: I am officially declaring a boycott of the Pain Olympics. It doesn't matter what brought you to the stirrups or the donation rooms: Lying naked in a cold room with a full bladder and only a thin sheet of paper for a blanket sucks. So does trying to masturbate into a cup while a disgruntled nurse in orthopedic loafers clears her throat and taps her foot outside the door. It's no better to have to reduce your life to a few short paragraphs in order to create your "Dear Birth Parent" letter—a letter that determines whether you're considered for adoption by an expectant parent.

The fact is, infertility is one of the great equalizers of the world, and everyone here could use all the support they can get.

In an ideal world, that's all that would need to be said. But until this world, and this island, become ideal, you'll need to know what you'll be dealing with. Therefore, let's take a walk through each neighborhood so you can get your bearings and settle into yours. Pay attention, keeping in mind that you may end up moving to a new neighborhood before leaving the Land of If—many do.

Primary Infertility vs. Secondary Infertility

Generally speaking, Iffers who do not yet have a child are considered to be experiencing "primary infertility," and those who do have children are experiencing "secondary infertility."

If you think that sounds simple enough, think again. After all, how do people describe themselves if they have a child through adoption but are now trying in vitro fertilization (IVF) to add to their family? It will be the first *pregnancy,* so is it primary? It will be the second *child,* so is it secondary? How about those who are looking to have a second child but conceived a first child with the help of fertility treatments? What about people who lost their first child to stillbirth? If they are attempting to become pregnant again, are they experiencing primary or secondary?

Now you're probably getting a sense of how muddy these labels can be—and how detrimental to those experiencing infertility—when they are used to determine treatment or coverage by doctors or insurance companies.

The main difference between primary and secondary is the existence, in most cases, of a child who must be taken into consideration during treatments or adoption. There are advantages and disadvantages to both sides. Without a child to take care of while on posttransfer bed rest during an IVF cycle, those experiencing primary infertility can enjoy more flexibility—yet they may also have more fears if they don't know if they'll ever reach parenthood. Those experiencing secondary infertility can enjoy the comfort of a child when they have a failed cycle—but they also know what they're missing, since they've experienced parenthood. It can be difficult for those experiencing secondary infertility to do fertility treatments discreetly when they need to arrange childcare for existing children. In addition, because they have been successful before, those experiencing secondary infertility might not receive much sympathy or support from friends and family, even though they are going through the same painful fertility treatments as primaries.

Who has it better? No one. So forget about it. Besides, telling other people that their grass is greener doesn't do anything to perk up your own patchy brown lawn.

Biological Infertility vs. Situational Infertility

These categories are rarely discussed but often come into play in terms of treatments. And, like the previous two categories, these also have an overlapping gray area.

People experiencing biological infertility need assistance to reproduce because they have a faulty reproductive system. People experiencing situational infertility need assistance in order to reproduce for other reasons. Those in the "situational infertility" neighborhood include the GLBT community, single parents by choice, and those of advanced maternal age (AMA).

The gray area? Here are a few examples: someone who was born with ovarian function but lost it due to cancer treatments. Or someone who had a hysterectomy but wants to add to her family. Or someone with a genetic trait such as balanced translocation—a chromosomal disorder that can be a cause of pregnancy loss.

Are they biological or situational? And does it matter? A speculum causes the same cramping sensation, and adoption paperwork is still lengthy—regardless of the circumstances.

THAT'S JUST SEMANTICS

The Latin prefix "in" usually means "not," which technically makes the word "infertile" mean "not fertile," which in turn is a synonym for "sterile." However, most people diagnosed with infertility are not actually experiencing sterility. In fact, many people diagnosed as infertile eventually become pregnant, either unassisted or through treatments (or sometimes unassisted *after* treatments). So should we be using the term "subfertile" more often?

"Infertility" can be used to describe a moment in time (before you become pregnant, you are "infertile," and afterward, you are "subfertile" or "fertile") or a lifelong diagnosis. Even though Josh and I were successful once, I still consider myself infertile, and I will continue to do so long after I finish building my family.

In this book, I use "sterility" to refer to problems that medicine cannot circumvent, and I use "infertility" to refer to problems that medicine could possibly circumvent. I leave "subfertile" for those who like to argue etymology. Most of us have better things to do.

Nevertheless, "situationally infertile" is a controversial concept. There are those who think that situational infertility somehow "doesn't count," since GLBT or AMA conception can be seen as a choice. This argument is reductive and dismissive of the big picture. Building a family is a choice, but sexuality is not, nor is early menopause.

And there are those—such as people in same-sex relationships, or single parents by choice—who are situationally infertile by my definition, but don't consider themselves infertile in any way. That's fine. There is no problem when someone doesn't wish to be labeled infertile. But there is a tremendous issue when those who *do* classify themselves that way are being told by an outside source that they aren't (see the sidebar "Access: Denied," in this chapter). The situationally infertile definitely get the short end of the stick when it comes to insurance coverage and thoroughness in treatment—even though they have the same strong desire as everyone else stuck in the Land of If: to get out of here.

Infertility vs. Recurrent Pregnancy Loss

Some women can conceive but experience recurrent pregnancy loss. On the one hand, they can get pregnant, but on the other, more important hand, they cannot carry to term. Recurrent pregnancy loss is part of the medical definition of infertility, and Resolve, the national infertility organization, includes "multiple miscarriages" in its definition of infertility.[2]

Unfortunately, those experiencing recurrent pregnancy loss have to contend not only with the terrible losses but also with a lack of support from insurance companies and doctors. They must be diligent with their healthcare providers and insurance companies in order to ensure that the proper tests are being run, and that future losses are being prevented. For more in-depth information about pregnancy loss, see Chapter 7.

Female-Factor Infertility vs. Male-Factor Infertility

Though infertility is often portrayed as a female problem ("She's got lady troubles . . . "), the reality is that infertility affects both men and

SECONDARY INFERTILITY

If you're arriving back in the Land of If after an earlier bout with infertility, you have likely brought with you equal amounts of coping mechanisms and fear. After all, you now know what to expect, so you're not fumbling around in the dark. On the other hand, you now know what to expect, so you can't hold the same blind hope you may have had the first time around.

If this is your first time in the Land of If, you may be shocked to find yourself here, especially if you had your first child or children with relative ease. You might have been positive that the boat that brought you here would eventually realize its mistake, turn around, and take you back to the mainland. It may have taken you a long time to actually feel comfortable stepping away from the dock and exploring the island.

Either way, having children in the picture brings a bit more complication. Every option needs to be weighed with your existing child(ren) in mind. For example, if you went the donor route the first time, do you choose the same donor again? If your first child came to your family through adoption, how will his or her experience change if a sibling comes via IVF?

Also, it can be a little more difficult to keep things under wraps when you have a child (see the sidebar "Talking to Kids About Infertility," in Chapter 4). Some clinics don't take a stance on whether children can be in the waiting room, but it would certainly behoove you to leave your children at home. It can be very difficult for a person experiencing primary infertility to have to spend time in the waiting room around a baby or toddler. So childcare may be necessary.

When arranging care, I do recommend at least some disclosure, simply because you want the person you're relying on to understand that these appointments *cannot* be missed. You don't need to divulge all if you don't want to. When you get home, just say, "Geez, I'm so glad I can leave all those details back at the clinic/agency and have my home just be a place to relax." Then wink and offer a margarita.

women. It breaks down to be about 40 percent diagnosed with female factor, 40 percent diagnosed with male factor, and 20 percent diagnosed with unexplained infertility or a combination of both female- and male-factor infertility.[3]

Receiving a partner-specific diagnosis can be both a blessing and a curse. On one hand, once you know the issue, you can treat it, or you can choose a path that circumvents the problem. At the same time, having a diagnosis often brings with it a terrible emotion—guilt.

Believing that you are the cause of the situation can be upsetting. In my own relationship, our infertility issues fall squarely on my shoulders, and even though my husband carries the weight with me as our shared problem, I can't help but feel responsible knowing that the money spent, the time away from work, and the emotional ups and downs are all due to my wonky body and hormone levels.

This emotion is far from helpful, and though I don't always live

---

no. 0001
THE LAND OF IF VISITORS BUREAU

TIP: If you are currently reading this book due to your partner's infertility diagnosis, I beg you to tread lightly, knowing that those who hold the diagnosis usually hold a great deal of shame. Make sure you clearly differentiate anger with the situation from anger at the person, and clearly support your partner in seeing infertility as a problem you share together.

this advice, I am here to lecture you: Remove the self-blame and see infertility as a problem of the couple, rather than of the individual, if you are in a relationship.

Believe me, I know it's so much easier said than done. But no one chooses to be infertile, and "fault" is an ugly, misused word in this case. Take blame for the things you can control and accept that there are things that will just happen to you—and that those things may affect other people you love, too.

Unexplained Infertility

What if you don't have a diagnosis? What if you've been through multiple IVF cycles with fine-looking embryos and no discernable reason why you're not getting pregnant or maintaining a pregnancy? It is frustrating and anxiety-inducing to not have a reason for your situation, and it can be maddening trying to make decisions when you have no idea what's wrong.

Unfortunately, even after going through the entire gauntlet of tests, you may still walk away without answers—and that is one of the most upsetting aspects of unexplained infertility. It is impossible to know when "enough is enough" if every cycle is explained as "just bad luck." Therefore, those diagnosed with unexplained infertility need to be vigilant about setting stopping points (see Chapter 3 for more information on doing this). If not, the path out of the Land of If can twist back on itself again and again . . . until it merges with the path to insanity.

Age-Related Infertility

When we speak about infertility and age, we are usually referring to women, even though male fertility declines after age thirty-five as well. A 2003 report in *Fertility and Sterility* looked at the time it took for men over forty-five to impregnate a woman. There

ACCESS: DENIED

All people may have been created equal, but all patients are definitely not treated equally. Hopefully, you will never run into a doctor who will deny you treatment, but three groups are particularly targeted by discrimination: single men and women, GLBT, and those labeled with "advanced maternal age," or AMA (which is usually determined to be thirty-five or older).

In August 2006, *Mother Jones* published a survey (conducted by *Fertility and Sterility*) of fertility clinic directors. The results were shocking: 48 percent of clinic directors said they'd turn away a same-sex couple seeking a surrogate, 20 percent said they'd turn away a single woman, 17 percent said they would deny treatment to a lesbian couple, and 5 percent said they would turn away a biracial couple.[4]

While doctors should stop patients from undergoing risky or unnecessary medical procedures, aiming to control access to parenthood or making judgments on what is in the best interests of a future child is *not* their job. After all, obstetricians hardly quiz prospective fertile parents in their office on their parenting beliefs and household structure. There is a stronger case to be made in the case of AMA after the age of forty-five or fifty-five, because there are age-related limitations to egg production and the ability to carry a pregnancy to term in a healthy manner, respectively. Just because it *can* be done does not mean it *should* be done. (See the section called "Age-Related Infertility," in this chapter.)

Garnering support from online and face-to-face sources becomes doubly important if you are being denied treatments. You need to educate yourself fully on your rights. Turn to the Resources section to connect with groups that are working to ensure that parenthood is the right of every individual, regardless of marital status, race, gender, or sexuality. And age. Within reason.

was a fivefold increase in time after the men turned forty-five, as opposed to thirty, pointing toward a decrease in fertility. It took forty-five-year-old men on average thirty-seven months to impregnate a woman.[5]

A woman's fertility starts decreasing at thirty, with a sharp decline after forty-five. Only 5 percent of women forty-five and older can still conceive without medical intervention.[6] Therefore, doctors have a difficult time classifying a woman over forty-five as "infertile," since fertility should naturally decrease with age, and therefore, this is simply a fact of nature, rather than a problem with the body. At the same time, medical intervention that can extend fertility does exist, and the debate continues about what the age cutoff—if any—should be to utilize it. The popular ideology recommends using one's own gametes until age forty-five (when fertility decreases significantly) and using donor eggs until fifty-five (the end age in the average menopause spectrum of forty-five to fifty-five).

Having AMA (advanced maternal age) stamped across your file can be salt on the wound, especially if the timing of trying to conceive has been out of your hands. It's not just life's choices that keep people from reaching parenthood at a younger age—it's also a matter of life's randomness. We can't control when we meet a partner, or when we decide that we're finished waiting to meet a partner, or when we lose a partner.

Therefore, it can be very upsetting to be over the age of thirty-five and trying to build your family, and be met with a lack of empathy, as well as attitude, from doctors who believe you should have started trying to conceive at a younger age. Many women existing in the "gray area" of AMA—generally speaking, ages thirty-five to forty-four—need to be assertive in order to receive treatments without being judged on their deservedness to parent.

Last Thoughts

You didn't necessarily choose where to settle down on the island; most likely, the neighborhood chose you. And you may fit in with many groups here: People rarely belong to only one neighborhood—which is often what causes bridges to spring up, connecting each neighborhood and each person's story, building understanding and support across varied experiences.

My own infertility journey began in primary and now continues in secondary. We have female-factor and biological infertility. There are some neighborhoods I've never lived in on this island, but that doesn't mean I don't empathize with and support the people living there. They may be grappling with issues very different from my own, but at the core, we are all banging our heads against the wall as we try to build our families so that they match the image we hold inside our head.

It doesn't matter whether the obstacle is your life situation or your wonky uterus—when you want to build a family and you cannot do so without help, it is very difficult to swallow. Therefore, the same respect and empathy should be allotted to everyone, across the board, as soon as they step off the boat and onto this wretched island.

Back in Siena, they slam the gnocchi down on the table when you wander into the wrong neighborhood. But my hope is that we can be more gracious and create a welcome table for everyone disembarking onto the island. After all, everyone needs to eat, and there's plenty of gnocchi to go around.

Chapter 2

Navigating the BERMUDA TRIANGLE

AS YOU MIGHT already suspect, paying a visit to the Land of If is not for the faint of heart. In addition to the challenge of navigating the various, confusing neighborhoods, the island is smack-dab in the center of a Bermuda Triangle, a vortex where physical, financial, and emotional hardship converge—so it is incredibly easy to founder if you don't stay informed and vigilant.

The Physical Point

Many of those living in the Land of If need to navigate the physical aspects of infertility on a daily basis. Not only do many of the causes of infertility pose a physical effect in and of themselves (endometriosis, for instance, is pretty damn painful) but those pursuing diagnostics and treatments are also enduring painful procedures, injections, blood draws, and surgeries in order to conceive.

The physical pain of infertility shouldn't be belittled or dismissed. I think because so much of treatments and diagnostics takes place within a clinic or an office, people are always shocked by the amount of physical discomfort and recovery time, as well as by the risks involved. If you were undergoing surgery in a hospital, no one would expect you to return to work that day, but if you are undergoing an invasive procedure in an office, you may think you can get to that afternoon meeting after the anesthesia wears off.

Even if you are taking the path of adoption or living child-free, you're not exempt from physical pain. The stress that comes from these options has a very real physical effect, such as tense shoulders, back pain, migraines . . . this list goes on. Stressful situations can cause physical pain, and being proactive about this goes a long way.

Life Preservers for the Physical Point

It is important to make sure that your sole physical identity is not completely tied up in treatments. Find a source of exercise, such as swimming or basketball, or another physical outlet, such as gardening, that fits your treatment plan. High-impact running may not be the most sound idea if you're experiencing hyperstimulation, but you can still walk or do yoga. Try to allot at least a half hour every day to this activity.

Be gentle with your body, and listen to its wisdom. When you are hungry, pause and eat. When you are tired, take a nap—even if you had eight hours of sleep the night before. Just as marathoners are acutely aware of addressing their needs while they're in training—not pushing themselves past endurance—those living in the Land of If need to be aware of the harsh conditions here and take care of themselves accordingly.

USING THE
THEORY OF RELATIVITY
TO YOUR ADVANTAGE

Anytime you hear "catheter" used in conjunction with your cervix, that should be your heads-up that something's going to be uncomfortable. I've never heard anyone say, "Catheters feel great!" or, "I barely felt it at all!" When you have a catheter and speculum inside of you, you *know*. So let's begin with the idea that anything involving a catheter starts out at at least 1 on the discomfort ladder.

"Cramping" is also one of those trigger words. I don't know about you, but when I have cramping with my period, I take pain medication. The point is that cramps are painful, and therefore, we try to get rid of them with two Tylenol and a heating pad. If cramps were nothing, we wouldn't treat them. So anything that causes some cramping should be bumped up at least another rung on the discomfort ladder.

Of course, pain is subjective and relative, and so many factors go into determining whether a procedure will be painful—from the skill of the technician to the tip of the uterus. And some people are simply more physically sensitive to pain than others. It has nothing to do with strength or weakness. So don't be upset when someone else rates her hysterosalpingogram a 3 on the 1-to-10 pain scale and you give yours a 9.

I am a firm believer that doctors should become scaremongers when it comes to explaining an imminent procedure. I'd rather my doctor tell me it is going to hurt worse than anything I can imagine (but it turns out to be some light cramping) than tell me that it won't hurt a bit (but I end up in tears by the end of the appointment). Doing the former and eschewing the latter leaves the patient feeling like a rock star at the end of the appointment, whereas diminishing the pain factor leaves the patient feeling like a wuss.

In this book (and in particular, in Chapter 8), take my descriptions of procedures with a grain of salt, knowing that I'm only trying to make you feel like a rock star.

The Financial Point

This is the way I explain the financial point to non-Iffers:

What if, during your eighth month of pregnancy, you were told by your obstetrician that in order to get the baby out, you would have to shell out the equivalent of a year of college tuition?

"But I thought I'd have eighteen years to save!" you'd exclaim, staring down at your belly, where the child you've been dreaming about for the last eight months waited.

Alas, you need to cough up the cash . . . immediately.

You somehow gather together and fork over the money, but your doctor stares at the wad of cash and says, "Sorry. I guess I wasn't clear. This money was just for me to think about it. You'll need to come up with double this to get me to actually do anything."

Once again, committed to having a child, you pull together the money . . . only to discover that there are more hoops, more bills—and not one of the payments you make will result in the absolute promise of a live child.

By the time you're ready to enter treatments or adoption, you—like those already expecting—are committed to the idea of parenthood. It's a strong impulse to procreate and/or raise children. Either you have that impulse or you don't, and if you have it, it is not something you can talk yourself out of or fulfill with a puppy.

Fertility treatments are expensive. Even with insurance covering everything but the copayment, each cycle can run well into the hundreds of dollars, with the constant blood draws and ultrasounds.

Of course, most insurance plans do not cover infertility, and few states mandate coverage at all. According to the American Society for Reproductive Medicine (ASRM), the average IVF cycle costs $12,400.[1] And that money comes with no guarantee. (Imagine putting down cash at an auto dealership without knowing if you'll be one of the lucky customers who actually drives away in a new car.)

Adoption is an equally expensive option. According to Resolve, the national infertility organization, adoption can range from free to $2,500 for a foster-to-adopt situation, to upward of $40,000 for domestic or international adoption. But on average, the cost of adoption is between $20,000 and $25,000.[2] While tax credits on the back end can ease some of the burden, a person still usually needs a hefty chunk of change to come to the adoption table.

Yes, there are free and inexpensive options for treating infertility or adopting. But these options may not fit every person or couple, nor do they always lead to parenthood. So for some people, the astronomical cost of treatments or adoption places their dreams of parenthood out of reach. Others manage to afford treatments or adoption only by cutting every other cost out of their life and making huge financial sacrifices.

Life Preservers for the Financial Point

So how do you get the money to cover treatments if you don't have insurance coverage? First off, there are loans that can be obtained for treatments or adoption. Clinics or agencies often have information about these loans, as well as financial counselors, and you can ask to meet with someone from the clinic's financial staff one-on-one.

Also, you can take a good hard look at your budget and cut out anything not considered necessary. You can forgo birthday gifts and holiday gifts, putting all extra money toward a baby fund. You can refinance any property or cars, start working a second job, or sell cookies door-to-door. People have found unique ways to slowly but surely add to their family-building fund.

As with all high-ticket items in life, it pays to make a financial plan. Rather than jumping headfirst into treatments or a clinic, do research on success rates and cost. (The success rates for many clinics are posted online at www.sart.org.) Because fertility treatments do not come with a promise—you're paying for the chance, not the child—some people come up with a palatable number for themselves, taking into account a treatment's success rates when determining its worth against a predetermined limit.

Also, be up-front with your doctor. Though she's holding your chart, she may not have any clue about your financial situation. Doctors focus on the medicine; the financial department focuses on the billing. Ask your doctor directly if there is anything she can do to make treatments affordable. Some clinics have a refund program for IVF, usually called a "shared risk" program (see tip 1, Chapter 8, page 18), and others will negotiate special payments for patients in need. No one likes to talk about money, but once you've lost all modesty by putting your legs up in the stirrups or by producing a sperm sample in the clinic's bathroom, admitting that you need a leg up in producing the thousands of dollars necessary to do IVF is a little less embarrassing.

Some people turn to friends and family for financial assistance. This can be a tricky maneuver, because the financial side of infertility is grossly misunderstood, and too many times I've heard people say, "Well, if they can't afford parenthood, they should take that as a sign that they shouldn't parent." This may be true if you can't afford *parenthood,* but those pursuing fertility treatments or adoption usually *can* afford the child, just not the infertility solution. It may take additional explanation before an outsider can fully understand your needs and the steps you're taking to parent, but it's worth the trouble to explain if they can make the road a bit more manageable. See Resources to get listings that will give more detail on the financial end of infertility.

The Emotional Point

The emotional point of infertility may be the trickiest waters—that's why this section is so much longer than the others.

First off, not everyone feels the same way about their own infertility. There are those who navigate easily in this area, never succumbing to the strong waves that break on the shore. But there are also those of us (myself included) who go in with great intentions, determined not to be bowled over, but get sucked under the surf, regardless. It's understandable. After all, we are talking about a problem that not only affects your life today but also changes your future. And with far-reaching effects comes sweeping emotion.

It's easy to see how unique each person's emotional landscape is when it comes to infertility. Sadness, frustration, jealousy, anxiety, guilt, hope, excitement, anger, and despair all mix together. That's a pretty wide variety. And at the same time, you need to factor in additional variables: the development of your coping mechanisms, the perceived amount of support (or pressure) from your family and friends, and the perceived amount of time left before it's "too late."

In addition to sampling the full spectrum of emotions, you may feel more than one of them at the same time. For instance, you may be full of hope and yet weighted by despair at the start of a new cycle. You may be happy for your friend but jealous as well when he or she announces impending parenthood. You may wish you could leave trying behind, but also feel this overwhelming frustration to keep going, no matter what, until you beat infertility into submission.

And then there are the sudden swings from one end of the emotional spectrum to the other. You may wake up one morning feeling at peace with the state of things. Then, on the elevator ride up to your office, a colleague pulls out pictures of his one-month-old, and all of a sudden, your emotions are ricocheting off the walls.

Just as emotional effects can long outlast physical pain, the emotional point of infertility has the power to drag people under even if they're doing a great job navigating the physical and financial points. Therefore, these are the waters that demand your closest focus. You can remain vigilant by utilizing common outlets, such as therapy, journaling, and support groups. But those outlets don't serve all types of people; not everyone has the ability or desire to discuss feelings. For such people, therapy, journaling, and support groups might be akin to being covered in fire ants. If this is you, remember: Gaining emotional support should not be a source of even more struggle, so do whatever you know you need to do, not what you think you're supposed to do. Other outlets may be to distract yourself with another activity, to go out dancing, to get some acupuncture, or to volunteer.

Do whatever helps. But remember: "Help" does not mean "complete relief." In our culture, we are accustomed to having things work well. If we take a pain reliever, we expect that the headache will disappear entirely. Emotions, of course, are different. They cannot be put to rest entirely—even by getting a full-body massage, or by dancing the Macarena until sunrise, or by chopping enough wood to get you through a Siberian winter. It's important to keep this in mind, because the impulse, when things don't work *entirely,* is to say, "It's not worth the effort." But it is. You may never find a solution that removes all pain from your heart, but keeping up with these helpful activities will bring you a modicum of much-needed relief.

RAINDROPS
KEEP FALLING
ON OUR HEADS

Living in the Land of If can put strain on a partnership for several reasons, the most common of which is a difference in emotional reactions to certain events or news. It can be strange to be living in the same house with someone who has partly cloudy skies overhead while you're in a tropical thunderstorm. But every person processes words and actions differently. What may devastate one person will merely disappoint another. When we process our emotions, we are taking into account not only the event at hand, but our past experiences as well. Sometimes we don't even know why something is upsetting us to the extent that it is until we start unpacking our baggage and see that our feelings about a long-forgotten event have crept into our processing of a current event.

No one should be judged for their emotional response. Just as your partner cannot ask you to change your feelings, you cannot ask your partner to change his or hers. If your partner tries to nudge you toward different weather, simply take yourself out of that situation by explaining your side and by acknowledging your partner's feelings. But too many times, we try to explain ourselves when we're upset. Make sure to take the space you need in order to calm down. If you do not do well speaking your thoughts, write them down and then read them aloud. State your needs clearly, since partners are not mind readers and may not know what they need to do in order to meet you halfway.

You may need to accept that you won't always be on the same page. One person may feel fine about going to baby-centered events, while the other cannot bear to step near a baby shower. Couples therapy is an excellent space for loosening whatever tension exists within the relationship that is keeping movement from occurring. Just as you are seeing a doctor to help with fertility, you sometimes need to seek a professional to help with emotions.

Life Preservers for
the Emotional Point

When it comes to coping, it doesn't matter whether you're a crier or a compartmentalizer—everyone needs a strategy. Here's a great piece of advice my sister once gave me (she is a brilliant therapist, so you know this is good advice):

> *Do whatever you need to do to get through this—*
> *as long as you're not creating more problems to deal*
> *with on the other end.*
> —MY BRILLIANT SISTER

WEIGHING THE RISKS

My sister's advice may seem obvious at first. But look closer, and you'll see the brilliance is in the simplicity of it. Let's take a couple of examples, putting the advice into effect.

> *I am anxiously waiting at home for my doctor to call*
> *and tell me my beta results. I can:*
> - call him and bother him, *or*
> - wait and possibly not get my beta results today.

> *What do I do? Well, for me, the impact of annoying the*
> *doctor is less than the impact of the emotional stress I*
> *will feel as the minutes tick past the time he'd told me*
> *he would call, and the chance of receiving the results*
> *that day dwindle. He may think I'm annoying or high*
> *maintenance, and he may go home and joke about*
> *me to his family. But how do those things affect me*
> *overall? Having people laughing at my expense is not*

fun, but it won't undo me. Not receiving my results will
undo me. Therefore, I call the doctor.

Not everyone would make the same choice, but that's because everyone, as we've covered, has a different emotional landscape when it comes to infertility.

Here's another example.

I receive an invitation to my cousin's baby shower,
and I really don't want to go and have to listen to
every family member coo about her burgeoning belly.
What do I do? I can:

- turn down the invitation and state honestly why I'm not going, *or*
- turn down the invitation with an airtight excuse, *or*
- accept the invitation, have a good cry on the way to the party, and know the whole thing will be over and done with by 3:00 PM.

I need to think about this in terms of my own family.
They are pretty understanding, so I could probably just
admit that I can't do this emotionally, and everyone
would roll with it. If my family were less understanding
and my anxiety about the event would keep me from
making it to the end of the party unscathed, I may come
up with an airtight excuse at the last minute ("I woke up
with a stomach virus") and send my gift on with another
family member. Of course, the other side of this is the
third choice. If my actions will create more problems
down the line—a damaged relationship with my cousin,

an angry conversation with my aunt, a lack of people

coming to (hopefully) my own future shower—

I may make the decision to go to the party, though I'll

certainly put coping mechanisms in place.

You may discover down the road that your choice didn't have the outcome you expected, or that you ended up making more problems for yourself than expected. Try not to anguish. After all, you made the best choice based on the information you had at the time, and that is all any of us can truly do within decision making.

HOW TO INSTITUTE YOUR OWN
EMOTIONAL RATIONING SYSTEM

While you're going to need to save your actual money for treatments or adoption, you're also going to have to wisely ration your emotional goods while in the Land of If. The cost of living here tends to fluctuate so quickly it could make your head spin, and problems start cropping up when you haven't rationed out this precious resource.

All island living requires forethought—there are lags of time between each of the ships bringing dry goods and nonisland products; therefore, islanders learn how to ration. And you are going to need to ration your emotional goods—namely, peace of heart.

When you have a lot of peace of heart, it's easier to get through the day. When you have a little, small problems become huge issues. Building your stores of emotional goods takes planning and forethought, with an eye to the fact that the weather here is so unpredictable that you never know when you're going to have to dip into your emotional goods and deplete the supply.

Ration out your emotional energy and keep within your means. You can't utilize goods you don't have, and you can't use emotional energy you haven't gathered. If you're feeling depleted, address that and no. 0002

THE LAND OF IF VISITORS BUREAU

TIP:
GOOD EXCUSES FOR
MISSING A BABY EVENT:

* We're so sorry—we have tickets purchased for that day (plane, concert, etc.), and it's been on the calendar for months.

* I threw up this morning, and I'm really scared to come around the baby right now.

* I'm sorry that I didn't make it; my friend got locked out of her house, and I had to drive the keys over. By the time I could get on the road to you, the party was almost over.

EXCUSES THAT INVITE MORE QUESTIONS OR ARGUING:

* I have to work that day.

* I can't afford to fly out there right now.

* I would love to come, but we're busy.

work to protect your heart. When making decisions, ask yourself how much of your stores you will need to use up and then weigh whether it's worth the price.

If you know there's a chance that you'll have to go to a baby shower for a cousin during the same month that you have one for a coworker, you may decide that your emotional goods are better spent on family than on an acquaintance and give yourself an out for the coworker's party.

THE THREE
LITTLE HAIRS

I love it when I receive email forwards that give a little tip not on how you can live a *better* life, but on the way you should view hardships in your life. In such emails, there are no practical instructions on how to achieve the proposed goal; there is only the underlying message that everyone beyond Mother Teresa needs an attitude adjustment.

One of my favorites is commonly called "the attitude of the three hairs." In this story, a woman wakes up and discovers she has only three hairs left, and she says, "Great, I'll braid them!" The second morning, she wakes up and sees that she has only two hairs, and she says, "Fantastic, I *love* a middle part!" The third day, she wakes up and sees that she has only one hair. So she smiles and says, "I look great with a ponytail!" The fourth day, she wakes up and laughs at her hairless head, saying, "I can sleep a few extra minutes, because I don't have to do my hair!"

And the moral of the story is that we should all be thankful for baldness.

I know this makes me sound bitter and cynical, but I don't believe we can change who we are. We can only work with what we have, and telling someone to see the world in a different way is not only condescending and infuriating but also just bad advice. Telling people they "shouldn't feel bad" is only going to make them feel bad about feeling bad. That's when the snowball effect starts rolling (feeling bad about feeling bad about feeling bad . . .), which often ends up causing serious depression and low self-esteem.

Does this mean we should all aim low and never try to better ourselves? Not at all. But there is a difference between striving to be "the best you" and striving to be "the best character from a sugar-packet parable."

At the same time, during a period when your emotional storage bin is overflowing, it may be a good time to go above and beyond in bringing out the peace of heart so people will excuse you for the lean times. If you're feeling up to it, go do all of your baby-gift shopping for the year in a single trip so you won't have to step into the toy store when you have no emotional stores down the road.

Recognize that everyone else out there has limited emotional energy, too, and they need you to be sensitive to their own lack of goods from time to time.

In the same way that sleep begets sleep and money seemingly begets money, emotional health creates more emotional reserves. We take care of our reproductive health by seeing an endocrinologist or a gynecologist, but it is just as important to address our emotional health. If you are noticing that you consistently are unable to stock your emotional stores, consider seeing an infertility therapist. Recommendations for an infertility therapist can be obtained through your local Resolve chapter (see the Resources section). While a therapist cannot wave a magic wand and instantly bring the peace-of-heart ships to the dock, a good therapist can help you ration out your emotional energy, as well as see the world from a different angle. Talking it out, joining support groups, leaning on friends and family, and/or generally releasing the pent-up feelings that accompany infertility can go a long way in staving off the depression inherent in any life crisis.

It's Your Party, and I'll Cry if I Want To

If you're a woman, every once in a while, you're going to open up your spanking-new mailbox on this island and find a pink or blue invitation in there, sent either by someone back on the mainland or by another Iffer asking you to attend a baby shower/baptism/bris/first birthday. You will stare at this book as if I can see you and plead, "Melissa, do I really have to go?"

TIP: Here are a few extra tips on surviving baby-related events.

* To avoid shopping for gifts on a hard day, go onesie and stuffed-animal shopping on a strong day, and purchase multiple gifts to keep in the closet. Wrap them and slap on a note with details about the contents on the outside. It's grab and go.

* Make sure you do something nice for yourself beforehand: Get yourself an expensive cup of coffee, listen to your favorite music in the car, work in a quickie with your partner before hitting the road.

* If you can go with another person—especially one who knows what you're going through emotionally—all the better.

* For the times when you need to travel alone, figuratively bring a friend in your pocket. If you can have a friend write a note to take along, making it specific to you and your friendship, all the better. If you feel shy about asking someone to write you a love note, xerox the one in the appendix, called "From Me to You."

The quick answer is no. Frankly, people just don't notice or care about things as deeply as we worry that they do. Most people are quite understanding and do not take offense when someone can't attend an event. After all, most of us lead busy lives, and sometimes we have prior plans. We get sick. We get stuck in traffic. We send a gift, write a lovely apology note, beg to see photos from the event, and then move on.

The longer answer is maybe. If the person is a work acquaintance whom you would never be in touch with if she left her position, skip the event. If she is a friend, neighbor, or community member—in other words, someone you will run into again—you can beg off with a conflicting engagement.

The more difficult cases are ones that involve close friends and family. You can still get out of some of these, but the gains need to outweigh the work you will need to do—on the front end or back end—to appease and assuage feelings.

Dealing with Pressure

There are three types of pressure you're possibly facing: internalized pressure (what you wish you could do, or cursing yourself for what you're about to do), recipient pressure (verbalized or nonverbalized pressure coming from the guest of honor), and familial pressure (coming from other friends or family members who are invited to the event and want you to be there, too).

The internalized pressure is probably the worst. No one beats us up better than we do ourselves. No one kicks us harder than we do when we mess up, and no one has higher expectations. I can't remove that self-inflicted pressure for you, but I can ask you to view it through this lens: If you are following my sister's brilliant advice, you are doing the best you can do in this moment in time.

TIP: Just as every person needs a good sport jacket or little black dress, everyone should have a set of standard answers to situations that make them uncomfortable.

If baby-related announcements and news about children make you uncomfortable, you need to take a moment to think up something vague and congratulatory that you can use every single time you bump up against someone else's good news. Practice it and own it, turning it into a reflex. Someone pops their pregnancy announcement on you at the next cocktail party? Swallow your mini-quiche and say, "How *nice* for you!" or, "Well, *that* doesn't suck!" or, "I'm speechless!"

Just pretend you live on the set of a hilarious sitcom about an infertile person surrounded by baby bumps, and that these words are your catchphrase. Get good enough at this, and you can start to hear the laugh track in your head.[3]

Recipient pressure is the least difficult, because you can easily look at it in this manner: Other people's craziness is other people's craziness. You don't have to live their life, and they don't have to live yours. If they choose to be angry with you and you've acted with the best intentions and apologized for any gaffes, it's on them. You can't change anyone else's mind—if you're like me, you can't even really change your own most of the time—so there's not a lot you can do. The worst-case scenario would be if people, as a result of your not attending, decided to remove themselves from your life entirely. If you can deal with that particular loss as a possibility, you have your answer. Do take into consideration what these people have done for you in the past. If these people were always there for you when you needed them, or if you were slated to be a person of honor (such as a godparent) in the life of that child, you do need to be there for them, within reason.

The last type of pressure, familial, is the most slippery: parents who want to make sure you're going to be close to your cousins, siblings who want you to show up to an event if they have to be there, in-laws who are going to stop speaking to you if you're not attending someone's wife's sister's cousin's baptism. Many times, they're putting the pressure on you because they will have to face some pressure themselves if they don't deliver the goods—namely, you as a guest.

The final thing to consider is your own future and a return to how you want the world to look down the road. If you skip all events, you need to be prepared for people to skip your own. Personally, it was never an issue, since I wasn't going to have a baby shower, but I did want people to come to my children's birthday parties. This meant that sometimes (not always), I had to squelch my feelings, have a small cry on the way to the event, and smile brightly as I watched the little ones break yet another piñata.

TIP: Luckily, more and more people are realizing that email is a great medium for giving sensitive news—though that doesn't always mean that they deliver it sensitively. It's hard to be sitting at work and have an email pop up on your screen with the subject line "Big news!" Or open a message to be confronted by a sonogram picture embedded in the text box with the message "Twins!" That said, I'd rather get an email than deal with such news unexpectedly during a phone call or in person.

If you feel the same, instead of asking people point-blank to send you an email when they have good news (which can be awkward and can require further explanation), hint about this preference during random conversations about the Internet, or mention how grateful you were when an announcement arrived this way. Most people pick up on it quickly and follow suit when they have good news.

HERE THERE BE MONSTERS

When it comes to infertility, no emotion gets discussed as often as "hope." And no positive emotion gets more bad press. People discuss it as if it were as unappetizing as week-old sushi.

"WHY CAN'T YOU JUST BE HAPPY FOR ME?"

When you're down in the dumps, it can be hard to hear how great another person's life is going. It's even harder when people share their good news with the expectation that it's going to make you feel better. After all, if *they're* feeling this ecstatic, why wouldn't *you?* Some will even go so far as to surprise you with their good news—you know, so you can feel the same rush of elation that they experienced when they first found out.

Lest I sound like a crotchety old cynic, other people's happy news doesn't create a pit of despair in my heart. But being happy *for you,* and for your good news, does not necessarily make me any happier in my own life.

When you do find yourself head-to-head with this situation, I hope you will be able to explain this dichotomy to the listeners. Their good news is great, and you can be happy for them while simultaneously being sad for yourself. And just as you don't expect them to change their emotional landscape to match your own, you can't be expected to change your emotional landscape to match theirs. They can be sad for you, and you can be happy for them, and then they can retreat to friends who can currently bask in their pool of sunshine, and you can retreat to friends who will share their umbrella.

Why the sneers? Well, hope is what generates the *what ifs,* and *what if* is the electricity that powers most of the island. The *what ifs* are necessary, especially in the sense of making decisions and continuing on a path. But it can be nerve-racking to have so much riding on something outside of your control. To top it off, hope is as elusive as Nessie, the famous monster of Loch Ness—when you want to find it, you can't. It pops up on unexpected days, and when you see it, you want to tell your friends and family all about it. And as a result, it can sometimes make you feel like a fool.

Instead of looking at hope as a taunting beast, try seeing it as the energy that propels you forward, helping you put one foot in front of the other and keep chipping away at the problem. And the reality is that so many of the greatest things in life require a leap of faith. Just as you shouldn't go into a marriage bracing yourself for everything that could go wrong, you shouldn't go into treatments, or adoption, or even pregnancy and parenting, focused on all the ways things could go wrong.

Last Thoughts

In dealing with hope, in dealing with the Bermuda Triangle of Infertility, in dealing with everything that is going to be thrown your way while on this island, keep remembering you will always have your life vests and your life raft, and you will always have your own internal compass. You'll need all of those things if you're going to get around the island without being dragged out into the murky waters that surround this place.

PLANNING
~YOUR~
ITINERARY

Chapter 3

THIS BOOK, AS you've noticed, is set up similarly to a travel guide-book. Why? Well, travel and infertility have a lot in common—not the least of which is this: Planning ahead ensures a smoother trip. Efficient travelers always chart a route and weigh out the pros and cons of each leg of the journey before hitting the road.

So, planning your stay here means you're going to be making some choices. And there are a lot of choices to make. Part of living on this island is that you need to choose your path *off* the island, as well as make several other decisions *within* that path . . . including when to give up on one path and try another.

This chapter will provide you with the practical tools you need to be as strategic as possible in making decisions during your stay in the Land of If.

The Decision List

We usually think of choice as a good thing, but having too many choices can leave us immobilized. Nipping at the heels of this situation is the fact that treating infertility is usually time-sensitive and very expensive—hence the pressure to make the *right* choices.

The first choice you'll have to make is whether you want to seek assistance or not, and if so, when. In my and my husband's case, we were walking the line, feeling as if we were treating the problem too soon *(what if we just waited and lucked out and got pregnant on our own?),* but also as if we were wasting important time *(what if we waited and learned that my hormone levels had meanwhile taken a turn for the worse?).*

This is where the middle school teacher in me came through: I made a "decision list." I used this concept to help some of my students who were immobilized by the enormous decisions before them. The decision list is a great way to choose a Plan A for exiting infertility, and it can be reworked every few months, as new information rises to the surface, to chart a new course if need be.

Let's begin learning how to make a decision list based on one of the larger decisions you'll have to make: which path you want to try, in this moment, to leave the Land of If. I qualified that with "in this moment" because you may end up taking more than one path over the course of your journey. This decision-list technique can also help you know when it's time to switch paths.

If you have a partner, each of you should fill out the decision list on your own and then compare lists to see where you match up in terms of addressing your needs. Make sure you are being honest with yourself and open with your partner in order to make choices together with peace of heart.

The Eight Factors

Each time you need to make a decision, you'll need to write down a list of factors to consider. I've started by placing what I think are the eight most important factors to consider when choosing your path out of the Land of If.

You may be able to think of additional factors that are unique to your situation. For example, if you were adopted as a child, you may also have feelings about adoption, or if you have a known donor that you would like to use, it may be something you weigh to bring you onto the third-party reproduction path. Certainly, when you start using this method to make decisions within a particular path, you will need to come up with your own factors for each unique decision.

COST

This factor takes two things into consideration: the cost of the path and your personal financial situation. I know it feels wrong to boil down parenthood to money, but remember: The money pays for the family-building *process,* not the child. You do need to be realistic in what you can afford, because it will not be helpful to enter parenthood severely in debt. That said, finances are easier to work around than other limitations, because there are a plethora of ways to finance treatments and adoption.

The expense on each path will vary greatly. Treatments may be prohibitively expensive for a person with no insurance living in Maine (a nonmandated state), whereas they may be inexpensive for someone with insurance living in Maryland (a mandated state).

CERTAINTY OF REACHING PARENTHOOD

This factors in how certain you can be to reach parenthood on a particular path. If becoming a parent is the most important factor for you, there will be paths that you should consider over others—especially if you are balancing out this factor against personal finances. If you have the financial ability to try more than one path, you may want to consider all of the choices below. If you have severe financial limitations, you may want to jump directly to a path that ensures parenthood.

Sureness of Leaving Infertility (IF)

This factors in how sure you can be to leave this island and not live forever in limbo. For some, the pain of infertility weighs heaviest as a factor. Truly, there is only one path that gives you absolute certainty that you will exit out of infertility, and that is living child-free. It is the only path entirely within your control.

Possibility of a Genetic Link

You may not be able to articulate why you want to pass along your genetic material to your child, and if this factor is at the top of the list, it should not be dismissed. Like cost, it can be embarrassing to admit how much this factors into your decision making, and like cost, it should not be something that you squelch for the sake of appearances. If it's important to you, it should factor into your decision, and you should never feel the need to defend its inclusion. Of course, on the flip side, there are also people who specifically *do not* want to pass along genetic material (for instance, in the case of being a carrier of a genetic disease).

Possibility of a Biological Link

While this option is open only to women, it may also factor high on a man's list if he wants his female partner to carry the child. If you are a woman, experiencing pregnancy may be very high on your list. If you utilize donor eggs or embryos, a woman can still be the biological parent if she carries the child, and that time period contributes (like genetics) to the life of the child.

Amount of Control over Prenatal Health

The reality is that much of what happens in life is out of our hands.

But there are certainly paths that afford more control over choices that can affect the outcome. Control can come in two forms: knowing the health history of the gametes and being able to make decisions about the in utero environment.

Average Speed of Resolving Infertility (IF)

This is tough to account for, because within a given path, time varies so much. Some people will conceive during their first IVF cycle, and others will conceive during their fifth cycle. With domestic adoption, some people will be matched after three months on the books, and others will still be on the books two years later. You just can't know. Time refers to two things: how quickly you need to exit the Land of If and knowing when it will happen. If all paths are open to you, some have a shorter timeline, due to logistics; some, at the very least, have a set timeline, so you can predict the future.

Importance of Maternal Age

Your biological clock is important, and some paths are more time sensitive than others. While you can enter living child-free at any age, treatments utilizing your gametes may not be open to women beyond a certain point (for the most part, only the woman's age is considered when determining age cutoffs). Clinics and adoption agencies also sometimes have cutoffs, and if they are not hard-and-fast cutoffs, they are certainly guidelines meant to also save you time on a possible dead-end path. If you are under thirty-five and do not have a diagnosis in hand that precludes the use of one or more paths, you'll probably be ranking age as the lowest of your priorities.

How the Factors Apply

Now that you have a sense of what is important to you (as well as what is important to your partner, if you have one), you can look at the multitude of paths out of the Land of If and see which one best fits your needs. It may be that you are choosing based on current factors in your life, and the list will be recalculated later on in the journey. Each path is explored in greater detail later in this book (for trying unassisted, see the Monitoring Your Fertility section in the appendix; for the others, see Chapters 8 through 11).

There is a table on the opposite page to show you, at a glance, how each factor applies to a particular exit from the Land of If. A deeper exploration of the factors follows below.

Treatments

For the sake of clarity, I use the term "treatments" to refer to using any form of assisted conception with your genetic material. Donor-gamete cycles (which also utilize treatments) have been separated out into their own sections, below. Treatments can be noninvasive, such as the oral medication Clomid, which requires little intervention beyond taking a pill, or very invasive, such as in vitro fertilization (IVF), which requires constant monitoring, injectable medications, and surgical procedures. The whole of Chapter 8 is devoted to utilizing treatments of all sorts.

Therefore, *cost* will range drastically, depending on the route you are taking. Treatments with your genetic material will always cost less than introducing donor gametes (in which case you pay for the treatment *and* the gametes), and insurance coverage varies not only from state to state but from person to person, even within the same insurance company. Add in the fact that each clinic sets its own price standard for procedures, and the fact that treatments can run anywhere from several hundred dollars to well over $10,000 for a single cycle. Treatments have a higher *certainty of reaching parenthood* than trying without assistance does, though even advanced procedures such as IVF carry a success rate of less than 40 percent.

| | | Third-Party Reproduction | | | Adoption | | | Living Child-Free |
| | Treatments | Donor Gametes | | Surrogacy | Domestic | Inter-national | Foster-to-Adopt | |
		Donor Eggs	Donor Sperm					
Cost	Medium	High	Medium	High	Medium to High	High	Low	Free
Certainty of Reaching Parenthood	Medium	Medium	Medium	Medium	High	High	High	N/A
Sureness of Resolving IF	Low	Low	Low	Low	Medium	Medium	Medium	High
Possibility of a Genetic Link	High	Low to Medium	Low to Medium	Low to Medium	Low	Low	Low	N/A
Possibility of a Biological Link	High	High	High	Low	Low	Low	Low	N/A
Amount of Control over Prenatal Health	High	Medium	Medium	Low	Low	Low	Low	N/A
Speed of Resolving IF	High	Medium	Medium	Medium	Medium	High	High	N/A
Importance of Maternal Age	High	Low	High	Low	Low	Low	Low	Low

TRYING
UNASSISTED

Being diagnosed with infertility doesn't put you immediately on a path to assisted conception or adoption without passing go. In fact, I don't think anyone should pass directly to treatments without first considering their feelings about those two options. When it comes to assisted conception, the importance of the loss of privacy and intimacy should not be minimized. Beyond the fact that it makes some people feel physically squeamish, there are also people who are not comfortable with assisted conception, due to religious or cultural beliefs. Plus, adoption is a huge undertaking, not to be entered into lightly (à la "Why don't you 'just' adopt?").

Even though it isn't covered directly in this book, trying without assistance is a very legitimate path out of the Land of If, and it's a common way of resolving infertility, especially when you are without a clear diagnosis. It's certainly one of the least expensive options, even if you add in tools that help pinpoint ovulation and home pregnancy tests at the end of each cycle. However, the certainty of reaching parenthood is low, and the longer you try beyond the first year without success, the more likely it is that a problem exists that needs addressing. However, trying without assistance, when successful, assures a genetic link and a biological link. There is total control over prenatal health and the in utero environment. But this is a slow and uncertain way of addressing infertility. Trying without assistance is not the best use of time if a person has been trying to conceive for over a year and is over thirty-five.

It holds no particular *sureness of resolving IF*—it is simply too easy to keep trying procedure after procedure, to no avail. Treatments provide the *possibility of both a genetic and a biological link*, as well as the optimum *amount of control over prenatal health*. This is because in some cases, such as when genetic testing is utilized, a parent may exercise an even higher level of control, choosing only to transfer embryos that do not carry a certain genetic illness. *Speed of resolving IF* does not differ greatly from that of trying without assistance, and there is no way to predict how many cycles a person will need before she conceives and carries to term. At the same time, *maternal age* does play a factor: Treatments are more successful when the woman is under thirty-five than when she crosses over that threshold, and some doctors will not work with patients over the age of forty-five.

Third-Party Reproduction

Third-party reproduction can be split into three distinct paths: using donor eggs, using donor sperm, and using a surrogate. This path is covered in detail in Chapter 10.

DONOR GAMETES

When it comes to *cost,* not only is donor insemination less expensive than donor eggs, but the actual insemination can sometimes be done at home. Donor sperm itself costs between $200 and $600 per cycle (and obviously, it could even be free if you have a known donor). Donor eggs, on the other hand, are much more expensive, because the removal of eggs (as opposed to sperm) is much more invasive. In addition, a woman needs to do IVF in order to utilize donor eggs; therefore, the cost per cycle will add up to between $15,000 and $20,000.

When compared with utilizing treatments alone, using donor gametes does not truly add a higher level of *certainty of reaching parenthood* (unless the woman is over thirty-five, in which case it takes her a step closer toward the likelihood of parenthood). It also doesn't provide true *sureness of resolving IF*. Of course, donor gametes remove the *possibility of a genetic link* to at least one parent, and in some cases both parents. Yet even though using donor eggs involves a loss of genetic connection to the baby for the woman, she still will have *a biological link*. This, in turn, provides a modicum of *control over prenatal health,* because she will have control over the in utero environment, if not the hereditary factor. The *speed of resolving IF* is similar with any treatment, though it can take a bit to choose a donor. Donor insemination is the faster route, while donor eggs tack on additional time as you wait to be matched, then to have your donor screened, and then to cycle. Yet donor gametes—especially in the case of donor eggs—can buy back time in terms of the *importance of maternal age.* A woman over forty has a greater chance of conceiving with a twenty-five-year-old's eggs than she does with her own.

SURROGACY

The other category of third-party reproduction, surrogacy, has its own set of pros and cons in terms of the eight factors being considered. The *cost* of surrogacy can be very expensive, depending on 1) whether you are using a known surrogate and 2) whether you are using gestational surrogacy (your gametes in the surrogate's womb) or traditional surrogacy (the surrogate's egg and womb). In the United States, surrogacy can cost between $40,000 and $60,000. Surrogacy is one of the most common forms of "infertility tourism," with India being a popular destination. Leaving the United States to pursue surrogacy can lower the cost to around $15,000, though there are drawbacks (see the sidebar "Reproductive Outsourcing," in Chapter 10).

Surrogacy holds about the same *certainty of reaching parenthood* as that of any other fertile person in the world trying to have a child. The surrogate may not be infertile, but she still has only around a 25 percent chance of conception each cycle. Therefore, surrogacy doesn't bring absolute *sureness in resolving IF*. If traditional surrogacy is used, the intended mother loses both her *genetic* and *biological link*. If gestational surrogacy is used, the intended mother loses only her biological link.

Surrogacy brings a low amount of *control of prenatal health*, since the in utero environment is controlled by the surrogate rather than the intended parents (though well-written contracts help bring this level to a medium). If this is a known surrogate—perhaps a family member—you may feel as if you have a bit more control than with an unknown surrogate. However, again, as with donor gametes, there is no promise about the *speed of resolving IF*. Surrogacy is certainly a longer route to parenthood, since it takes time to find a surrogate, to go through the requisite testing and legal work, and then to cycle and conceive. Of course, especially with traditional surrogacy, *maternal age* is not a factor at all. Technically, an eighty-year-old could have a child via traditional surrogacy, though she may have trouble finding a surrogate and a lawyer who are willing to make her dreams come true.

Adoption

This path also has so many variables that it make it difficult to place on the financial continuum. When it comes to *cost,* the least expensive form of adoption is foster-to-adopt, especially when adopting a special-needs or older child. In some cases, with tax laws in place on the back end of the process, adoption can be virtually free. International adoption is usually the most expensive, at $20,000 to $30,000. In the middle is domestic adoption of a newborn, which has a wide range of fees, depending on whether you use a full-service agency or do some of the legwork yourself. Domestic adoption can run, on average, between $10,000 and $25,000.

Adoption has the most *certainty of reaching parenthood* out of any of the paths, because the child is not only conceived but also born before the parents step into the picture. The majority of people who pursue adoption end up adopting, but not everyone does, giving it just a medium level of *sureness of resolving IF*.

Yet with adoption, you lose the *possibility of a genetic link or biological link,* and you relinquish any *control over prenatal health.* The average *speed of resolving IF* via adoption varies greatly, but is typically within two years (though it may be longer with some international programs). And within some limits, *maternal age* is not a factor with adoption.

Living Child-Free

This is the least expensive way to resolve your infertility: It's completely free of *cost.* There is also the highest level of *sureness of resolving IF*—it's guaranteed and possibly instantaneous. *Maternal age* is not a factor here: Someone who discovers she is infertile can take this path at age twenty just as easily as she can at age forty. The other categories aren't applicable to this path out of infertility.

All of Chapter 11 is devoted to the choice to live child-free.

A Sample Decision List

In the appendix is a page that you can copy to make a list of your own. Right now, let's look at a sample list and then walk through it. In this list, the lower the number, the higher the priority.

Erica is a twenty-nine-year-old teacher married to John, a thirty-three-year-old teacher; they have been diagnosed with female-factor infertility. As you can see, their ranking order is exactly the same—which makes things easier for them (and for me). I guess our fictional couple were just meant for each other.

	Erica's List	John's List
Cost	3	3
Certainty of Reaching Parenthood	2	2
Sureness of Resolving IF	6	6
Possibility of a Genetic Link	5	5
Possibility of a Biological Link	4	4
Amount of Control over Prenatal Health	1	1
Speed of Resolving IF	6	6
Importance of Maternal Age	6	6

The most important thing to them is control over prenatal health. They are vegetarian nonsmokers who want to have the ultimate control over their in utero environment. This is followed by certainty of reaching parenthood; they will stop at nothing. Next in line is cost. They hate to consider money, but they do have limited finances and poor insurance coverage. They realized while making this list that it is more important to them that Erica experience pregnancy than that they keep the child genetically related to her. Age, time, and sureness are low on their list because they are relatively young and willing to stick with each process until they become parents. They also assume that sureness of resolving their infertility will follow once they become parents.

Since control over prenatal health is the highest priority, their first pick, other than trying unassisted, is treatments—the only path in the table that has a "high" in this category. (When considering your highest priority, anything that is ranked "low" should be dismissed automatically.) They can then move to the second priority: certainty of reaching parenthood. The only option that is ranked "high" in that category is adoption, but that has been ruled out automatically, because adoption is ranked "low" for Erica and John's highest priority. Of the paths ranked "medium" for certainty of reaching parenthood (treatments and third-party reproduction), treatments are the better option, because third-party reproduction ranks only "low" or "medium" in their first-priority category (amount of control over prenatal health). After realizing this, the couple weigh their two top priorities for a minute and decide that "control" still trumps "certainty." Treatments are currently in the lead.

As they move to their third priority, cost, it becomes clear that treatments are the best path for Erica and John. It may not be the fastest route or the most certain route, but it is definitely the one that fits their needs right now.

Creating a Choice Web

Choice webs also take all of the "what ifs" out of your head and place them on paper to allow your mind to let go of the circular, anxious thinking that can happen when big decisions need to be made. They can be used to make small choices within the path you've chosen through the decision list. In addition, however, a "choice web" can be utilized to figure out when to return to your decision list and choose a Plan B.

The choice web is also a technique I taught to my middle schoolers and then borrowed for my own decision-making process.

ESCAPE ROUTES vs. BRICK WALLS

For some people, it feels scary to look ahead at Plan B or C—as if it might jinx their Plan A. This, of course, is magical thinking. It's sort of like going to the movie theater and declaring that you don't want to know the nearest exit—for fear you'll have to use it. But knowing the location of the exit doesn't change the flammability of the building. It does, however, mean that your chances of survival are greater for knowing how to get out quickly, and that you're not going to have to think on your feet if flames do start trailing down the aisle.

Sometimes a person intends to find escape routes, but what they're really doing is building brick walls. Here is the difference:

An escape plan is not a STOP button. It's a segue into the next step or path. Escape plans are feasible and enticing in their own right. Even if they weren't your first choice, they are your best choice. And even if they are not choices that bring you joy, they are choices that bring you peace of heart.

Walls, on the other hand, serve a dual purpose of keeping things out and keeping you in. Limits cause more panic—the internal promise, for example, that this is the *final* IVF attempt.

Where limits bring about second-guessing, escape routes bring about re-lief. The relief may be mixed with other emotions—guilt, sadness, longing—but it is relief nonetheless.

How do you know if you are building a wall or finding an escape route? Walls have limits and negatives built into the phrasing: "I will never . . ." or "We will stop . . ." or "We can't do . . ." whereas escape routes follow an if/then forma-tion. *"If* the RE thinks I have a low chance of conceiving with my eggs, *then* I will start with donor eggs."

If you still feel uneasy about those alternative, backup plans, try this: Set up your next steps—then tuck them away somewhere and revisit them only when the time feels right. It can be freeing to know that a Plan B, C, and D exist, but it can feel overwhelming to focus constantly on those future plans, too.

The first one I ever made had to do with deciding how I wanted to spend the cycle prior to my first appointment with the reproductive endocrinologist (RE). My OB-GYN was giving us the option to try another round of Clomid and progesterone under his guidance. This may seem like a no-brainer—take the Clomid while you wait. But we also knew that we would have limited tries with the Clomid, and we didn't know if we wanted to use one (and maybe waste it) before going through testing with the RE. Making a choice web helped us see that trying another round of Clomid during the wait was the best option. Of course, it seems a little silly, looking back on this web now, that I was worried about using up my Clomid rounds, but during that time, with the information I had on hand, it was an important choice.

The point of a choice web is to literally place all of the possibilities out in front of you, in black and white. You begin with the option at stake inside the main circle. Each line leading off the circle provides a "what if," and the web shows the implications and consequences of each decision.

Let's take my first choice web as an example. We had used the decision list and decided to go the treatments route. I was twenty-eight years old and had already done three rounds of Clomid. The recommendation was to do no more than six rounds of Clomid.

I began by placing the option inside a bubble:

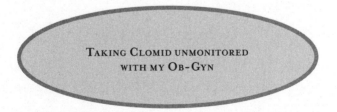

I then drew multiple lines between additional bubbles depicting all of the "what ifs" that could happen by taking this path.

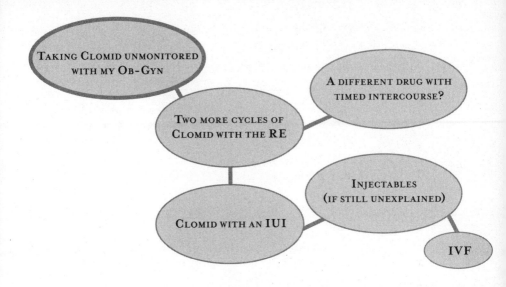

Once I could follow out the consequences of my decision to their ends and see that even the farthest end result sat well with me, I decided to take the Clomid with the OB-GYN while I waited for that first appointment.

In this next example, a hypothetical couple named Amanda and Jesse are given the diagnosis of azoospermia after a third semen analysis.

They place the diagnosis inside the central bubble:

Each line off the central bubble follows out a certain possibility. In making the web, Amanda and Jesse felt that they had three main choices: donor insemination, adoption, or surgery followed by treatments. They didn't include living child-free, because they both determined that they wanted to utilize one of the other paths if possible.

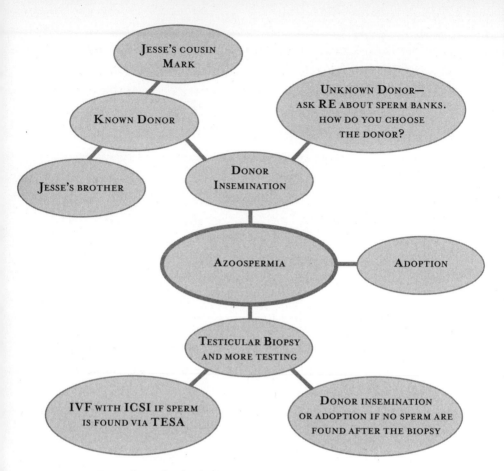

Donor insemination broke down into two choices: known donors (Jesse listed his brother and cousin as possibilities) and unknown donors. Adoption wasn't explored deeply but was placed on the list as an option. The testicular biopsy led to two possibilities. In one, sperm would be found, and they would need to utilize IVF in order to use it. In the other, the surgery was performed and no sperm were found, and they would need to use either donor insemination or adoption in order to become parents.

Once Jesse and Amanda had created the web and could both stare down at the possibilities in black and white, they started to have a conversation, debating the pros and cons of each "what if." In the end, based on their religious beliefs, a fear of nonlifesaving surgery (and the possibility of needing to recover from surgery without the promise that sperm would be found), and a desire to avoid IVF, they went with donor insemination, which they could do with an IUI. They decided to try the known-donor route first, after they created yet another choice web exploring the pros and cons of known versus unknown donor insemination.

Plan Bs and Cs and Sometimes Even Ds

Knowing the right time to move on to another path—or even to take a step further on your current path—is challenging. Choice webs and decision lists can help, but remember: They are only guidelines. Stick to them only as it feels right to do so. Some people recommend making a financial cap or cycle limit, but I think these brick walls bring more anxiety than comfort. It can be very stressful to be facing what you know is your final cycle. At the same time, it's too easy to keep hacking away at the problem without seeing results and driving yourself deeper into debt in the process. Rather than setting a single number, set a range for when you'll revisit the decision to continue, with markers built into the journey. For instance, decide that you'll revisit the idea of continuing treatments every three cycles or every $5,000, and gauge whether you believe it is worth it to go on.

Last Thoughts

Mindful decision making rarely leads to regrets. Frustration and sadness, possibly, but at least you can knock regrets off the table. The point is to always make your decisions while being true to yourself and your needs. After all, you know yourself best and how you would rank the factors in your personal decision list. Go forth and decide with peace of heart.

THE IFFER'S
BILL OF RIGHTS

In Chapter 1, I compared the mainland's adoption agencies, insurance companies, hospitals, and clinics to an out-of-touch colonial government that imposes its rules and taxes on us islanders. Well, here is my response to that tyranny, the Iffer's Bill of Rights. There are three main things you deserve as someone seeking assistance in family building:

1) YOU DESERVE ANSWERS.

If you have questions, you deserve answers to them—and in a timely manner. In the case of treatments, you deserve to be told test results—not just that a beta is positive or negative, but the hCG levels. In the case of an adoption agency or donor program, you deserve to have someone return your call and give you the information you desire.

Unless you are an RE yourself, you must admit that you know less about reproductive endocrinology than the person on the other end of the stirrups does. At the same time, they should be educating you—and you should be educating yourself—so you can help guide your treatments. I certainly don't have a medical degree, but I obviously know a great deal about hormone levels and menstrual cycles. Some of that is from reading and research, but a lot of it is from my very patient and wonderful RE, who took the time to explain the procedures and choices. And this leads to your second right.

2) YOU DESERVE TO BE A PARTNER IN YOUR JOURNEY.

Part of this right depends on your being well read and educating yourself on family building and fertility. The other part of this right depends on the professionals who are aiding you in your process.

Each time your infertility professional lays out the options and lets you help choose the path, you are empowered by knowing you are the most critical member of the team. My RE was great about doing this. To be honest, being so in charge made me feel more responsible for some of the failed cycles . . . but it also made me feel more responsible for the successes. It's true that the doctor or agency is more experienced with the process and probably has more knowledge and information than you—but you also know your head and your heart better than anyone.

It sometimes happens that an infertility professional encourages IFfers to make a decision they're not ready to make. What then? It's a hard call, because if you trust your professional, you know that your best interests are at heart, and that he or she is really just trying to save you heartache or bring you closer to your ultimate goal. However, at the same time, you are not only balancing reality and your medical needs—you are balancing strong emotions about how you envisioned yourself reaching parenthood. There is no easy answer in this situation, except to listen to your doctor's thoughts . . . and then trust your gut. If your gut agrees, fantastic. If it doesn't, you may wish to seek a second opinion. Regardless of what you decide, your infertility professional should be supportive of your decision . . . which brings us to the last point.

3) YOU DESERVE TO BE TREATED WITH RESPECT.

The two other rights also deal with respectful interactions, but what I mean here is that you deserve to have your privacy taken into account, to not feel ridiculed or bullied, and to have your concerns taken seriously.

That said, you also deserve someone who is not going to put you through the wringer simply because you ask to be put through the wringer. You may be rip-roaring ready for IVF, but you (hopefully) also want a doctor who will practice due diligence and walk you through the testing—and ensure there is an actual *need* for IVF before you take the risks inherent in the procedure. Making sound, conservative decisions is part of respecting the patient.

(continued . . .)

IF YOU'RE NOT GETTING these things from your infertility professional, walk over to the phone and call your local Resolve chapter to get a recommendation for a different doctor in your area (see Resources for contact information).

Okay, so essentially firing your doctor or agency isn't easy for everyone. If you're like me at all, assertiveness is not your strong suit. And it's difficult emotionally to leave a clinic midway through treatments, but sometimes it is the best decision a person can make if the clinic or RE is causing stress on top of the normal anxiety fertility treatments involve. If it helps, remember: You're not just sticking up for yourself in this situation—you are also sticking up for your future children.

Remember: Infertility is a consumer industry. Shop wisely.

Chapter 4

REGARDLESS OF WHETHER you've ever openly expressed an interest in children, once you hit your twenties or thirties, the questions (silent and vocal) will come about family-building. It doesn't matter if you are young or old, single or married, gay or straight—people are nosy, and the topic of family-building often arises when you least expect it. The form it takes—telling a married couple that they should get on with the baby making, or mentioning to a single woman that she should freeze her eggs for the future—differs from situation to situation. But outsiders' curiosity about plans for parenthood is something that every person gets to enjoy.

The Four Approaches

There are essentially four approaches to addressing these unspoken and verbalized questions.

- Be PROACTIVE, and talk about the situation *before* being asked,
- be REACTIVE, and talk about the situation *after* being asked,
- be EVASIVE, and avoid talking about the situation after being asked, or
- just LIE through your teeth.

All four are equally valid responses, but each comes with advantages and drawbacks.

The Proactive Approach

This is my own standard approach, probably because of my open personality (I have no qualms about discussing any of my foibles, from my inability to ever master theorems in geometry to my phobia of mayonnaise) and because of my strong belief in passing on useful information. You never know—you may unwittingly be confiding in another secret Iffer, who could end up as a great source of understanding and inspiration.

This level of openness comes with a lot of advantages. First off, you don't have to worry about having your privacy breached with intrusive questions if you bring up a topic first—it's kind of like a preemptive strike. Also, since there are so many in the know, you have a wide selection of people to choose from when you need to vent about a particular frustration. You may be pleasantly surprised by the level of support—logistical, emotional, and even financial— you have without even asking for it. (For example, my mailbox is often stuffed with unsolicited article clippings about the latest in fertility technology.)

But there are drawbacks to being so open. You may feel as if you have little or no privacy. Even if you're a person who generally doesn't mind that, there will probably be days when you *do* mind, and when you just don't want to talk, or even think, about your infertility. But, based on the precedents you've set, people may think they can bring up the subject anytime, anywhere. In addition, news—both good and bad—may be spread before you're ready to share it. (For example, even if you wanted to keep a pregnancy under wraps for a few months, it will be hard to keep it a secret if everyone knows when you're awaiting your beta results.) Lastly, the slew of unsolicited advice, though well intentioned, can get annoying, even for the most patient people. (For good advice on handling bad advice, see Chapter 5.)

The Reactive Approach

This tactic bears many similarities to the "don't ask, don't tell" policy of the U.S. military: You provide the information only if someone provides the question.

With the Reactive Approach, you get many of the same advantages of support as with the aforementioned Proactive Approach, but fewer people end up knowing your business. And although you'll have a few curious bystanders whose inherent nosiness means they learn the intimate details of your last sperm count or are knowledgeable about your wonky ovaries, for the most part the people who ask about your progress toward parenthood are people who actually care about whether you reach your goal.

But probably even more disadvantageous than the Proactive Approach is that with the Reactive Approach, you don't really get to spread the news on your own terms. When you wait for people to ask, they essentially get to choose the timing of when the information is released to them. And it could be perfect timing (such as at an intimate coffee date at your place) or not-so-perfect timing (such as during Cousin Lisa's Bat Mitzvah). Either way, the "when and where" are out of your hands . . . unless you push off the questions until later, which brings us to the next approach.

TALKING TO KIDS
ABOUT INFERTILITY

If you are experiencing infertility and you already have children, you're probably going to have to make a decision—or a series of decisions—about how much to tell them. After all, children are very intuitive and notice pockets of stress. Chances are, there's going to be some explaining to do. Whether you're honest about it or not is up to you: Only you know what's best for your family in the given situation. If you do decide to let them in on what's going on, here is some advice I came up with—unfortunately, through trial and error with my own family.

- Rather than dumping a lot of information in their laps, let them ask questions. This allows them to guide the conversation to fulfill their own needs. They may not actually want to hear about your woes and are asking only that you assuage their fears.
- When it comes to talking about future brothers or sisters, avoid making any promises you might not be able to keep.
- Reassure them that you love them and you're not attempting to replace them.
- Avoid using the word "secret." That word usually connotes something shameful, scary, or wrong. You can frame it as "home information" (something we talk about inside our home, when guests aren't visiting), as opposed to "outside information" (something we discuss outside the home).
- Pay attention to your body language. Breathe deeply through the conversation to make sure that the information is coming across clearly and matter-of-factly— so that it doesn't become overwhelming for a little listener.
- If you're too emotional to have the conversation when they ask, make sure you explain 1) why you don't want to speak and 2) when you will sit down with them to talk about it.

- Check that your children understood the conversation by asking them to repeat back what they heard. This is a chance to correct any misunderstood information.

Even if you do all this, and do it well, you can expect that questions will pop up at random times, and that you will need to field them with aplomb. As for me? Well, I can't promise that my children will emerge unscathed by their knowledge about my infertility . . . but they seem to be doing a fine job so far.

The Evasive Approach

Some people are naturals at this maneuver, which involves tricks such as answering questions with questions, changing the subject, or coming up with vague responses that actually reveal nothing. Others, however, have to practice. If this is you, see below for some sample evasive responses to prying questions.

The advantages are pretty obvious: If you play your cards close to your chest, you risk less and have more freedom to lead, rather than react. You can go to a family dinner without fielding questions about your latest IVF cycle. When you're hurting after a negative beta, you don't have to spread the news by repeating the story to twelve different people. In the end, if privacy is your major concern, this is the approach you should take, because you can always reveal more later. In fact, it can be very useful to employ the Evasive Approach until you know how you feel about people knowing the intimate details of your anatomy.

However, this method can backfire. Iffers who utilize the Evasive Approach tend to get more questions in the long run, because many people are nosy. They also make hurtful assumptions, such as "Since I don't see you making babies, you must not even care about starting a family." It can be frustrating to hear these words when you know how hard you have been trying to become a parent.

TIP: If you like the idea of the Evasive Approach but aren't particularly practiced in the art of avoidance, here are some responses to get you started:

- "That is a really interesting question! Actually, before I forget, did you know that X is pregnant?"
- "Why? Are you trying?"
- "That requires a long answer. Actually, I wanted to hear about your new job."
- "Babies . . . I guess spring makes everyone think about babies. I was at the post office the other day, and . . . "

The Liar's Approach

I truly believe there are instances in life where lying is the preferable option to telling the truth. And when it comes to talking about your infertility, there are plenty such instances. The only cases where lying about infertility is *never* condoned is when it's to someone in the situation with you, such as a partner, surrogate, medical professional, or adoption agency employee. Otherwise, the choice is yours. If evasive techniques have not worked and being honest would bring more stress than support into your life, *I give you full permission to lie.*

Of course, lying means that you need to remember a random

story and false details and possibly invent more lies in the future. It means that if you are found out, you can lose face and possibly lose trust. But seriously, sometimes these disadvantages are worthwhile, especially when the person asking

- has inflexible beliefs or opinions—and feels the need to remind you about them;
- has a personal agenda regarding your fertility situation;
- is hypercritical by nature;
- is liable to steal the Follistim you're storing in an unmarked brown paper bag in your refrigerator.

Sometimes, the Liar's Approach is for the benefit of the person you're lying to, not you. Let's say you didn't tell Grandma initially about your donor gametes because you thought she might discourage you or tell you it was abominable. When and if you do decide to tell her, there is no need to insult her. Instead, go with a reason that is about you instead of the person you're telling.

An example might be "We always wanted to tell you, and we could have used your support years ago, but we wanted the baby to be the first person told." If you're not waiting to tell your child first, another excuse that works is "We wanted to wait until we were sure about everything, until we were holding our child in our arms. We know you probably would have said that everything would be fine, but we simply weren't comfortable letting go until we were parents."

The fact is, you never owe someone all the details about your life. But that doesn't mean that someone won't act emotionally or be deeply hurt when they discover you've withheld important information. If a white lie makes them feel better and allows them to accept the information, that's all that matters. The point, as always, is to do what you need to do without creating more problems to deal with on the other side.

TIP: Here are some sample fibs you may find useful at some point during your stay in the Land of If.

SITUATION: You're sore after a retrieval, and someone asks you why you're walking so gingerly.
LIE: "I pulled a muscle in my back."

SITUATION: You have to go upstairs for a few minutes to give yourself an injection.
LIE: "Excuse me, I have to go make an important work-related phone call. My boss is so annoying."

SITUATION: At a big gathering of family or friends, you are suddenly experiencing an early loss and have to go to the hospital.
LIE: "I think I ate some bad shellfish earlier today; I'm going to the doctor."

The last lie—food poisoning—has a bonus effect. If you have to return later that day to the gathering, you can retire to your room, knowing full well that no one wants to be near someone who smells like vomit. And it's good for other situations. Use it to get out of the house for a transfer if family members have descended on your house midcycle. If you come down with ovarian hyperstimulation syndrome, use it to explain why you need to be cooped up in your room. Use it to get out of a baby shower at the last minute. The point is to come up with an excuse that makes people want to leave you alone, no questions asked—though they may start wondering where you're eating if you claim "food poisoning" every cycle.

Which Approach to Use, and When

So how do you know which approach is best for you overall? Well, you may end up with a blend of all four choices. After all, your tactic will probably vary on a case-by-case or person-by-person basis. You may tell many people in one area of your life, behave reactively in another, evade the question at work, and lie through your teeth to your nosy aunt.

When considering which approach to use in a certain situation, remember these things:

• IT IS NOT YOUR RESPONSIBILITY to satiate another person's curiosity. There needs to be something gained by telling, and while it may be a gain for both parties, it definitely needs to be a gain for you. It also needs to be a personal choice, and telling should never be a response to outside pressure.

HANDLING NEWS
IN PUBLIC

Most of the time when you're receiving IF-related bad news (and hopefully good news), you will be receiving it during business hours, since those are the times when offices are open. Unfortunately, it is also the time when you are probably at work. Which means you need to find a way to deal with your subsequent emotions without having to explain sperm counts and hCG levels to your coworkers.

Some people are excellent at compartmentalizing their emotions and dealing with them later. I'm not. I'm a cry-in-the-moment-and-get-it-out sort of person. But crying leads to questions. Even if you can hide your tears, it's hard to hide puffy eyes and a red, stuffy nose. If you're a prep cook at a restaurant, you might be able to say you were chopping onions, but it's a lot more difficult to explain away if you work in IT.

The fastest solution is to exit the bathroom holding a box of allergy medicine in hand, sighing as you pass each person in the hallway and grumbling about your sinuses. A slower solution is to drink a lot of water to flush out your system (and by the time you consume a liter of water, the swelling will have gone down on its own). Press cold water against your eyes, since cold shrinks and compresses puffiness. Better still is to find cold milk in the office refrigerator, soak two cotton balls, and place them on your eyes for a moment (perhaps bring the drink with you to the bathroom if you have the forethought before the cry).

And the last option, which may be the best option, is simply telling the truth. Explain that you received some bad news but don't want to talk about it. People can understand the concept of bad news and the lack of desire to discuss it, and you may find that you gather more empathy and space by being forthcoming from the start.

- **TMI IS IN THE EYE OF THE BEHOLDER.** What's considered to be "too much information" varies from person to person. Private people often prefer that everyone else operate on the same level of privacy, and may be uncomfortable if you start sharing your estrogen levels with them at a dinner party. Conversely, people who tell even the cashier at the supermarket their own health woes may not understand why you don't want to do the same.

- **ALL CONFIDANTS ARE NOT CREATED EQUAL.** When choosing whom to tell and whom not to tell, you obviously need to consider who's asking the question—especially if you are expecting something in return, such as thoughtfulness, a shoulder to cry on, a cheerleader . . . or a zipped lip. Consider the person's abilities and desires. If they're not the sort who can be supportive, they're not a good well from which to try to draw support, plain and simple. And gossips probably will not be able to keep the news to themselves, no matter how much they swear up and down that mum's the word, and no matter how much they actually want to keep your secret. Bottom line: Don't expect people to change just for your situation.

Some Iffers find it easier to tell acquaintances and strangers on the Internet than family members or close friends, simply because the expectation is different. After all, a lame reaction from your father is a lot more devastating than a lame reaction from HopefulMama2009.

And just because you told your sister doesn't mean you have to tell your brother. And just because you've told half the world online anonymously doesn't mean that you need to share the same information with family and friends face-to-face. (Just remember to weigh whether you'll be creating more problems for yourself down the road.) If you are being open with only some people in your life, and not others, you may want to make it expressly clear that the information should not be shared with anyone else. (Incidentally, I suggest saying "anyone else" as opposed to getting specific by naming those to be excluded. It's clearer that way.)

How to Break Your IF News

Although it's memorable to share your news with others by hiring a singing telegram or buying a JumboTron announcement, most Iffers elect to bring up the topic of their infertility through more traditional methods of communication.

- FACE-TO-FACE DISCUSSIONS are advantageous in that they give you immediate feedback, as well as clues from body language. But they also require both speakers to think quickly on their feet, and you always have to consider the possibility that you will be interrupted, or that the topic will be changed before you can communicate what you want to.
- PHONE CALLS give you a modicum of personal space within the conversation. The other people can't see you cry or doodle pictures of them with X's through their faces. But they still contain the same drawbacks of a face-to-face conversation.
- EMAILS OR LETTERS are the perfect medium for people who need time to shape their thoughts. But with these mediums, you have to wait for a response . . . for who knows how long. Plus, the person you wrote may not respond at all, necessitating a strained follow-up "Didn't you get my message?" note.

With all three mediums, start the conversation or note by *asking for attention*. Phrases such as "I have something to tell you that is really hard for me to talk about" give the listener or reader the heads-up to get serious and prepare themselves for important information.

Next, *state your expectations* before you give the information. You'll state some of them again later, when you end the conversation or note, but take a moment in the beginning to tell them why you're telling them. It may be because you want support, or because you think they could benefit from hearing about your situation. By stating your expectations, you're giving the person a chance to fulfill them and to respond appropriately. An example would be:

> *I don't want you to try to solve my problem or offer solutions; I just want you to listen, because I need a lot of support right now. And I want to ask you to keep this discreet. I don't mind if you tell Uncle Paul, but no one else.*

Next, *impart the actual information*—that you're starting treatments, that you used donor sperm, that you've decided to pursue adoption, whatever. If you think it will help, you can make it easier for them by telling them that you know it's a difficult subject, and that you understand if they're a little floored by the information.

Finally, *repeat your expectations as needed* at the end of the conversation or at the end of the note. You can even spoon-feed them their response by telling them exactly what you need to hear in return. If you're sending an email and you definitely want at least some kind of reply, include a small note explaining that you don't need a long response; you simply need a note to let you know that they received and read your email.

Last Thoughts

Even in the best of circumstances, you're bound to be disappointed by a reaction every once in a while. The bad reaction can go numerous ways.

They might act as if you've never confided in them, avoid the topic completely in future conversations, and even feign memory loss over this thing that may have been excruciatingly difficult for you to say in the first place. They may diminish your feelings or tell you to put your problems behind you. They may pass judgment, telling you how they feel about your choices or trying to change your mind about decisions you've already made. They may not keep your confidences. In worst-case scenarios, they may distance themselves from you, reject your children, or say hateful things to end the relationship. The scale of disappointment is vast and varied.

On the other hand, they may become too involved, asking more questions than you're comfortable answering. They may want to help you make decisions. Both situations can be very difficult: It's no easier to be suffocated with help than it is to be drowning without a lifeline.

What do you do when someone disappoints you? Well, obviously, you can either address it or keep silent. If you already stated your expectations and people haven't stepped up to the plate, you can decide whether you think they would be more receptive to the message if you repeated it. If not, it's best to move on and remain more circumspect with them in the future—their lack of reaction or their breach of trust is their loss of information.

Remember, you are trying to get through this by doing what you need to do and not creating more stress for yourself along the way.

Luckily, there will also be a lot of people who surprise you: who say the right thing or give you great advice or show up at your door with a pint of ice cream the day you get a negative, just to keep you company. The fact that a good experience is equally possible is what makes me open my mouth and tell people time after time.

Chapter 5

THE
ROAD TO HELL
IS PAVED WITH
"JUST RELAX!"

ONCE PEOPLE HEAR that you've moved to the Land of If, they'll start telling you about *other* people's travels through infertility, regardless of how related these stories are to your experience. Chances are that among the excellent information, you will also receive plenty of information that is ignorant, hurtful, or just plain strange. Chances are that people will speak without thinking. Or they *will* think, but will still end up saying insensitive things. Or they will give terrible advice—over and over and over again—as if it gets more helpful or charitable with each repetition.

This chapter is all about the stupid things people say to Iffers. And although my own impatience, frustration, and snarkiness pervade this chapter, I want to just let you know that I know, all too well, that no one is perfect, and that we have all done our fair share of putting our foot in it. The key to surviving this bit of your adventure in the Land of If is in how you respond.

The Three-Strikes Approach

The verbal bomb has been dropped, the moment of silence follows, and now you need to respond to the advice that was just served up like a skunked beer.

When it comes to your response, speech does have the distinct advantage that it can't be read over and over again by the person, inciting more anger with each run-through of your words. The disadvantage, however, is that once spoken, the words are gone and cannot be dredged up as proof of your incredible politeness and impressive rationale in the face of such uncouth commentary. If the offending person decides to complain to others about your ungratefulness in the face of their excellent advice, you'll have no hard evidence to back you up.

When the unwanted advice or hurtful comments come in spoken form, the challenge is greater, since you need to think on your feet. If you're anything like me, this is tough. When I get emotional, I get tongue-tied. That's why it's a good idea to keep a few sample responses in your figurative back pocket, so you can pull them out at the appropriate moment.

The point is to nip the unwanted conversation in the bud. But more than one attempt may be required. Here's how I recommend you proceed:

1) Start with kind.
2) Move to firm.
3) In the event that #1 and #2 fail to solve the problem, you have two choices: walk away . . . or bump the conversation up to the "free-for-all" level.

PICKING YOUR BATTLES

By the time I got to treatments, I'd already gathered a huge amount of information on infertility. I had read the books, clipped the magazine articles, and watched every *Oprah* episode covering any aspect of the subject. I'd quizzed pregnant women at the grocery store, begged my doctor for tests, and posted three thousand questions on bulletin boards.

During that time, I got a lot of great information from others who had done or were currently doing time on this island . . . but I also got a lot of terrible information from people who had never been there even once. Let's just say that advice is best given by someone who has experience in the area, rather than someone who has read a single article and now thinks that she can biopsy your testes or thread a catheter through your cervix.

You can try to be proactive about this problem by informing people who know about your situation what is and isn't okay to say—what you don't want to hear, and what you do want to hear.

Of course, you never want people to feel as if they have to walk on eggshells around you—after all, you do want their love and support, and that's hard to get if your friends and family keep you at arm's distance for fear of upsetting you. And sometimes, no matter how explicit you are about what you consider helpful and what you consider hurtful, chances are that someone, somewhere, sometime is going to say something that will be worthy of a full blog post to muse on the fact that you can't *believe* they said that.

Throughout your stay here, you're going to need to remind yourself to be forgiving, because everyone makes mistakes. But most of all, remember to clearly distinguish the intentional stings from the unintentional mistakes. It always sucks to be on the receiving end of a hurtful question or comment—but don't let the unintentional mistakes carry the same emotional weight as the intentional ones. It's a hard journey, and you're going to need all the support you can get.

Of course, as your island etiquette adviser, I am going to officially recommend that you simply walk away from the matter and ignore any further attempts from said person to engage you on the subject if the first two attempts fail. Unofficially, I encourage you to respond in any way you wish (short of the criminal, perhaps), as long as you're willing to accept the consequences.

What You May Hear, and What You May Say

Now let's take a look at the most common pieces of advice or commentary passed along to inhabitants of the Land of If. For each type of idiot comment, I've given you sample responses for each step: first time, kind; second time, firm; third time, free-for-all.

"If You Just Stop Trying, It Will Happen."

Despite the all-American "winners never quit" attitude, people in this country love to offer the advice of "stopping" as a cure-all for infertility: "I know someone who quit treatments, and the next month she became pregnant—with twins!" Or: "Just stop thinking about it so much, and it'll happen." Or, one of my all-time favorites: "What you really need is a vacation." As if the entire medical community were participating in a massive conspiracy to make innocent people undergo ICSI, when all they really need to do is go scuba diving.

The "stop trying" mentality is the same sort of magical thinking described by "a watched pot never boils." But, as we all know very well, a pot—whether watched or not—will never boil if the stovetop isn't *working*. The most insidious aspect of this kind of statement is that it places the blame squarely on your shoulders: Instead of a low sperm count or polycystic ovaries, your inability

THE LAND OF IF VISITORS BUREAU

TIP: I know I've said that bad advice usually comes from people who have never even once stepped foot onto the Land of If. But don't dismiss all advice just because it doesn't come from an insider to the experience. After all, you may be speaking to the world's wisest and most empathetic fertile person.

Also, keep your ear to the ground for any non-IF-related advice that could be applied to your own situation. Remember back in Chapter 2, where I gave you that great advice that my sister gave me? Well, what I didn't say then was that she said that not in regard to my infertility, but in regard to my dating angst. Sometimes, nuggets of wisdom can be applied elsewhere to great effect.

to have a child is now due to your ridiculously overwrought neurotic tendencies. Nice.

KIND: "I wish it were that easy."

FIRM: "I guess that might help if there weren't actual medical issues at hand."

FREE-FOR-ALL: "I never thought of that. Probably because I got a C+ in Magical Thinking 101."

"Aren't You a Little Old?"

Conception is a catch-22: if you're under thirty-five, people can't push you into Strollerville fast enough. If you're over thirty-five—especially if you're passing forty—the question "Do you think this is a good idea?" is asked with the same nose scrunching that accompanies asking someone if they think that the milk smells funny.

If it took a long time for you to find a partner, if you're choosing to start a family on your own later in life, or if you waited to start your family because it was the right choice in your relationship, it can be incredibly frustrating to have your wish to become a parent second-guessed—as if life and time were entirely within your control. Questions and comments such as "Aren't you worried the baby won't be healthy?" "Do you really want to be sixty when your child graduates?" or "I heard you're more likely to have multiples or miscarry at your age" are just plain rude.

KIND: "Well, isn't that sweet of you to be concerned, but no, I'm not worried at all."

FIRM: "That's not helpful for me to hear. I've obviously already made my decision."

FREE-FOR-ALL: "Eh? What's that? I seem to be losing my hearing in my old age."

"Why Can't You Just Be Happy with the Kids You Have?"

Those experiencing secondary infertility (either on the heels of primary infertility or after an easy time conceiving the first) are between a rock and a hard place. They are asked questions that no one would *imagine* posing to someone who can conceive easily: "How can you focus on fertility treatments/adoption when you have kids who need you?" and "Aren't you happy with what you have?"

Of *course* you're happy with what you have—that is precisely why you are willing to try things such as treatments or adoption in order to build your family. What you need are offers of baby-sitting, or meals dropped off at the house. What you don't need is someone questioning the love you have for your family just because you wish to expand it.

This is a great time to pretend to hear your child calling for you. But if that doesn't work and you need to respond to this inane line of questioning, remember to move through the three tiers: kindness, firmness, and then a free-for-all—which may or may not include siccing a teething toddler on the offending person for good measure.

KIND: "I love my child(ren). That's why we're working so hard for another."

FIRM: "Definitely appreciative, but I shouldn't have to defend my reasons for another child."

FREE-FOR-ALL: "Well, I really wanted a second husband/wife, but a second child is *so* much cheaper."

"It Could Be Worse."

This nasty type of comment is an unwelcome invitation to enter your recent loss into the Pain Olympics. It usually comes in the form of stories comparing your situation with someone else's:

"I knew someone who had *three* miscarriages!"

(Spoken after you've told someone about your second loss.)

"My coworker lost a child at *twenty-five weeks*—that would be *so* much worse."

(As if an early loss were somehow lucky.)

"My friend has been trying for *eight years* and has gone through *five* IVF cycles! Can you *imagine?"*

(As if four years and two IVF cycles were a walk in the park.)

These types of comments often elicit an even deeper emotional response than most. The reason is simple: No one wants their painful feelings to be dismissed. No one wants to open their heart and share what they are feeling with another person and have the response be an invalidation of their emotions.

We Iffers do enough damage to ourselves by minimizing our own situations internally, and by beating ourselves up for feeling the emotions of infertility or loss so intensely. We certainly don't need others to do that too, and this human trait of telling people, "Cheer up, it's not that bad!" can have a terrible impact on the mourning process. Feel what you feel without allowing the other person to make you feel guilty about your emotions. Your response may need to be a figurative closing of the door if the other person is not going to respect your world.

KIND: "That is terrible/wonderful for *them."*

FIRM: "That is a terrible thing, but I'm not sure how what happened to someone else affects my situation."

"Maybe I'm not the best person to hear these stories. It feels as if my situation is being minimized."

FREE-FOR-ALL: "I assume it always makes you feel good when someone dismisses your feelings? That's why you're doing it to me?"

"But the Baby Looks Absolutely *Nothing* Like You!"

Those who don't know you've used donor gametes will often point out this fact as they play everyone's favorite baby game: who does he/she look like? Even those who do know that you've utilized donor gametes may bring this up. It works best to steer the conversation away from physical traits and point out the similarities you do have in common.

KIND: "He may not look like me, but he certainly has my sleep habits."
FIRM: "You know what, we prefer not to focus on who he/she looks like and instead allow our child to be his/her own person."
FREE-FOR-ALL: "We're just grateful that the baby doesn't look like you."

"Since You Chose to Live Child-Free, You Must Have Not Really Wanted to Be a Parent."

This is one of the huge myths that cast a shadow on this path: that the lengths you're willing to go equal the amount you want to parent. The truth is that it takes a lot of emotional fortitude—as well as a great deal of self-knowledge—to not put on the infertility blinders and be led through cycle after cycle after cycle. There are those who do treatments—many treatments—mindfully, fully aware of their intent and what they are enduring. There are others who continue cycling because they don't know how to stop. Being willing to stop does not make you less committed to the idea of parenting. It simply places you as equivalent to the former group, yet on a divergent path. Both groups are led by mindfulness rather than reflex.

I don't think there is a proper kind or free-for-all response to this statement. There is only the simple, firm remark "Well, you have that completely wrong" that can meet this level of misunderstanding.

"I Know You Said You're Living Child-Free. But It Could Still Always Happen!"

Living child-free is not about inactively trying. It is about consciously moving away from the goal of parenthood and focusing energy on other aspects of life. People may not understand this at first, and may make statements like this because they think they give you hope. Gently correct their way of thinking by moving from kind to firm to a free-for-all.

KIND: "Oh, I think you misunderstand; we are moving away from trying entirely, and we are living child-free."
FIRM: "No, it couldn't. We have chosen not to try anymore."
FREE-FOR-ALL: "Not gonna happen—unless you secretly poke holes into the condoms we're now using . . . and then I miraculously become fertile again."

"I'm Sorry You Miscarried. But You Can Always Try Again!"

The future—a point that is not emotionally painful—is a favorite place for people to direct you toward when you tell them about your loss. Gently remind them that you're not looking toward the future yet; you're just here in the moment and you're in a lot of emotional pain. You aren't certain whether you'll try again or not. For now, you're focusing on what is happening in the moment, instead of on what you may or may not do in the future. Lastly, remind them that one pregnancy does not replace another. People are irreplaceable.

KIND: "Perhaps, but that is beside the point right now."
FIRM: "We're focused on mourning this loss, not thinking about future children."
FREE-FOR-ALL: "I didn't know you viewed people as entirely replaceable."

"It Wasn't a Real Baby"

I'm not sure how much more "real" babies can get, since they're all composed of skin and organs and blood and bones. Some people may bring their political viewpoints to the discussion, and those who think it's an appropriate time to tell you when they think life begins are probably not the best people to look to for comfort during a crisis.

KIND: "We don't see this in the same way at all, so perhaps we shouldn't discuss it."
FIRM: "It's pretty cruel to say something like that to me when I am obviously in mourning."
FREE-FOR-ALL: "I always forget that you put your political views before people's feelings. I need to get a tattoo as a reminder so I don't make the mistake of opening up to you again."

"It's Morbid to Keep Focusing on the Loss. You Need to Move On."

Focusing on the loss and not living life are two separate issues in my book. A parent may still honor and remember a lost child many years down the line. There may be moments of sadness as you go about your day, and you may have an overwhelming need to speak about the lost child for months or years after the loss. These are all normal responses. I think it is healthier to deal with the emotions than to sweep them under the rug. No one should rush you through the mourning process.

KIND: "I need to mourn on my own timetable."
FIRM: "We have very different definitions of 'morbid,' and I think we see 'moving on' in a different way, too."
FREE-FOR-ALL: "Have you considered writing a book about the mourning process, since you have such better ideas than those other hack psychologists?"

"Maybe This Is Nature's Way of Telling You Something."

Yes, everyone knows how wood nymphs are notorious for smiting the unworthy with infertility. But with so many unplanned teenage pregnancies—and so many unwanted pregnancies in general—one has to wonder whether there's any rhyme or reason to their system of justice . . . or whether they really just want to make sure that *Jerry Springer* stays on the air for all eternity.

The reason this kind of statement really sucks is that it's probably something you've already mulled over on your own. Who doesn't wonder whether they're somehow being cosmically punished for stealing gum at age five? Even if your rational mind knows that's ridiculous, your emotional heart might present a very strong argument, dredging up past transgressions galore.

Allow me to intercede: You are *not* being punished, by the wood nymphs, by Mother Nature, by the universe, by Krishna or the Earth Mother or G-d. If you do believe that there is a larger plan in place, it may be helpful to reframe this thought as *I'm still en route.* My mother is fond of saying, "All will be fine in the end, and if it's not fine, it's not the end." This may be the route you want to take in addressing this statement. Here are some other sample responses.

KIND: "Who could possibly know what the bigger plan is?"
FIRM: "Ouch. Do you really think an unwed pregnant teenager deserves parenthood more than I do?"
FREE-FOR-ALL: "I know. It sucks. If I had known that G-d was going to kill all of my babies, I wouldn't have peed in Mrs. Casper's flower garden."

"Aren't You Worried about Having a Litter?"

Back when we were trying the first time, as my consolation prize for not being able to maintain a pregnancy, a friend bought me a gift certificate for a massage at a fancy-shmancy spa. As I was lying on the table, the masseuse asked if I had any problem areas, and I warned her that my stomach was bruised and sore from injectable medications. As she kneaded my shoulders, temples, and back, I received a fifty-minute lecture—on how I was going to "end up with seventeen children" from fertility treatments. Soooo relaxing.

The media loves the dramatic—octuplets and IVF-gone-wrong horror stories. After all, it just doesn't make for good TV to do a feature story on a nice couple who wanted a child and did IVF and ended up with a singleton and lived happily ever after. As a result of the media, the typical noninfertile person's understanding of IVF is somewhat sensationalized. The masseuse (a typical noninfertile person) had no other frame of reference, and therefore could only visualize the opposumization of me—probably even with a bit of excitement and satisfaction about the punishments that come to people who play around with fertility drugs.

KIND: "We'd be happy with whatever we get."
FIRM: "I think you know that isn't at all possible."
FREE-FOR-ALL: "Can't fit that in a minivan, can you?"
"I'll warn my doctor to transfer only sixteen embryos."

"Why Don't You Just Adopt?"

Whenever I hear this question, I immediately picture myself throwing one of those heavy adoption books at the perpetrator and yelling: "If it's *just* adoption, that shouldn't cause too much of a bruise, right?"

Even if you haven't begun exploring this path yet, you've probably gotten a sense by visiting online communities that there is no "just" in adoption. It is a very difficult process—emotionally, financially, and physically—and there are very real people with very real

TIP: As I've stated elsewhere, during your stay on the island, you may hear the same rude comment, question, or advice—again and again and again—from different people. For example, if you're in a relationship, you will at some point probably have to field the ever-offensive question "Whose fault/problem is it?" That's why, to clear up any confusion, I often wear a T-shirt that says ASK ME ABOUT MY WONKY OVARIES.

"Fault" is such an ugly term that divides an undividable situation into right and wrong. Instead, take the united-front approach and keep repeating, "It's our problem" or, "Our diagnosis is simply infertility." No one is entitled to know the medical reason behind the joint diagnosis.

emotions involved. This is a situation that requires a long-term commitment and should be explored only with wide eyes and an open heart. In other words, it is never a quick fix to parenthood, nor should it be treated as such.

Even worse is the horribly self-righteous "How can you do treatments when there are so many children who need homes?" Parents are not saviors—they are merely people raising children. And all parents or parents-to-be should be afforded the right to build their family in a way that works for all members. Without an outsider's input.

KIND: "I can tell you don't know the ins and outs of adoption. Do you want me to point you toward some good websites so you can understand better?"

FIRM: "It doesn't sound like it would be helpful to get into this conversation with you. Why don't we talk about something else?"

FREE-FOR-ALL: Smile brightly and say, "We would *love* to adopt, but we're awful people."

Yet another variation on this is "Once you adopt, you'll get pregnant." (Are they insinuating that you should adopt just so that you can conceive?!) Tiresome as it is, this is a statement that demands that you educate the guilty party. People who make statements like this aren't exactly the type of people who like to research their facts, so tell them yourself: There is *no* connection between adoption and pregnancy. The number of those who conceive after adoption is the exact same as the number of those who are infertile and conceive without treatments after not adopting: around 8 percent.[1]

"What If They Grow Up and Want to Find Their Real Mom/Dad?"

I am making this huge leap and assuming that you are not a robot or a blow-up doll (if you are, please skip this section because the question may be valid), and therefore you are . . . real. Yet those who adopt or build their family through third-party reproduction hear this question all the time. The obvious answer is that you are the real mom or dad. After all, it takes someone real, someone made of flesh and bone, to take care of a child. There is space in your child's world or history for a multitude of people, but you are the mommy or daddy. Take a deep breath before you try to answer this one.

KIND: "Then they'll find me in the living room. I'm their real mom/dad."

FIRM: "Using the term 'real' implies that I'm somehow fake. Is that what you meant?"

FREE-FOR-ALL: "What if *your* kids grow up and want to find a better mom/dad?"

"I Know *Exactly* How You Feel."

True, it might blow his mind, but even a stoned college freshman considers how *his* blue might not be the same as *your* blue. So how can sober, rational, grown-up minds truly believe that they can definitively know what something is like for another person?

"I know exactly how you feel" comes from a place of empathy. It is human nature to want to empathize with people in pain and make them feel less alone. Yet there are some things we need to walk alone, and one of these things is grief. The grief inherent in infertility and loss is personal and unique to each individual.

KIND: "I know you're trying to understand."

FIRM: "You couldn't possibly know, and that's okay—I don't truly know how you feel when things happen to you, though it's good to sit together and try to understand."

FREE-FOR-ALL: "I totally forgot about all of those miscarriages and D&Cs you went through, Uncle Jack. I mean, before they took out your uterus."

"You're So Lucky You Don't Have Kids."

I cannot tell you how many times people tried to make me feel better about my childless state by complaining about their children. If it wasn't about how much they wanted to strangle their offspring, it was statements like "You're so lucky that you can travel whenever

"MY PSYCHIC
   SAID . . ."

The polar opposite of when people disregard your feelings is when they take them deep into the future, promising that this cycle will be the *one,* that the *next* phone call will be from your adoption agency, saying, "Congratulations!" or that you will be a parent soon—simply because they feel it in their bones.

Statements such as "You two will be next!" or "I just know that this cycle is going to work" are like candy—they taste great, but they have no nutritional value and often make you feel crappy later. Every once in a while, this kind of statement can be just what you need to hear. When you need a dose of hope, comments like these are perfect. But when you just need to lick your wounds, hearing things like these can be infuriating.

I recommend that you remain in the "kind" zone with these. Stave them off by saying, "We're just taking it one day at a time" or by gently correcting them, emphasizing the word "hope":

THEY SAY: "I just *know* you're going to be parents by the end of this year!"
YOU SAY: "We *hope* that we're going to be parents one day."

THEY SAY: "This cycle is the one! I feel it in my bones."
YOU SAY: "I *hope* that this cycle works."

It is always good to have hope, and it is always good to work hard at your goal. But part of this process is also knowing when you need to turn off hope, and people who wish to support you need to understand that, too.

you want" and "Spend a day with my kids, and you'll run screaming from that fertility clinic."

While it may be true that the children of your friends and family are complete nightmares, it's strange to be called "lucky" when you're doing nightly injections and shelling out thousands of dollars to achieve what they did so easily and freely. And it's hard not to feel bitter when confronted with braglaining—that nasty combination of bragging and complaining: "I just wish I didn't have *aaaaaaaall* of this money to spend. It is just *sooooooooooooo* exhausting to be *sooooooooooooo* rich."

While it may be a little numbing and difficult to be so rich—in children or money—since you don't know, you'll have to simply run through the three responses instead.

KIND: "That sounds really hard."
FIRM: "If being a parent is so bad, why'd you have a second child?"
FREE-FOR-ALL: "I'd be happy to take little Tommy off your hands. Should we go upstairs and pack a bag for him? Do you have any diapers you can lend me until I can do a Target run?"

"I Don't Understand How She Could Give Up This Baby."

This is not dissimilar to "This baby is so lucky to have you." Both of these comments are meant to point out your greatness as a parent, and both are hurtful in their own unique ways. The truth is that we can never know how it felt for that particular person to create an adoption plan—even if we are birth parents ourselves. Each person is unique and goes through his or her own emotional process. A family *is* lucky to come together, but the phrase above implies that the child was somehow unlucky to be born into that first family. Each family has its own foibles and strengths. Children are not lucky or unlucky when it comes to their family.

KIND: "I can't even begin to imagine how difficult it was for her."

FIRM: "I'm sure you meant to say 'create an adoption plan,' which conveys the difficult decision, right?"

FREE-FOR-ALL: "It's funny that you don't understand how she gave up her baby, because I don't understand how you could say something so outrageously insensitive."

"Why Don't You Just Have a One-Night Stand and Be Done with It?"

This question negates the sanctity of your relationship if you're in one, and it's downright dangerous and irresponsible if you're not in one. Honestly, this is one of those questions that doesn't warrant the kind or firm response. I would just jump directly to feigning deafness.

"Let Me Show You How" . . . and Other Kinky Ideas

In the grasping-at-straws category, some people may offer these overtly inappropriate suggestions:

"Lose weight!"

"Gain weight!"

"Start exercising!"

"Stop exercising!"

"Have sex more often!"

"Have sex less often!"

"Have you tried it doggy-style?"

"Have you tried it with the woman on top?"

"You know, the chances of conceiving are much greater if the woman has an orgasm. Are you having an orgasm each time?"

"Just let me know if you want to use some of *my* swimmers."

Some of these suggestions or comments may be mortifying, touching on your own insecurities or fears. Make sure you return the favor with the most embarrassing answer possible—after you get past the kind and firm stages, that is.

KIND: "Thank you, but that wouldn't really fix our problem."
FIRM: "We're so deep in this now that we're only taking advice from our doctor."
FREE-FOR-ALL: "Are you serious? Yes, I'd love to use your sperm. I'm actually ovulating right now, so let's get this started. Make sure you give me an orgasm, too!"

Emailed Advice and Other Missives

Especially because of the popularity of email, you'll undoubtedly get plenty of unsolicited advice in written form. In many ways, written advice is easier to handle. First, you can afford yourself the pleasure of writing back the way you *really* want to, no holds barred—including as many curse words and biting insults as you wish—and then not sending it. (Please don't send it. No matter how good it felt to write, I promise it will not continue to make you glow when you have to deal with the fallout. So erase it, tuck it away in a drawer, file it somewhere unsearchable on your computer, and sit down to write a new note.)

When responding in written form, remember: The more information you give, the more they'll try to come back with something else helpful. You took the time to explain the intricacies of IVF? That must mean you want them to fully understand the situation so they can better help you. If your intention is to educate, and you think the person will be receptive to the message, by all means, educate—but know that your correspondence may become long and drawn out. If your intention is to simply ensure that you won't receive a similar email next week, you need to nip it in the bud. In the following examples, I am assuming that you will want to receive one email, return one email, and make that the end of the advice giving.

The idea here is KISS—Keep It Simple, Stupid—and it is meant to remind you to use the least amount of words to get across the idea. Try to think of every unnecessary word or sentence as adding fuel to the fire.

It's also good practice to use the "sandwich technique"—which means presenting a kind sentence, slipping the rejection in the middle, and tying up the paragraph with some kind words again. Here is a sample kind response:

> *Dear Aunt Jane,*
>
> *That was really sweet of you to pass along this story about your neighbor's daughter's pregnancy after drinking pineapple juice three times a day during her IVF cycle. Unfortunately, fertility treatments, like all other areas of medicine, don't really work with a one-size-fits-all approach. If it were that easy, no one would cycle more than once. We're really comfortable with our doctor and our clinic, and, coming from an insider's perspective, we're really comfortable with the protocol he set up to address our situation. Sorry to be vague with our protocol, but to explain it would turn this into a forty-page email! And the point is not our situation but just how kind it was for you to think of me.*
>
> *Love, Me*

Even if you're not truly thankful, you will have less cleanup to do if you go with this approach. And notice the use of the word "kind" in the letter: People who think they're being helpful like to see the word "kind," because it confirms their idea of themselves as thoughtful, generous beings.

Now, let's just pretend that first note didn't do the trick, and Aunt Jane writes the following week with a story about her hairdresser's cousin's son's friend who is creating an adoption plan for her baby. At the end of her letter, she asks if she can pass your information through the chain so this pregnant woman can know all about your heartbreaking tale of infertility and baby lust. Your firm response might go something like this.

Dear Aunt Jane,

Again, it's really sweet of you to think of us, but I think it would be best if we took the topic of infertility off the table. We aren't comfortable with you sharing our information with other people. Your emails are meant to be helpful, and we know you have our best interests at heart, but they're not being heard in the right way right now. It would really be best if we both stopped talking about it for the time being. We'll share good news with you when we have it, but just assume until that point that we're blazing our own trail and are only taking advice from our doctor. Thank you, Aunt Jane. We can't wait to see you at Cousin Jill's wedding!

Love, Me

Of course, sometimes the Aunt Janes of this world come back with a third note, even after the blunt requests in your second response. This is when a person must pull out the free-for-all.

Dear Aunt Jane,
Even though you have a degree from a major university, as well as forty-seven years of experience with the

English language, it seems as if the message is being
lost in these various email exchanges. I'm not sure I
can state this more emphatically: Stop talking about
my wonky uterus/nut sack. I don't mean to pee in your
Cheerios, because I know you think you are being
incredibly helpful. But you're not. At the same time, I
hope you're having a wonderful vacation with Uncle
Jack, and we'll see you at the next family reunion!

Love, Me

Ah, if only we lived in a world where it was a good idea to send the free-for-all response. Though your masterpiece will never see another person's inbox, it's still important to vent. The responsible advice is that if things get to this point, keep in mind that not every letter and email needs to be answered. If you do think that something needs to be done, consider asking a friend or family member to act as the go-between, but do whatever you can to minimize fallout and to allow the other person to save face even as you draw a firm line—and then move on. You've got bigger issues to deal with.

Last Thoughts

It is really hard to hear some of these comments and questions, and they can have a negative effect on your day; but whenever you need to untangle yourself from these words and leave them behind, remember that unless you are getting a vibe otherwise, these words were spoken because the people either care about you or simply don't know that their words are offensive. It doesn't make it okay, but it does give you the space in which to close the door and forget about them while you still walk your own path.

Chapter 6

UPON ARRIVING, SOME immigrants to the Land of If have no problem answering the custom official's question "Reason for visit?" These people get a firm stamp on their passports, right away or after a quick jaunt through inspections: AZOOSPERMIA . . . LACK OF FALLOPIAN TUBES . . . UTERINE ANOMALY . . . SITUATIONAL INFERTILITY. But for others, diagnosis gives the slow reveal, coming together like pieces in a puzzle.

I fell into the latter category. It took a long time and a lot of phone calls to get any sort of conclusive answer as to why we couldn't conceive. (And for some strange reason, I received many of my diagnostic calls outside the same supermarket. I will forever equate my infertility with melting ice cream and sweating heads of broccoli.)

Even though it took me a long time to get diagnosed, I shaved months off my treatment plan by becoming as informed as possible.

I was taking my basal body temperature and had months of charts to show my doctor before he could ever suggest it. I impressed my new OB on the first visit by knowing to ask for a progesterone test. I didn't let people take a wait-and-see approach when I knew that waiting and seeing weren't going to bring about desired answers.

This chapter will let you know what to expect when you begin your diagnostic workout. It is also for people already diagnosed who want to learn about tests or blood work they may have done during treatments.

The medical information here has been checked by a doctor but has been simplified and kept to a minimum, on purpose. My desire is to give you the confidence and vocabulary you need to discuss your infertility and to know what questions to ask, so that you can make informed decisions. It is not to give you enough knowledge to perform your own testicular biopsy. Once you are ensconced in the diagnostic process, you can use this chapter as a springboard to catapult you toward more detailed information, along with the books and websites listed in the Resources section.

My hope is that this chapter will save you time and hassle and move you out of customs quickly so you can start your stay in the Land of If and catch a boat off the island at an earlier date.

First Steps

Unless a clear issue—such as a lack of menstruation, or a genetic disorder that causes sterility—is apparent before couples start the conception process, most doctors will not begin fertility testing on a woman younger than thirty-five until she has completed a year of well-timed intercourse (or, in a same-sex female relationship, a year of well-timed inseminations) without protection; if she is older than thirty-five, the doctor will typically begin testing after six months.

Unless there is a secondary health issue that could affect sperm production or quality, the man isn't given his first semen analysis until the woman is going in for her workup.

Reproductive endocrinologists (REs) are specialized obstetrician-gynecologists (OB-GYNs) who focus on conception issues. Gynecologists are doctors who specialize in when things are going *right*. They may be trained to triage small problems, or to diagnose large ones in order to get you to the correct specialist, but REs have additional training that gynecologists do not—namely, a three-year fellowship specifically in reproductive and hormonal disorders.

This doesn't mean that a gynecologist can't run some basic blood work or exams. Your gynecologist may be the one who starts you down the road to your RE by running day 3 blood work, trying out a Clomid cycle, or checking progesterone levels in the second half of your cycle. But once a problem has been determined, or soon after the one-year mark of trying to conceive, you should switch to an RE in order to treat the underlying issue efficiently. Unlike gynecologists, REs are equipped to treat male-factor infertility, especially as it pertains to the reproductive health of the couple, but your RE may also refer you to a specialized urologist or andrologist, especially if male-factor infertility is diagnosed from the first semen analysis.

Diagnostics for Men

As you'll see, this section is exceedingly small—not because the problems are not just as large, but because so much of conception takes place inside the woman's body.

The men's workup begins with the semen analysis. But there will also be a spoken component to the exam, where your doctor gathers your history, including how long you've been trying, your sexual history, and your past health issues. Your doctor should know about past sexually transmitted diseases, any surgeries you've had, medications you take, and the age you experienced puberty. It's a lot

UNEXPLAINED INFERTILITY

While this chapter is about diagnosing female-factor and male-factor infertility, we need to also look at a large population on the island: those with unexplained infertility. There is a reason why they can't conceive, but technology and diagnostics simply haven't caught up to reality.

Women or couples with unexplained infertility are usually treated with the same procedures as those with female-factor infertility, though treatment comes with the frustration that it isn't pointedly addressing an issue. The lack of diagnosis can also make knowing when to stop treatments difficult. After all, without a clear reason, a person can continually believe that the next cycle may be a successful cycle (it has to happen sometime, right?). But "unexplained" doesn't mean "for no reason"–it just means that science hasn't quite caught up with understanding every reason for infertility. Therefore, be extra vigilant about creating stopping points where you'll reassess whether treatments are the best option. Otherwise, you may be in limbo for an unbearable amount of time.

of personal information, but it's important that the doctor have the full picture in order to make a diagnosis.

There is also usually a physical exam, which includes a prostate exam and a check for undescended testes (as well as undescended testes that have been treated), which can cause infertility. The doctor will also be checking for a varicocele, which is a dilated varicose vein that runs around a testicle—it's one of the most common issues affecting male fertility (see the section on varicocelectomies, later in this chapter).

TIP: When providing the sample, you'll need to make sure that you do not ejaculate in the forty-eight hours preceding the exam—but you'll also need to make sure that you *have* ejaculated in the five days prior to the exam. If that is confusing, follow this simple rule: Have sex on Monday, and give your semen sample on Thursday.

The Semen Analysis

The semen analysis provides the doctor with basic information and helps to weed out any obvious problems. According to the American Society of Reproductive Medicine (ASRM), your doctor should be looking for the following things in your sample:[1]

- a *volume* of over two milliliters (and under six milliliters)
- a *count* of over forty million sperm (the average being eighty million)
- a *concentration* of over twenty million sperm per milliliter
- at least 50 percent *motility* after one hour (meaning half of the sperm are still swimming in a forward motion)
- at least 30 percent normal *morphology* overall
- at least 14 percent normal morphology for the *Kruger morphology* test (which looks only at the sperm head)
- *liquefaction* (transforms completely into a liquid) within one hour

- *appearance* and *consistency* (not too thick and not too thin)
- a *pH* of 7.2 to 8.0
- fewer than one million *white blood cells* per milliliter

So what happens if your semen analysis comes back and you're outside one of those ranges above? To rule out a fluke abnormal reading, your doctor should run two separate semen analyses before making a diagnosis.

The thing about the semen analysis is that it's sort of like online dating: The initial profile, in both cases, can help you know if there is a potential problem or if things look good on the surface, but you have to do some deep exploration (i.e., several "dates" with the doctor) to actually discover the true situation.

Here are some of the terms you may hear if there is a problem with your semen analysis:

Azoospermia means there are no sperm to be found within the sample. There are many reasons why there might be a lack of sperm, and the reason for the absence of sperm is important in knowing whether or not azoospermia can be overcome. Sometimes, it could be due to a blockage; other times, it could be due to the body's inability to create sperm. There could be congenital abnormalities, such as hypospadias, a condition in which the urethra opening is not in its correct place, or CAVD (congenital absence of vas deferens, also known as CBAVD, or congenital bilateral absence of vas deferens), which is most often found in men who carry the cystic fibrosis gene (in other words, while they may not have the condition themselves, they are a carrier of it). An important thing to note is that if there are no sperm within the sample, there may still be sperm being produced within the body.

Oligospermia means there are a reduced number of sperm in the sample. In other words, the situation is not as dire as azoospermia, but it still needs to be addressed. The same things that can cause azoo-spermia (blockage or an inability to create sperm) can lead to oli-gospermia, and the same means (including some less invasive ones) can be used to correct it.

Asthenospermia means the sperm are there, but the motility is reduced. These sperm do not swim forward.

Aspermia means that there's a problem with the prostate and seminal vesicles—the glands that produce seminal fluid. Aspermia means there is a lack of semen (as opposed to azoospermia, which refers to the number of sperm in the sample).

---

no. 0011
THE LAND OF IF VISITORS BUREAU

TIP: Some doctors will allow you to collect your sample at home. Unless you have some kind of weird fetish, masturbating at home is usually preferable to doing it in a public restroom, but in my opinion, the stress of keeping the sample at the correct temperature and getting it to the office in the set amount of time can create more anxiety than it's worth. (Then again, I've never had a doctor demand that I masturbate on cue, so I may be wrong there.) In any case, if you would prefer to collect your sample in the privacy of your own home, ask your doctor—it may be a possibility.

Additional Tests

If a problem has been found in the initial evaluation, more tests will be run. As you've probably guessed, to get a proper diagnosis, the tests become more invasive. From the semen analysis, you can determine only that a problem exists; you can't know what is causing the problem until you examine the reproductive tract.

---

no. 0012

THE LAND OF IF VISITORS BUREAU

TIP: If you're going to give your sample at the doctor's office, they will either have a set room specifically for that purpose, or—if you're a cheap bastard, like our first doctor (just kidding, Doctor!)—you'll have to use the bathroom.

And if you're squeamish about touching . . . . used . . . . magazines, you may want to bring your own porn. Actually, even if you're not squeamish, it's a good idea to BYOP. What they have to offer may not be your cup of tea—in which case, you'd have to take a page from Lady Hillingdon's journal by closing your eyes and thinking of . . . . well, if not England, then something more titillating than a tiled bathroom.

TESTICULAR BIOPSY

A testicular biopsy is used to determine whether the testes have the ability to create sperm when none (or a low amount) are found during the semen analysis. This is an outpatient procedure that uses local anesthesia. A sample of tissue is removed and sent to a lab for examination. Discomfort afterward, as there would be with any surgical procedure, is normal, and the scrotum may be bruised for several days after the biopsy. This test can tell your doctor many things. If there are sperm in the testes that aren't making it into the ejaculate, your doctor can determine that there must be a blockage—which, of course, leads to more testing, this time of the vas deferens.

Going hand in hand with the testicular biopsy are methods for removing sperm that can be used later during treatments. *Microsurgical epididymal sperm aspiration* (MESA), *testicular sperm extraction* (TESE), and *testicular sperm aspiration* (TESA) are three techniques used to retrieve sperm to use for IVF (but not IUI, which requires a large sample; these three surgical techniques usually retrieve a small amount of sperm). These sperm are better used for ICSI in conjunction with IVF. With MESA, sperm are surgically removed from the epididymis. TESE, on the other hand, is similar to a testicular biopsy. In fact, the sperm are removed from tissue taken for the biopsy (or a surgeon may test several areas, looking in the testes for sperm). Lastly, TESA involves using a needle to withdraw fluid (and hopefully sperm) from the testes.

VAS DEFERENS BLOCKAGES

There are numerous ways in which the vas deferens can be examined, and each gives the doctor different information about the type of blockage. Saline may be injected into the vas deferens, or a catheter may be threaded. A small sample of fluid may be removed and examined to check whether sperm are present. And a *vasography* usually follows a testicular biopsy if the biopsy itself shows normal sperm cells. In a vasography, the doctor will inject contrast dye into the vas deferens and examine the flow of the dye to determine the blockage. But vasography can actually cause a blockage, strangely enough, so it is usually done in conjunction with *microsurgery*. Microsurgery is simply surgery performed with a microscope; the two most common forms of microsurgery used in conjunction with vasography are *vasovasostomy* and *vasoepididymostomy*. Both surgeries are used to bypass a blockage in the vas deferens. All of these procedures cause a great deal of discomfort and pain, and you should make sure that you speak to people who have undergone the procedure before you're on the operating table. Doctors are great, but unless they have been through the same operation, they generally can't tell you the fine details that come from going through the experience yourself.

ULTRASOUND

An ultrasound may also be used to examine internal structure. Ultrasounds can be done either abdominally or transrectally. Abdominal ultrasounds have the transducer outside of the body. They can be used to see the testes inside the scrotum. A *transrectal ultrasound* (sometimes abbreviated as TRUS), where the transducer goes inside the rectum, is used to examine the genital tract, especially structures that affect fertility, such as the vas deferens and seminal vesicles. CAVD and CBAVD (mentioned earlier in this chapter) can both be diagnosed when vas deferens are not seen during a transrectal ultrasound. While transrectal ultrasound is not painful, per se, the sensation can be surprising and uncomfortable. Again, it helps to speak with someone who has had one prior to your appointment.

VARICOCELECTOMY

The surgery to correct a *varicocele* is called a varicocelectomy, and while the scope of its helpfulness has been debated, many doctors believe that the procedure increases fertility. Varicoceles can cause problems with sperm quality because they're impeding correct blood flow to the testes; therefore, the veins are treated either by cutting off the blood flow completely or by reducing it by introducing a blockage to slow down the flow. Some varicocelectomies are done by laparoscopy, and others require surgery to open the scrotum. In both cases, varicocelectomies do not require an overnight stay in the hospital. If you have this procedure done, treat the pain afterward with a prescription painkiller and rest—no strenuous activities for about four weeks. Don't be surprised if you see a lot of bruising; this is normal and will go away as the incision site heals.

HORMONE LEVELS[3]

Blood work can test for hormone levels during your initial workup and can determine whether sexual organs are functioning correctly. I didn't include a worksheet in the back of the book, as I did for women's hormone levels, because blood work for males does not happen monthly. At the same time, you should record your blood test results here in the margin or request a copy of your test results.

Testosterone

Because testosterone is responsible for the development of male sex organs, a lack of it can cause a multitude of fertility problems, including affecting the production of sperm and the ability to maintain an erection. Doctors are looking for testosterone to be between 300 and 1100 ng/dl.

Follicle-Stimulating Hormone (FSH)

FSH controls the production of sperm and generally doesn't change

BOXERS
OR BRIEFS?

Everyone can point to the chain-smoking, bike-riding, brief-wearing coworker who has easily fathered ten children and think that some of these "lifestyle precautions" are bunk. But the reality is that 1) they can't hurt and 2) they could help.

- Don't allow your testes to get too hot (no saunas, no hot tubs, no wrapping heating pads around your testicles . . . if, for whatever reason, you did this).
- Riding a bike recreationally is probably okay, though limit the length of your bike ride.
- Don't smoke cigarettes, cigars, or legal smoking products. And absolutely no illegal substances, including marijuana. Marijuana stays in the testes for up to two weeks! So put down the joint and take up a sport for relaxation (just not bicycling or hot-tub football).
- Limit caffeine intake to one cup of coffee or 100 to 150 mg of caffeine per day.
- Limit alcohol intake to one or two drinks per week.
- Make sure you're getting enough vitamins. Males seeking to optimize fertility should make sure they are getting daily: vitamin C (500 mg), vitamin E (200 IU—but not more), selenium (200 mcg), folic acid (800 mcg), and zinc (no more than 20 mg).

Why do people talk about boxers or briefs, and why does it even matter? The thought behind your choice of underwear is that boxers allow the testicles to hang away from the body, allowing them to maintain their core temperature, which is actually slightly lower than your overall body temperature. Not having them up against the body, with their temperature slightly raised from the transfer of heat, allows them to keep trucking along, producing sperm. In the end, according to one doctor at the Baylor College of Medicine, it doesn't truly matter which one you wear: Boxers and briefs have no impact on infertility.[2] For more information on unproven but popular alternative methods of boosting fertility, see the sidebar "Alternative Fertility Boosters," in Chapter 8.

drastically at different points in the month, as FSH does in women. Doctors are looking for FSH to remain between 4 and 10 mIU/ml.

Luteinizing Hormone (LH)

Men do not want high LH levels, which can indicate a problem with testicular function. At the same time, low levels can indicate a problem with the pituitary gland. Doctors want to see male LH levels in the 2- to 18-mIU/ml range.

Prolactin

High prolactin levels (the hormone in women that produces breast milk) can affect sperm production and may also indicate a tumor on the pituitary gland. Men should not see prolactin higher than 20 ng/ml.

POSTEJACULATORY URINALYSIS

If a low amount of ejaculate is collected during the semen analysis, the doctor may order an additional test called a *postejaculatory urinalysis* to check for retrograde ejaculation. *Retrograde ejaculation* is when semen—which you would expect to be released with the orgasm—actually gets sucked back into the body and pools in the bladder. Sperm can actually be removed from the bladder or urine and then treated to use with an IUI or IVF.

Some doctors treat retrograde ejaculation by having men take a simple over-the-counter cold medication, because ingredients in those medications help the bladder sphincter close tightly (the loosening of this sphincter is the problem, since it means urine goes out with the ejaculate, and the ejaculate goes back into the bladder).

ANTISPERM ANTIBODY TESTING

Men who have gone through the initial gamut of fertility testing without finding a cause may have an additional semen analysis performed

BOYS DON'T CRY

There are two myths out there that need to be addressed before we start talking about male infertility.

One myth is that infertility testing and treatments are nothing for men, because *all* they do is "produce a sample" (a clinical euphemism for "masturbation"). I emphasize the word "all" because I think this myth is in the same vein of offensiveness as "just adopt." The other myth is that men in heterosexual relationships actually enjoy infertility because they get to have a lot of sex.

Let's tackle these, shall we?

Any person who tells you that men enjoy infertility has about as much sense as a bag of hair. Male infertility causes the same range of emotions as female infertility: anger, guilt, frustration, sadness, and jealousy. Men and women need to remember this: Differences in outward expression are not a reflection of differences between inward emotions. Men and women both feel emotional pain about infertility, and others (including partners!) need to keep that in mind. No two people will express their frustrations about infertility in the same way.

Men may enjoy sex just as women enjoy sex, but no one enjoys sex when it takes on the urgency of an army maneuver. More sex doesn't equal more enjoyment. Beyond that, some men diagnosed with male-factor infertility face many a painful procedure (on top of the more embarrassing ones, such as masturbating inside a room with everyone in the hallway knowing your business).

So let's dispel these two myths once and for all: Men may express their feelings about infertility differently than women do, but they find the inability to have a child when they want one frustrating and upsetting.

to check for *antisperm antibodies*. Antibodies attack foreign cells, though they can also go awry and attack healthy cells. This test may also be run without special cause in men who have had a vasectomy reversal (which is a leading cause of the production of antisperm antibodies). Sperm washing (a process that removes dead sperm and mucus from the sperm sample, leaving behind the sperm with the best motility) and medications may be able to remedy this problem.

GENETIC TESTING

While you may have initial genetic testing done before you begin trying to conceive if you fit into a high-risk category for a certain disease (for example, those of Ashkenazi Jewish origin may be tested for eight disorders that commonly occur in Eastern European Jews), a second level of genetic testing is done when infertility is suspected, or after multiple losses (or failed IVF attempts). Genetic testing and the karyotyping of chromosomes can tell two people whether they are compatible fertility-wise, as well as whether they are carriers for or affected by different genetic conditions, including cystic fibrosis, Klinefelter's syndrome, or problems on the Y chromosome.

Male-Factor Diagnoses

Beyond the problems already listed within the testing section, such as varicoceles, antisperm antibodies, and hormone deficiencies, the conditions below may be diagnosed as the reason for infertility.

Conditions that inhibit fertility include the aforementioned *Klinefelter's syndrome* (when the man has an extra X chromosome), *Kallmann's syndrome* (which creates a lack of GnRH, an important hormone related to sperm production), and *Sertoli-cell-only syndrome* (where there is a lack of germ cells, and therefore no sperm can be produced). Those who are carriers for or are affected by cystic fibrosis may have a lack of vas deferens, therefore keeping sperm from exiting the body during orgasm. *Erectile dysfunction* and *anejaculation* (the inability to ejaculate even if an erection can be maintained), of course, can both be a cause of infertility. While both conditions can come as a side effect of another situation, other times, they occur on their own.

Diagnostics and Monitoring for Women

The infertility workup for women begins with a physical exam, similar to the physical exam you get yearly at your pap smear (wait, you *do* go in yearly for a pap smear, right?). You will be asked about your medical history, including the age you began menstruating, the dates of your last few periods, and the reproductive history of your mother and even grandmother. Blood work will be drawn on the correct day of your cycle, which means that you may need to come in for a second appointment once your next cycle begins. The first day of your period is the start of a new cycle (also known as cycle day 1, abbreviated to CD1). Most blood work for diagnostic purposes is run either on the third day after your period begins (CD3) or seven days after ovulation occurs. On CD3, a doctor may also order an ultrasound to check for antral follicles (the small follicles that are resting at the beginning of a cycle, just waiting to grow and hopefully pop out an egg).

Blood Work

Blood work is usually the starting point—it's noninvasive, and checking hormone levels at certain points in the cycle can give doctors a lot of information. Usually, they are looking at your blood to discern hormone levels. Some of these tests are run just once or every few months. Other tests are run several times each cycle. And still others are a one-shot deal used for diagnostic purposes. There's a lot to cover with blood work, and some of it leads directly to a host of female-factor diagnostics.

TIP: For information and help with monitoring and tracking your own fertility— including charting your basal body temperature (BBT) and using ovulation-predictor kits (OPKs) and fertility-monitoring machines—see the appendix section called "Monitoring Your Fertility." For more information on using alternative methods of boosting fertility, see the sidebar "Alternative Fertility Boosters," in Chapter 8.

Your doctor is going to be interpreting the results, but it's still good to have a sense of "normal" so you can ask questions. There is generally a good reason when a doctor dismisses a low or high number, but *you* should understand that reason, too, if you want to take an active role in your treatment.

The following are the most common blood tests, the days they are taken, and the ranges for results. Keep in mind, different labs have different ranges for the same test. These are just a general guideline. I've included only the most common tests.

Remember to always record your hormone levels so you can play an active role in your own treatment and refer back to these numbers when asking questions during future cycles. Even if you never have a second cycle because you're pregnant after the first one (or walk away from treatments altogether), it's nice to have all the information about your body that everyone else knows. There are two worksheets in the appendix where you can record hormone levels—either on the treatment worksheet or on the specific day 3 worksheet.

THERE WILL
BE BLOOD WORK

Oy, the blood work. Can we all just complain for a moment about this? The annoyance of blood work gets short shrift when it comes up against the more painful procedures. True, it's certainly not painful in the grand sense of the word, but many people have a problem with needles—myself included (see more about injections and needles in Chapter 8). Men have blood work, but women have Blood Work with a capital B and W—in other words, while men may have a single blood draw or two, women who are in treatments will have blood drawn several times each cycle.

If you're afraid of needles, the main thing is to recognize your fear—then do something to address it rather than dismiss it. The point is to get yourself in the phlebotomist's chair with a minimal amount of stress, because you're going to be going through this a lot, unless you get pregnant on the first try.

If you quake in fear of needles as much as I do, take this advice:

- Drink plenty of water beforehand. Even a little bit of dehydration makes veins difficult to work with, as they tend to "roll" when the phlebotomist attempts to insert the needle. The remedy? A simple twelve ounces of water on the way to the appointment or while you sit in the waiting room.
- Consider using an anesthetic topical cream, such as EMLA, to numb the area.
- Ask the phlebotomist to use a butterfly needle, the smallest. Not only do they hurt less, but they can get into a thin, scarred vein more easily than the larger needles. (Constant blood draws can cause scarring, especially when the same vein is used over and over again.)
- Be assertive. After a while, you start to know your arms better than the phlebotomists at the lab. Tell them which veins have been the easiest for drawing blood. Do all phlebotomists appreciate having the patient tell them how to do their job? No. But when you're pregnant, or moving on from treatments, you can write the phlebotomist a nice card or drop off some homemade cookies.

CD3 Blood Work[4]

Let's start with the most common day for testing, CD3 (remember, the third day after the full-flow start of your period). Sometimes other hormone levels are checked on day 3, but these six are the most common.

Follicle-Stimulating Hormone (FSH)

Doctors use this test as one of the predictors of egg quality and quantity. On average, a doctor is looking for a test under 10 mIU/ml. Anything under 6 is great. Between 6 and 9 is good. The tipping point is 10, with 10 to 13 signifying a problem. Anything over 13 is usually labeled "poor responder." Doctors are also looking for a 1:1 ratio with LH (next).

Luteinizing Hormone (LH)

Since you want it to have a 1:1 ratio with FSH, you want it to be under 6 mIU/ml. One sign of PCOS (polycystic ovarian syndrome) is an LH level that is higher than the FSH level.

Estrogen (E2)

Estradiol (E2) is the specific form of estrogen that doctors examine in pre-pregnancy cycles. There are three forms of estrogen, but for clarity, when using the umbrella term estrogen in this book, I'm always referring to estradiol. You want low estrogen on CD3 in order to have better ovarian stimulation later on. (Estrogen levels will rise as you move toward ovulation.) Anything between 25 pg/ml and 75 pg/ml is fine. You're going to have E2 levels taken throughout the cycle, so this is just the starting point for CD3.

Prolactin

This hormone can interfere with ovulation; therefore, doctors want to make sure that it is under 24 ng/ml on CD3. High amounts can make you anovulatory and can indicate a tumor on the pituitary gland.

Progesterone (P4)

Progesterone should be extremely low at the beginning of the cycle. Doctors want to see below 1.0 ng/ml on CD3. After ovulation, progesterone should go up. Doctors usually want to see over 10 ng/ml later in the cycle.

Thyroid-Stimulating Hormone (TSH)

Doctors are looking for TSH between .4 and 4 uIU/ml. High TSH can be a sign of hypothyroidism, which can affect fertility. If the TSH test comes back with an abnormal reading, T4 will be examined.

BLOOD WORK FOR A MONITORED CYCLE

If you are being monitored, your doctor will keep checking hormone levels throughout the cycle to keep tabs on when you're ready to ovulate or when you have optimal conditions for implantation. Therefore, blood work done later in the cycle looks at the following:

Luteinizing Hormone (LH), Again . . .

An LH surge comes prior to ovulation. Your doctor is looking for over 20 mIU/ml.

Estrogen (E2), Again . . .

Later on, immediately before ovulation, your E2 levels should be around 200 pg/ml per mature follicle. So do the math: If you have three follicles, your E2 level should be around 600. It could also be much higher than this—even having an E2 level in the 1,800 range (for three follicles) is still considered normal. But the higher the E2, the greater the chance for ovarian hyperstimulation syndrome (OHSS). Your doctor will check your E2 level several times during the first half of your cycle (the amount of times will depend on what type of treatment you're doing and the drugs you are taking).

Progesterone, Again . . .

This blood test is sometimes called a day 21 progesterone test. Yet the number 21 is a misnomer based on a twenty-eight-day cycle. This test needs to be performed on the seventh day after ovulation. Anything over 5 ng/ml shows ovulation, though, as I said above, your doctor is looking for 10 ng/ml or more.

The Beta (hCG)

Lastly, at the very end of a cycle, you'll have a final blood test—*the* Blood Test—the beta hCG, which is usually abbreviated just to "beta" (as in, "my beta is scheduled for next Thursday"). This is the test that measures the hormone that is produced when pregnancy is achieved.

"But wait!" you say (or you'll say in the future, when you read Chapter 8). "Isn't hCG the drug given to trigger ovulation during an injectable cycle?" It is, which is why a pregnancy test will show up positive if you pee on it right after a trigger shot.

The scheduling of the beta varies from clinic to clinic. Some test at fourteen days postovulation, counting the day of retrieval during IVF as ovulation. Some test as late as eighteen days postovulation. It's a fine balance—you don't want to test too early and see either the hCG left over in your blood from the trigger shot (it takes about seven days to fully leave the body) or a negative simply because it's before implantation, but you'll go crazy in those last few days waiting to see if the cycle is a success. See Chapter 8 (under "Ovidrel") for more information.

During a nonpregnant cycle, a woman will have a beta of under 2 mIU/ml. Defining a positive gets trickier. Most clinics consider anything over 10 mIU/ml to be "pregnant" and anything under that to be "not pregnant."

TIP: Although most clinics consider 10 mlU/ml to be the cutoff between a positive and a negative beta, some clinics set it at 5 mlU/ml, and may even phrase a beta of 3 mlU/ml as "under 5" or betas above 5 mlU/ml as "pregnant."

A word of advice: Ask for the specific number, and if you are receiving betas between 5 and 10 mlU/ml that are not being counted as pregnancies, ask your RE to explain what she thinks is the reason for these low betas. Numerous low betas, normal betas that fail to double, and unsuccessful IVF cycles should all be explored.

ULTRASOUNDS

While men may have one or two ultrasounds (also known as sono-grams), women will have transvaginal ultrasounds several times each cycle. The transducer is a long wand that is covered with a sheath and inserted vaginally in order to visualize the reproductive organs.

The first time you have a transvaginal ultrasound (sometimes called a "wanding" or a "dildo cam" if you're on the bulletin boards or blogs), it can be a little uncomfortable. But it is a sensation you quickly become accustomed to, and most consider it to be in the same vein as a teeth cleaning at the dentist's office: No one lines up and begs for it, but it isn't the kind of appointment people usually dread.

AFTER THE
POSITIVE BETA

So a positive beta tells you that you're pregnant. But you are infertile, so "pregnant" or "not pregnant" isn't enough, right? The thing is, a single beta doesn't tell a lot of information. There are low betas that produce healthy, full-term pregnancies, and there are high betas that produce pregnancies that end in miscarriage. This is why fertility clinics repeat the beta forty-eight hours later.

Every forty-eight hours or so, a beta should double. Some people will see it double in twenty-four hours, and others will see it double in seventy-two hours. I know, I know, you want your beta to double every twenty-four hours, because you think that is a sign that everything will be okay. But nothing is a promise about the outcome. Not even a great doubling beta. Now that I've snatched away your comfort zone, remember that statistics are in your favor, and it is more than likely that if you have a nicely doubling beta at the beginning, you will bring home a child in the end. I just want to be honest and not have you put too much stock in the beta being the be-all and end-all.

After your hCG levels hit 1,200 to 1,600 mIU/ml, the doubling time will slow down to between seventy-two and ninety-six hours. After 6,000 mIU/ml, it slows even more, to a doubling time of over ninety-six hours. But you'll probably never know that it slowed down, because most doctors draw only two or three betas in quick succession at the beginning of pregnancy. Production of hCG increases until it peaks, around the fourteenth week of pregnancy, and then begins to gradually decrease.

Something to keep in mind in regard to this test: You probably won't see a gestational sac or fetal pole—in other words, the early stages of the embryo—until your hCG is between 3,500 and 5,000 mIU/ml. If your doctor isn't giving in to your battiness and allowing you to come in for an ultrasound when you are twelve days past ovulation with a beta of 70 mIU/ml, here's an explanation: Nothing to see, people, nothing to see.

The ultrasound will be used to visualize the internal organs, count follicles (since you can't actually count the microscopic eggs inside the follicles), check for lining thickness in the uterus, and help guide the catheter during an IUI or IVF transfer, as well as work as a diagnostic tool when trying to find a cause for infertility, such as uterine fibroids, a lack of fallopian tubes, or polycystic ovaries.

SALINE SONOHYSTEROGRAM (SSH)

The saline sonohysterogram is a single test that goes by many different names, including a hysterosonogram, sonohysterogram, saline sonogram, and saline-infusion sonogram. Which can be a bit confusing, but all names refer to this examination, which is used to check the uterus for polyps or fibroids that can impede implantation, as well as the size and shape of the uterus.

The SSH can either supplement the information gathered from a hysterosalpingogram (HSG) or be used in lieu of an HSG, which is addressed in the next section. The SSH is sort of like a "hysterosalpingogram lite." It's certainly less uncomfortable than an HSG, and it has fewer risks than an HSG—but it also gives you less information. It's a lite experience all around. During fertility treatments, an SSH may be used with a mock transfer for an IVF cycle (more on that in Chapter 8).

When used as a diagnostic tool, an SSH should be done prior to ovulation but after the end of your period (in other words, in the first half of your cycle). If you still have your period, you should reschedule the appointment. Depending on when you normally ovulate, aim for CD7 through CD12.

I think any time a foreign fluid is injected into a reproductive organ, it's going to involve a modicum of discomfort. Consider preparing by taking some pain medication an hour in advance. In my unscientific but conscientious survey of other stirrup queens who underwent this procedure, the advice ranged from two to four Advil—so consider taking the middle road and popping three.

After removing everything from the waist down and hiking up your shirt (make sure it's not tucked under your bum, or your top will end up wet, too), your doctor will open up the vagina with a speculum and swab the cervix with a cleansing solution (if you're allergic to iodine, let your doctor know). A catheter will be passed through the cervix, and your doctor will use a transvaginal ultrasound to check the catheter placement (it will look like a white line across the sonogram screen). If the catheter is in place, the saline solution is squirted through the catheter, and the uterus is checked for abnormalities.

If you like, ask your doctor to turn the screen and let you watch as well. You'll see a pretty picture of your black, oval-like uterus filling with sparkling saline-solution bubbles. And who knows, it may distract you from any discomfort you might be feeling.

Some people have cramping or spotting afterward. But more than that—that is, pain and bleeding—is unusual and should be reported to the doctor. The general rule? If it feels wrong, it probably is wrong and should be reported. Better safe than sorry.

Hysterosalpingogram (HSG)

After you get past the initial blood work, the physical test most doctors start with is the HSG because it tells you something very important: whether or not there is a blockage in the fallopian tubes. Like the SSH, it is performed during the first half of the cycle.

The HSG is used to check for blockages in fallopian tubes, fibroids, scar tissue, and uterine anomalies. It is performed by a radiologist (usually with input by the RE) and closely follows the same structure as the SSH. A speculum opens the vaginal passage, a catheter is inserted, and dye is expelled into the uterus (again, if you are allergic to iodine, tell your physician or the radiologist). The radiologist takes x-rays of the reproductive organs. The whole test takes about fifteen minutes to complete.

Most women find HSGs more painful than SSHs. A lot of the pain comes from the shock of not knowing that the dye (unlike saline solution, which remains in the uterus) is extremely uncomfortable when it spills through the tubes. If there *is* a blockage, you face the possibility of some serious cramping and discomfort during the procedure. Like the SSH, people who tell you this test was a breeze usually took something preemptively for the pain. Most doctors will tell you to take a painkiller a half hour before the procedure. Others take it a step further and prescribe a relaxant, such as Valium or Ativan, to take prior to the test. These drugs not only relax the patient but also relax the uterine muscles (some of the pain of the procedure comes from tensing muscles in anticipation). Therefore, be prepared: Demand that a painkiller or relaxant be prescribed prior to the procedure. And then relax, knowing it can't possibly be half as bad as I've scared you into believing it is.

Your doctor should also prescribe a general antibiotic, to be taken for a few days around the time of the HSG; this is to stave off any infections that could come from the procedure. After all, you're introducing a foreign fluid into your uterus through an opening that is not meant to have tubes going in—sperm, yes, rubber tubes, no—so be sure to report any unusual postprocedural symptoms, especially symptoms related to infection, such as a high fever.

This test can also be emotionally difficult. For most, it is the first test performed when fertility treatments are started. Lying on that table, wondering how you got there and why you can't get pregnant, can be, frankly, scary. Don't let anyone make you feel bad if this test is difficult for you.

---

no. 0016

THE LAND OF IF VISITORS BUREAU

TIP: There is a common belief, supported by some REs, that the dye from the HSG itself can loosen a small blockage in a tube, thereby bringing about renewed fertility that cycle. Make sure you definitely try to conceive during the cycle when you have the HSG, and ride this one possible benefit to an otherwise miserable test.

HYSTEROSCOPY

After the HSG, if your doctor suspects that you have a uterine anomaly, he or she may order a hysteroscopy. A *hysteroscope* is a thin telescope used for looking at the inside of the uterus. This procedure may be used in conjunction with *laparoscopy* (see the next section), and it's impossible to state what kind of sedative or anesthesia will be used, since it varies from office to office and depending upon the reason for the procedure.

Hysteroscopes aren't used just to diagnose problems—they're also used to correct uterine anomalies once they are found. Doctors use them to remove fibroids or adhesions. As with many of these other procedures, the optimal time to have them performed is prior to ovulation and is usually scheduled around the eighth day in a cycle (CD8), give or take a few days. Because anesthesia may be used, you won't be able to eat or drink for a prescribed amount of time prior to the procedure.

After sedation and/or anesthesia has been given, the cervix is dilated and the uterus widened with either gas or a liquid. A light illuminates the inside of the uterus and the fallopian tubes, and the doctor can peer through the hysteroscope and look around inside. If surgery needs to be performed on the spot, instruments can be passed through the hysteroscope and used inside the uterus. Pretty cool, right?

Because anesthesia is used, you may need to wait a bit to recover before someone can drive you home from the office. If gas is used to widen the uterus, it can also cause pain in the shoulders. This procedure can lead to cramping and light bleeding afterward. Severe pain or heavy bleeding should be reported to your doctor.

LAPAROSCOPY

Laparoscopy, otherwise known as a "lap," is performed in conjunction with hysteroscopy; it can also be performed on its own. If it's performed with the hysteroscopy, it's usually scheduled for around the eighth day of the cycle. If it's performed on its own, it may be moved closer to ovulation.

It is used to treat a plethora of situations, including endometriosis, adhesions, ovarian cysts, and fibroids. This procedure may also be used to diagnose and/or treat an ectopic pregnancy (see Chapter 7 for more on ectopic pregnancies).

Because anesthesia will definitely be used, you cannot eat or drink the night before. You will also probably have a meeting with the doctor prior to the procedure, at which blood work and x-rays may be ordered.

Unlike the hysteroscope, which is threaded through the cervix, a laparascope requires a tiny incision beneath the belly button. Small incisions are also made above the pubic-hair line. Gas is pushed into the abdomen to move organs and create a clear line of vision to the reproductive organs. The laparascope and tools are slipped through the incisions and manipulated from outside the body. The laparascope provides a view of the internal organs, which are projected onto a screen. If endometriosis or adhesions are found, they are removed with a laser.

The recovery time is faster than that of traditional surgery, but there still is a recovery time. Some people may feel the side effects of the anesthesia afterward. If gas gets trapped in your body, you may feel shoulder pain until the gas leaves or is absorbed. Expect that you'll need at least a couple days to recover.

ENDOMETRIAL BIOPSY

This is one of those tests that gets billed as "not that bad" but then turns out to be surprisingly painful. Therefore, I'm going to go the opposite route and tell you that it's awful so you'll be pleasantly surprised by your own endometrial biopsy.

This test is scheduled toward the end of the cycle, usually more than seven days after ovulation. It is performed in the office and without anesthesia. You can help yourself tremendously by taking a painkiller that reduces swelling (such as Motrin or Advil) *and* Valium before the procedure.

To get the sample of the endometrium (uterine lining), the doctor will open the vaginal passage with a speculum and will thread an instrument called a pipelle through the cervix in order to suck off cells from the uterine lining. Ouch. Nerves run through this region, and you have to take the "not that bad" from the RE with a grain of salt. As the pipelle draws in cells by using suction, intense cramping can take place. Afterward, you may have continued cramping, as well as light bleeding. Heavy bleeding or a discharge should be reported to your doctor. Try not to do strenuous activity for a day or two following this test.

This test can show whether the uterine lining is optimal for implantation and can help in diagnosing a luteal-phase defect (see page 137, later in this chapter). Unlike some of the tests above, the information isn't immediately available—you'll need to wait a week to receive results from this procedure.

POSTCOITAL TEST (A.K.A. THE SIMS-HUHNER TEST)

This test isn't used widely anymore, but it can provide doctors with some valuable information. Sometimes it's called the Sims-Huhner test, and frankly, it's a little embarrassing. Essentially, you have sex at home (I know, this sounds really risqué) and then race to the clinic to have a sample of cervical mucus taken and examined under the microscope.

The reason for this test is that sometimes the cervical mucus looks normal but behaves like an acid, killing those poor little sperm before they have a chance to get to the egg. Doctors are looking to see if the sperm are still swimming in the fluid. This test must be performed right before ovulation, when there is an LH surge, so the doctor will be checking for the right kind of cervical mucus. (Cervical mucus changes during the woman's cycle, and the best environment for sperm comes only directly before ovulation. It is sometimes called egg white cervical mucus, or EWCM.)

Can this test stop you from getting pregnant that month? Unlikely. By the time you get to the doctor, the race is pretty much on. Think of it as a bus stop: The sperm collected by the swabbing are the commuters still waiting for the #31 downtown, not the ones that caught the express, heading nonstop to the ripe ovum.

Female-Factor Diagnoses

There are four main areas that serve as umbrella topics for the common culprits in female-factor infertility: hormonal, structural, growth, and age.

Hormonal Factors

Hormonal issues are tied to those hormones that we already spoke about earlier in this chapter. Hormone imbalance can lead to a number of conditions. There is *anovulation,* which means a lack of ovulation. All women have a cycle or two where they don't ovulate, for whatever reason. "Anovulation" is a term used to describe those cycles, but it's also used to describe a situation in which ovulation constantly fails to occur. Related to anovulation is *amenorrhea,* when a woman either never has her period or stops getting her period (usually for three or more months). There's a third term, *oligomenorrhea,* that is used to describe irregular menstruation.

POLYCYSTIC OVARIAN SYNDROME (PCOS)

One of the most common hormonal imbalances is polycystic ovarian syndrome (PCOS). Many tiny follicles form in the ovaries, and while these follicles may contain an egg, they remain immature, usually growing cysts.

According to the International Council on Infertility Information Dissemination (or INCIID, pronounced "inside"), 5 to 10 percent of women who are within childbearing age are considered polycystic, and up to 30 percent show some symptoms of PCOS, even if they haven't been formally diagnosed.[5] Symptoms vary—some women have irregular cycles or a complete lack of ovulation, while others have a normal twenty-eight-day cycle. Some women experience irregular bleeding with their periods, and others have unremarkable menstruation.

Symptoms

Big clues that point toward a diagnosis of PCOS are:[6]

- cycles over six weeks in length;
- lack of menstruation;

- irregular menstruation (long periods of bleeding);
- immature follicles;
- an overabundance of male hormones, including testosterone, androstenedione, and dehydroepiandrosterone sulfate (DHEAS);
- hirsutism (an unusual amount of body and facial hair, caused by the high level of male hormones);
- a tendency toward adult acne;
- enlarged ovaries (usually, one and a half to three times the normal size);
- weight gain focused on the abdomen;
- insulin resistance or diabetes;
- thinning hair.

If immature, tiny follicles are noted on an ultrasound (doctors are looking for eight or more cysts that are less than 10 mm in size), doctors will explore the possibility of PCOS by examining a hormone ratio on the third day of the cycle. If the level of LH is found to be twice that of the FSH, PCOS is often diagnosed (all doctors should confirm with blood work, because even nonpolycystic women have tiny follicles sometimes). Your doctor will probably also look at other hormones to see if the levels are elevated—namely, prolactin, testosterone, and DHEAS.

Treating PCOS

It's important to treat PCOS, because it can have long-term effects on overall health. Women with PCOS are prone to high cholesterol, high blood pressure, and diabetes. So even if you decide not to pursue fertility treatments after receiving a diagnosis of PCOS, it is important to work with an endocrinologist to treat this syndrome. If you are interested in pursuing fertility treatments after receiving a diagnosis of PCOS, see Chapter 8.

Whether or not PCOS requires fertility treatments beyond oral medications, most women diagnosed with the syndrome will control symptoms with one of three medications: Glucophage/Metformin, Avandia, or Actos. Glucophage/Metformin are definitely the most popular; more information on those two is provided in Chapter 8. Changes in diet—namely, moving to a low-carbohydrate diet—can also help control PCOS.

PREMATURE OVARIAN FAILURE (POF)

Women are born with all of their eggs and slowly lose them over time until the reserve is depleted with menopause. But in women under thirty-five experiencing POF, the reserve is depleted at an accelerated rate. This form of female-factor infertility is investigated when FSH is elevated on day 3.

LUTEAL-PHASE DEFECT

This is an umbrella term for various problems with the luteal phase, which is the second half of a cycle (the first half is called the follicular phase). After the follicle releases the egg, the follicle becomes the corpus luteum (which means "yellow body"), and it has a second job—it produces progesterone. In some women, the corpus luteum doesn't produce enough progesterone, or the body fails to utilize the progesterone and therefore doesn't thicken the uterine lining. In either case, an embryo cannot implant if the lining isn't perfect.

An endometrial biopsy can be used to diagnose this disorder, which is suspected when a progesterone test run seven days after ovulation (7 DPO) comes back abnormally low or when the luteal phase is consistently fewer than twelve days long.

LPD is treated by creating a better corpus luteum through fertility drugs that affect follicle growth, as well as by supplementing progesterone through suppositories after ovulation. See Chapter 8 for more information on this.

Structural Abnormalities

In addition to hormone imbalances, there can be structural abnormalities. Females: Back when you were in utero, between weeks nine and sixteen, your Müllerian ducts fused together to create your uterus—if you were lucky. In some cases, the ducts do not fuse properly, resulting in a host of *uterine anomalies*. Most people with uterine anomalies are not aware they even have this situation until they are being tested for infertility or recurrent loss. In some cases, the anomaly does not impede conception but may affect the pregnancy, and in other cases, it may keep an embryo from implanting.

There can also be *tubal anomalies* that are keeping the sperm from reaching the egg. Blockages can be congenital or can result from scarring—from an ectopic pregnancy or endometriosis or infection. This problem can be circumvented with IVF (see Chapter 8) or treated with surgery such as the laparoscopy (see page 131).

Growth or Scarring

And then there are the diagnoses that stem from abnormal growth or scarring.

Endometriosis

Endometriosis is when cells from the uterine lining grow outside the uterus. Usually, this abnormal growth is found on organs surrounding the uterus. It can cause inflammation of tissue and scarring, which can affect implantation. Treating endometriosis is a fine balance because some of the treatments—from Lupron to surgery—can impede or impair fertility.

Fibroids and Polyps

These are noncancerous growths that can appear in the uterus. The position of the fibroid or polyp can affect fertility—especially regarding the embryo's achieving and maintaining implantation. Fibroids or polyps are not usually removed unless they are impeding fertility or causing another health problem. Sometimes, doctors will first treat the fibroids with medication to shrink them before resorting to surgery.

Pelvic Inflammatory Disease (PID)

Bacterial infections such as PID can cause scarring and block fallopian tubes. PID is most often associated with sexually transmitted diseases, which is why all STDs need to be treated—even when they're asymptomatic. PID can also be a side effect of a D&C, which may be performed after pregnancy loss (see Chapter 7).

Asherman's Syndrome

In addition, D&Cs can cause a form of uterine scarring called Asherman's syndrome. This scarring must be surgically removed by laparoscopy if it is impeding fertility. In extreme cases of Asherman's, the uterine walls can stick together due to the adhesions.

THE AGE FACTOR: AMA

Lastly, there is the simple diagnosis of age. By mentioning this factor, I don't mean to say that there should be an age cutoff for trying to conceive with one's own genetic material. If hope exists, it should be grabbed with two hands. Sometimes hope gets away, and other times we end up with the happily ever after.

In Chapter 8, I'll address clock-rewinding DHEA supplements, but an ethical debate happening right now with reproductive health concerns age limits and treatments (both treatments using your genetic material and treatments using donor eggs).

Fertility does have an age limit. With aging come losses and gains. It is one thing to treat ovarian dysfunction, and another to treat ovarian reality. And it's a fine line, and one that should be defined by the patient and doctor, taking into consideration all the appropriate factors. It is not a line that should be defined by any arbitrary age cut-offs. Still, there does need to be a balance between treating fertility problems and treating fertility realities due to age.

That said, age is a weird limit because bodies differ from person to person. What your body is capable of doing at forty-five, my body may not be capable of doing at thirty-five. Until menopause is complete, a woman can technically conceive. And menopause comes at a different age for each woman. According to the Mayo Clinic, fertility declines between ages thirty and thirty-five, decreasing almost 20 percent below maximum potential. Fertility decreases again between ages thirty-five and thirty-nine, to being almost 50 percent below the norm. In the last phase, ages forty to forty-five, women's fertility drops dramatically, to 95 percent below normal levels. Which leaves 5 percent of forty-five-year-old women with their fertility intact.[7]

Your clinic may already have an age limit in place, or your doctor may decide your personal limit based on a number of factors, including overall health and FSH levels.

Last Thoughts

Diagnosis comes with a whole rash of emotions. Finding out the problem can be both a relief and a source of grief. It can come down to your feeling vindicated for getting angry all those years you were told to "just relax"; it can make you anxious about the realization that something could be wrong with your body without your even knowing it; it can bring deep sadness and mourning. However you react to a diagnosis of infertility, go easy on yourself. Review Chapter 2, and take a few hours, days, or weeks to digest the news before pushing on with any next steps.

Chapter 7

WHEN PEOPLE DIE, they usually leave behind all kinds of tangible objects that remind us of them. Photographs, clothes, and worn-out shoes can be comforts that remind us the person was once here, once existed, and touched our lives immensely. Oftentimes, those objects are attached to endless stories—or images, sounds, smells—keeping the person's memory vivid and close to our hearts. And when a person dies, the weight of remembrance is spread out over many people.

Pregnancy loss, however, is a strange and different type of loss. Especially if it occurs early on, the burden of loss may be known by only one or two people. But even if the loss occurs further along—and even if many people know about it—the deceased has not had any relationships with the mourners, no chance to create memories with them. Comforting tangible objects left behind are few at best—a sonogram picture, a hospital bracelet, a stick from a positive pregnancy test.

THE
TERMINOLOGY
OF LOSS

The following are terms related to the timeline of pregnancy loss.

For the first eight weeks of pregnancy, the baby is called an *embryo;* after that, the term *fetus* is used. *Pregnancy loss* is an umbrella term that covers a wide range of loss, from miscarriages to stillbirth, starting with a *chemical pregnancy.* This type of miscarriage takes place very early on—perhaps only a few days after a positive pregnancy test, and prior to seeing the gestational sac or heartbeat on an ultrasound. Though often given short shrift, chemical pregnancies are a definite loss and the epitome of the proverbial emotional roller coaster: the car ticks up the hill during the two-week wait, only to plunge into loss soon after reaching the goal at the top of the ride. To top it off, these losses are often mourned alone: Rarely do people know that you experienced a brief pregnancy.

At the other end of the loss timeline is *stillbirth,* in which the fetus dies in the womb after twenty weeks of gestation. (*Neonatal death,* a death that occurs within the first twenty-eight days of life, though technically not a pregnancy loss, is also discussed in this chapter.)

A loss that takes place within the first twelve weeks is called an *early pregnancy loss* or *miscarriage.* Between thirteen and twenty weeks, it is referred to simply as a *miscarriage.* After twenty weeks (the "age of viability," when the baby may be able to live outside the womb), it is called a *late-term loss.*

This differentiation between all of these unique terms is a sensitive one. People who have lost their child after the first trimester deliver the baby, and some are given the option to hold their child. While some who have miscarried earlier feel cheated that they missed out on feeling their baby move, others who have held their baby want that fact recognized.

Pregnancy loss comes with strange and unique kinds of pain: the feeling of failed responsibility as the carrier of another person's life, the frustration of never having had the chance to build that relationship, the anguish of mysteries that may be left unsolved: *Was it a boy or a girl? Would he have been short or tall? Would she have been good at math or at writing short stories?*

If you are currently experiencing or have experienced a pregnancy loss, my heart goes out to you. And I hope you find a some measure of comfort in this chapter.

Why Pregnancy Loss Happens

Because so many pregnancies end before they're even discovered, estimates of the frequency of miscarriages are just that: estimates. Doctors predict that between 10 and 20 percent of pregnancies end in miscarriage. That rate increases with age: Over thirty-five, it's up to 20 percent, and over forty, it's up to about 33 percent.[1]

While some doctors will look for the reason behind the miscarriage after one loss, others will wait until the medically accepted line of three losses has been crossed. No doctor should allow a patient to experience loss after loss without doing some testing.

There are several reasons why pregnancy loss occurs.

Genetic Abnormalities

At least 70 percent of miscarriages are the result of a genetic abnormality in the embryo.[2] Humans are composed of two sets of twenty-three chromosomes—one set comes from the egg, and one set comes from the sperm. The most common form of abnormality is a *trisomy*— which is a third copy of a single chromosome (as opposed to the usual two chromosomes each child receives, one from each parent). Some trisomies can be compatible with life, such as Down syndrome, otherwise known as trisomy 21. Other trisomies are not compatible with life and result in pregnancy loss.

Other genetic abnormalities are *polyploidy* (having a set of four chromosomes—an extra copy of the two usual chromosomes), *trip-*

loidy (having three complete sets of the twenty-three chromosomes), and *translocation* (part of one chromosome is transferred to another chromosome). More information on genetic abnormalities can be found in the books and sites listed in the Resources section.

Advanced Age

Thirty-five is the magic age most people know of as the starting point for the decline of fertility in women, but it is also the age at which genetic abnormalities increase, hence the reason genetic testing is usually aimed at women over that age. Chromosomal changes can occur in eggs as the eggs age. The most common genetic abnormality, Down syndrome, occurs in about 1 in 1,000 pregnancies for women under the age of thirty. By age thirty-five, it increases to 1 in 400, and by forty, it is found to be 1 in 105 (still less than a 1 percent chance).[3]

Structural Abnormalities

Fibroids (noncancerous uterine growths) and other structural anomalies of the uterus can lead to implantation problems. Problems with uterine shape (such as a bicornuate or unicornuate uterus), as well as with septums (a growth that divides the uterus), can cause miscarriage or preterm labor. Lastly, a weak cervix can open too early, causing a loss of the fetus.

Hormonal Imbalances

Hormones play an important role in preparing the uterus for the pregnancy, as well as supporting the fertilized egg. Low levels of hormones such as progesterone can lead to implantation problems or early loss. Other hormones have been tied to pregnancy loss, including thyroid hormones and prolactin.

Infections and Environmental Causes

Infections and environmental causes are two factors that can bring

A LOSS
FOR WORDS

We really don't have enough words and customs in our language to refer to feelings of loss. For example, what do you call the anniversary of a death date? Or an unfulfilled due date? What do you call that mixture of joy and grief when getting the opportunity to hold your child after his or her death? This dearth of words and customs related to loss and grieving is reflective of our society's underdevelopment in the realm of death, especially when it comes to pregnancy loss and neonatal death.

We all know what to do when a person is widowed. We attend the funeral, cook some meals, make sure the person is not alone during difficult times. But people rarely extend the same type of thinking to pregnancy loss. It's not really their fault: Our culture doesn't have a clear protocol in this situation, and so people simply don't know what to do. Do they bring up the loss or pretend it didn't happen? Do they attend an event or leave the mourning solely to the grieving parents? Do they inquire about the future or never bring up the topic of babies again?

Some people will know the right thing to say when you tell them about your loss. They'll give you a hug and ask the right questions and even follow up with concern weeks down the road. But others will be lost trying to help you mourn.

You just never know how people are going to react to the information. It may happen that the people you least expect to be compassionate become the ones who surprise you with the most thoughtful response, while the ones you thought would be at your front door with a pint of ice cream may be the ones you can't reach by phone for several weeks following your news.

You may not find people in your day-to-day life who can fulfill your mourning needs. Some find more solace in turning to others who have been through the experience. Pregnancy-loss groups—both face-to-face and online—are listed in the Resources section.

about a large amount of guilt. But assigning blame after the fact doesn't help anyone work through the terrible emotions associated with loss. (See also the sidebar "What Did I Do to Deserve This?" on page 156.) Rubella, cytomegalovirus (CVS), chlamydia, herpes, and toxoplasmosis—as well as toxins from chemicals, drugs, and alcohol—have all been linked to pregnancy loss.

Blood Incompatibility

Just as you probably know your blood type in terms of A, AB, B, or O, there is a second typing system called Rh that looks at how things adhere to red blood cells. In this case, you can be Rh positive (+) or negative (-). If a woman is Rh- (meaning her blood type is A-, AB-, B-, or O-) and the man is Rh+, the fetus could be Rh+ as well, and the mother's antibodies could cross the placenta, harming the fetus. The problem usually doesn't occur with the first child, but instead is a problem in subsequent pregnancies.

Immune Response and Clotting

Pregnancy is the only time foreign cells can live in a body without being attacked. This is sometimes called "the immunological paradox of pregnancy." The baby is a foreign group of cells, but the body doesn't reject it outright. In fact, it nurtures this group of cells and allows it to tap into the body's resources.

Except that this isn't what always happens, immunologists have discovered. In the case of recurrent loss, the body may be attacking and rejecting the baby. Those with recurrent pregnancy loss are sometimes found to have autoimmune (attacking one's own cells) or allopathic (attacking the embryonic or placental cells) disorders. Hematologists have also discovered clotting disorders that affect implantation and fetal growth.

If you have had recurrent loss, or if you have had multiple failed

TIP:

The following are a few practical things you can do for yourself, and ask of others, to help you get through the grieving process:

- Inform people of any dates you're worried about, and ask them to write them down and check on you when the time comes. Be mindful of holidays and other important dates on the calendar, and ask people to be understanding during those times.

- Give others tasks—things they can do for you— so they can feel helpful. For example, ask them to cook a meal or to run an errand, or simply to keep you company.

- Make a scrapbook or create a memory box to honor the lost baby. Fill it with any mementos you have or cards you receive after the loss. Anything you purchased specifically for that baby can go in the box as well, including onesies and teddy bears. If you didn't purchase items before the loss but you think it would help you to have tangible objects to hold and place in the box, consider purchasing or making something for your lost baby.

- Create your own ceremony or put together a small service. You could plant a tree or light a candle in memory of the loss, and ask others to join you. Some people release balloons outside—pink or blue—to commemorate their loss; others purchase a piece of jewelry, perhaps bearing the birthstone of the estimated due date, that can be worn daily to remind them of the baby.

IVF cycles, testing for these factors is worth pursuing. However, you may need to press your doctor to order the tests: This is a newly emerging field within reproductive endocrinology, and not everyone is onboard with it yet. Testing usually happens as a last resort because these disorders do not always affect fertility.

Testing usually involves looking at three different factors. *Thrombophilias* are inherited blood-clotting disorders such as MTHFR (a gene mutation that affects the way the body processes folic acid), Protein S and Protein C, prothrombin, and factor V Leiden. *Antibody testing,* on the other hand, looks at acquired thrombophilias and autoimmune issues such as antiphospholipid antibodies (APA), antinuclear antibodies (ANA), antithyroid antibodies (ATA), and anti-coagulant antibodies (ACA). Lastly, *natural killer cells* are cells that attack embryos.

There is a wide range of treatments for clotting factors and immunological issues, from a simple baby aspirin a day and Lovenox injections to stave off clots to the experimental IVIG, a blood product taken from people without immunological disorders and given intra-venously to combat the abnormal autoimmune response (see Chapter 8 for information on Lovenox and baby aspirin).

Complications

Though we've discussed the things that cause complications, now we need to look for a moment at the complications themselves. I didn't lead you to this part of the Land of If to scare the crap out of you, and if you find yourself becoming overwhelmed by the possibilities of what can go wrong, close the book and breathe for a moment. Can I promise you that these things will never happen? Of course not, because I don't make promises that I can't keep. But statistics are on your side: Many more people deliver healthy babies at term than go into labor prematurely or lose the child altogether. I included this information not only for those who may be affected in the future, but more as comfort and information for those who have been affected by loss. The subsections have been arranged chronologically, based on when they'd be diagnosed or occur during a pregnancy.

Molar Pregnancies

Molar pregnancies are extremely rare (about 1 in 1,500 pregnancies in America).[4] There are two types of molar pregnancies—a *complete mole* or a *partial mole*. With a complete mole, the placenta develops abnormally (it has the appearance of a cluster of grapes if you see it on an ultrasound) and no baby is present. In a partial mole, the placenta is abnormal, and while the baby is present, it is unlikely to survive until birth. In both types of molar pregnancies, the baby has too many chromosomes, as the egg was fertilized by two sperm.

A molar pregnancy is dangerous to the woman's health and requires a D&C (see page 159). A small portion of women will also develop a *choriocarcinoma,* a pregnancy-related cancer that may require chemotherapy. An even smaller portion of those women will have a hysterectomy in order to remove all cells from the mole (which may travel to other organs). Doctors need to monitor hCG levels for a yearlong period and make sure the mole does not return (in some cases, it does return, even after a D&C). Therefore, doctors universally prescribe a yearlong waiting period before a woman can try to get pregnant again following a molar pregnancy.

Ectopic Pregnancy

In one out of fifty pregnancies, the fertilized egg implants outside of the uterus—usually in a fallopian tube—creating an ectopic

PREGNANCY LOSS AFTER INFERTILITY

Another hardship particular to certain Iffers is returning to the mainland after a prolonged stay on the island—only to experience pregnancy loss. Although it is difficult to lose any pregnancy, a loss that occurs after fertility treatments or donor gametes also means that all the emotional, physical, and financial capital spent on procedures, injections, retrievals, and transfers was for naught.

These Iffers are stuck now on the mainland with a weighty set of baggage and plaguing questions: *How do I trust my body when it not only let me down during conception but now is letting me down during pregnancy? How do I find the strength to return to the clinic and try another round of IVF? And how do I afford to try again?* The answers to these questions, as you probably guessed, are unique to each person.

A loss that occurs after treatments should be examined in order to discover the root of the problem, because the answer can sometimes (but not always) assist in future conception. In addition, multiple failed IVF cycles should be taken as multiple early losses and examined in order to determine if the cause is simply chance or an underlying problem.

pregnancy.[5] These embryos must be medically treated or surgically removed in order to avoid a rupture and internal bleeding.

If caught early enough, before any damage has been done, a doctor may be able to remove the embryo without removing the fallopian tube. When removal of the tube is required, the woman suffers an emotional double loss: Not only is the pregnancy over, but it has taken her tube (and perhaps future fertility) with it.

While over 40 percent of women who have had a fallopian tube removed go on to have healthy pregnancies, ectopic pregnancies have between an 8 and 14 percent rate of recurrence.[6]

Placenta Previa

This complication occurs when the placenta lies over the cervix, rather than at the top of the uterus. Not all women diagnosed with placenta previa will have a problem. Depending on the type of placenta previa (there are multiple forms), there is a chance that this condition will fix itself. At other times, it can cause uterine bleeding toward the end of the second trimester, which can be fatal for both the baby and the mother. Women with placenta previa that does not correct itself will need to deliver their baby via C-section and may need to deliver their baby prematurely in order to control bleeding. This bleeding can intensify during and after the delivery and should be monitored closely.

Fetal and Uterine Abnormalities

Fetal abnormalities sometimes play a role in late-term loss. These abnormalities are often diagnosed using prenatal testing. See page 268 of Chapter 12 for more on prenatal testing, including the pros and cons of it.

Uterine abnormalities can also cause problems. A weak cervix can open prematurely, causing preterm labor. This condition can sometimes be circumvented with a stitch in the cervix, called *cerclage,* that is performed between weeks fourteen and sixteen in the pregnancy. Unfortunately, since the cervix isn't routinely tested during every pregnancy, most women do not know that they have a weak cervix until they have suffered through a late-term loss. Therefore, cerclage is generally used to treat a subsequent pregnancy.

Premature Rupture

In every vaginal delivery, the amniotic sac either ruptures naturally or is broken by the physician. But when the amniotic sac ruptures or leaks prior to thirty-seven weeks, it is called *preterm premature rupture of membranes,* or PPROM. PPROM can cause a premature delivery. Depending on the time of rupture and the progression of the pregnancy, some babies will not be able to live and thrive outside of the womb.

---

no. 0021

THE LAND OF IF VISITORS BUREAU

TIP: If you have experienced pregnancy loss, the best way to help yourself is to let others know your expectations and needs.

If you want to be left alone, explain to people that you'd rather not have visitors or go out to events. On the other hand, if you want company, let people know that, too.

If you don't want others to talk about it to anyone else, let them know. It's also okay to let them know not to try to discuss it with you again unless you bring it up yourself.

On the other hand, if you *do* want to talk about it, remind them that it would help you immensely if they asked about it from time to time. With some friends or family members, you may need to be firm and ask them not to change the subject when you bring up the loss.

Preeclampsia

This condition, also called *toxemia,* can be life-threatening for both the mother and the baby. It is characterized by high blood pressure and protein in the urine. Unusual swelling or weight gain can be a tip-off, so doctors should be contacted immediately. At the same time, some women with preeclampsia experience no symptoms prior to diagnosis. Preeclampsia can affect the flow of blood (and consequently nutrition and oxygen) to the baby. The best way to treat it is to deliver the baby, and there are times when it is necessary—in order to save the life of the mother—to deliver the baby immediately. If the baby can survive outside of the womb, this may not be an issue, but that is not always the case. Preeclampsia can cause many problems for the mother, including organ failure and brain damage, and these need to be taken into account when deciding whether to risk continuing the pregnancy. There are times when blood pressure can be reduced with medications, as well as bed rest, but these are decisions that should be left to a doctor.

Placental Abruption

When the placenta becomes detached prior to delivery, it is called placental abruption. It can cause severe bleeding for the mother, which in turn can adversely affect the growth and development of the fetus. Problems with the placenta can restrict the flow of nutrition and oxygen to the baby, causing long-term effects. In rare cases, if blood flow cannot be controlled after the delivery, the uterus may need to be removed in order to save the life of the mother. Once the placenta detaches from the uterine wall, the baby will need to be delivered immediately, regardless of the gestational age, since remaining in utero can lead to death for both the mother and the baby.

Umbilical Problems

There are several problems that can occur with the umbilical cord, the

WHAT DID I DO TO DESERVE THIS?

As you can see, things such as "negative thoughts" or "telling people too soon" or "punishment for having a morning cup of coffee" are not listed as reasons for pregnancy loss. Nevertheless, this kind of magical thinking affects some people, burdening them with a great deal of guilt.

Because the general public understands so little about why pregnancy loss occurs, those who experience it often think they could have done something to prevent it, and worry that they are personally responsible for the death of the embryo or fetus. This, of course, is not true. With the exception of a few situations, loss is generally outside the parents' control.

Pregnancy loss happens to good people. It happens to some not-so-good people, too. Pregnancy loss happens even if you do everything right, attend church twice a week, and eat only organic food. And it's important for you to hear this message: You did nothing wrong. Sometimes terrible things just happen.

Sometimes our hearts won't listen to our brains. If the guilt of pregnancy loss is eating you up even if you rationally understand the prior paragraph, please turn to some of the online and face-to-face groups listed in the Resources section.

narrow tube that connects the baby to the placenta. Most of the time, these problems cause no long-term damage to the developing baby. But in rare occurrences, they can be the cause of late-term loss.

The cord can be either too short or too long. It can compress or become knotted. It can be connected improperly to the placenta, affecting the flow of nutrition and oxygen to the developing fetus. A prolapsed cord can exit the vagina after the membranes break but before the baby is delivered; these babies need to be delivered immediately and via C-section in order to prevent stillbirth. Sometimes, the cord can be wrapped one or more times around the neck (called *nuchal loops*). While this looping may sometimes be harmless, at other times, it can cause death. The cord can also develop a knot that could cut off a baby's oxygen supply if tightened inadvertently.

Vasa previa is a serious condition in which blood vessels are over the cervical opening within the uterus. These blood vessels aren't protected (as they should be) by the umbilical cord and can rupture when the amniotic sac breaks prior to delivery. Vasa previa can cause life-threatening bleeding for the baby during the delivery if blood vessels are ruptured. When vasa previa is diagnosed, the baby must be delivered immediately by C-section.

Intrauterine Growth Restriction (IUGR)

Babies who experience IUGR are less than the tenth percentile for their gestational age. There are a multitude of reasons for IUGR, and many are connected to the placenta. When the uterus seems small for the gestational age, a doctor should carefully monitor the pregnancy with ultrasounds and nonstress tests. IUGR can lead to intrauterine death if the baby stops growing due to a lack of nutrition from the placenta.

Complications with the Amniotic Fluid

A woman may have too much amniotic fluid (hydramnios) or too little (oligohydramnios). When there is too much, the uterus can become distended, and the woman can go into preterm labor. When there is not enough, the baby's lungs may not develop properly, and the umbilical cord may become compressed. Both are serious conditions. Medications are sometimes given, or amniocentesis used, to remove excess fluid. At other times, the fluid level will be closely monitored and the baby delivered when it becomes necessary.

TIP: Delivering a baby who was born still and losing a child to neonatal death are particularly devastating tragedies. And unfortunately, hospital staff members are not always trained on how to deal with these losses sensitively. Worse still, a lack of hospital space may mean that the woman is laboring in the maternity ward, surrounded by the cries and sights of newborns and new parents. Later, there can be other painful reminders of the loss: The woman's body often does not "know" that the baby has died and behaves as if a live birth has taken place. Breasts may produce and leak milk.

When you're in the middle of this kind of crisis, it's impossible to think clearly. So, if you can, put someone in charge of being your advocate, and give him or her the following instructions:

1) Make sure all staff members entering the room know what has just happened. It is terrible to get a friendly visit from the lactation specialist to congratulate you on your new baby.

2) Make arrangements to ensure you will get time alone with the baby to say goodbye if you desire.

3) Take photographs.

4) Collect any reminders of the baby—footprints, handprints, or locks of hair can sometimes help later with the grieving process.

5) Help streamline the process of making funeral or cremation arrangements, consulting you only when decisions need to be made.

Remember, even if you think you will not want mementos from this time, you may change your mind, so it never hurts to make sure you have the option. Later on, you can always ask that the mementos be destroyed. Sometimes it can help to have these tangible reminders that this person existed and was loved.

Missed Miscarriages

A missed miscarriage is when the baby dies but is not expelled naturally by the body. It can be extremely traumatic to learn that the baby has died and to have to wait days until a D&C or a D&E can be performed.

D&C (which stands for dilation and curettage) and a D&E (which stands for dilation and evacuation) are two procedures used to clear the uterus of tissue after a pregnancy loss. With a D&C, the lining is scraped from the uterus. With a D&E, the lining is suctioned out.

D&Cs and D&Es are surgical procedures; therefore, general anesthesia is usually used (though some doctors will use a local anesthetic). A speculum, clamp, and rods will hold open the cervix, while either a scalpel or a hollow tube is used to remove the tissue from inside the uterus. After the procedure, you can expect light bleeding (heavier bleeding should be reported to a doctor), as well as cramping. Though it is a relatively quick procedure, the length of time should not fool someone into believing that the emotional scars will heal as quickly.

As hard as it can be to miscarry naturally, the finality of this surgical procedure can be heartbreaking. For some women, they would rather have their body pass the tissue than take an active role, or assign that active role to a doctor. For others, they feel it is better to move forward and have closure with the pregnancy—especially if they are seeking answers through tissue typing after the loss.

Medical Termination

Medical termination, also known as therapeutic abortion, is the termination of a pregnancy either to protect the health of the mother (in the event of a life-threatening situation, such as preeclampsia) or to euthanize the fetus. This is possibly the hardest decision a parent will ever make—and it is even harder when the termination comes after infertility. Those entering into this decision should seek counseling by medical professionals before and after the loss.

Selective Reduction

A subsection of medical termination is *multifetal pregnancy reduction* (MPR), more commonly known as "selective reduction." Yet the word "selective" is misleading, because selection gives the illusion of choice. And like many cases of medical termination, MPR is not a choice insomuch as it is a necessary step to ensuring the health of the mother and the remaining fetus(es). MPR is used when more than one fetus is in the uterus (it is usually done only on higher-order multiples) or when one baby's medical conditions are affecting other babies in the womb.

WHEN AND WHETHER TO TRY, TRY AGAIN

After experiencing the pain of pregnancy loss, not everyone chooses to get back on the proverbial horse and try again. Some may not have the money or wherewithal to go through it again. Those who seem to conceive with no problems but have trouble carrying to term may give up on experiencing pregnancy, and look toward adopting, surrogacy, or living child-free. There may be times that a couple is not in agreement on when or if to try again. The timing needs to take into account both people in a partnership, and it's best to postpone until both people are on board.

There are three schools of thought on attempting pregnancy again after a loss. One includes people who push forward into another cycle as soon as possible. Another includes people who decide to wait for an extended period of time. And the third includes those who choose never to risk loss again, by not trying. All paths are completely healthy and legitimate.

The doctor may put a medical timeline in place, requiring a certain period of time before the woman is medically cleared to conceive again. But once you are medically cleared to try again, the timing is entirely up to you. Everyone's emotional timeline varies, and a desire to try again doesn't mean a cessation to the mourning process. In fact, you may find yourself balancing two very different emotions—the excitement of trying again and the sadness of the loss. And certainly, fear plays a big role in trying again after a loss. You may worry that trying again is disloyal to the first baby, and that you need more time to pass between the loss and the new pregnancy. Some people prefer to wait until they pass their estimated due date before trying again. On the other hand, you may not have time to wait, or you may be anxious to be pregnant before that estimated due date.

Final Thoughts

There is not a right or wrong way to mourn pregnancy loss, stillbirth, or neonatal death. There is not a right or wrong way to remember the baby. You may find comfort through either face-to-face support groups or online discussion boards connecting you with others who have gone through loss. These are people who understand, who can nod, give you space to cry, and help you stand up if or when you are ready to move forward once again.

A WALKING TOUR

of Treatments

FERTILITY TREATMENTS (also called infertility treatments) cover a wide range of medications and technologies meant to either treat or circumvent a fertility problem. They can be as simple as oral medication and as complex as in vitro fertilization. Most doctors start small and ramp up to more-invasive procedures. (But that's not always the case; see the sidebar "Nixing the NyQuil Approach," in this chapter.)

Treatments have some advantages when compared with the other paths: Sticky legal questions are circumvented, and parents can maintain a genetic and biological link to their offspring. Depending on insurance coverage, treatments can be less expensive than the other paths.

But there are some drawbacks. Those undergoing treatments pay for the chance (not a promise) to get pregnant and carry to term, so it is hardly a sure thing—and the cost of treatments can really add

TIP: By "fertility treatments" I mean treating infertility with your own genetic material. Donor gametes also involve utilizing assisted reproductive technology (ART), and some people do noninvasive approaches, such as timed intercourse or alternative therapies. But for the sake of clarity, when I speak about treatments, I am talking about everything from medications and IUI to IVF, ICSI, PGD, and assisted hatching.

There is no possible way for me to address all of the fertility drugs on the market. Not only are there just too many, but the market is also constantly in flux: New drugs are being introduced all the time and are pushing older ones out of the marketplace. In this book, I address the most commonly prescribed medications.

up. They can also be fairly uncomfortable, they involve health risks, and they can control your schedule. The emotional ups and downs that come with fertility treatments must be taken into account as well.

In a partnership, both people need to be equally comfortable with ART (assisted reproductive technologies), and it's best to make decisions before you are in the moment and emotions come into play. Many people have found it helpful to create decision lists or choice webs (see Chapter 3) to gauge their physical, emotional, and financial comfort levels with different procedures and medications *before* the decisions actually have to be made. Some recommend establishing a financial cap or cycle limit, but I think these brick walls cause more anxiety than comfort. It can be very stressful to be facing what you know is your final cycle. At the same time, it's too easy to keep hacking away at the problem without seeing results and driving yourself deeper into debt in the process. Rather than setting a single number, set a cycle range for when you'll revisit the decision to continue, with markers built into the journey. For instance, decide that you'll revisit the idea of continuing treatments every three cycles and gauge whether you believe it's worth it to continue.

Noninvasive Treatments

First up are medications that can be taken orally, nasally, vaginally, or rectally. How many times in life do you have the opportunity to utilize four orifices for medical reasons in a single month?

Clomid

ALSO KNOWN AS: clomiphene citrate, Serophene
ADMINISTRATION: oral
KNOWN SIDE EFFECTS: hot flashes, headaches, fatigue

Clomid is handed out by everyone and their grandmother. True, it is a simple, noninvasive, and often helpful medication that works by inducing ovulation. But it also has a tendency to be misused, both by doctors and by patients. Unless an underlying and specific fertility problem has already been diagnosed (for instance, a lack of fallopian tubes), Clomid tends to be a first-line-defense drug thrown into battle without prior blood work.

To extend the war analogy, whereas injectable medications are like guns, Clomid is like a bomb. Gunfire can be controlled: It can

TIP: Some clinics offer a "shared-risk plan," and without arguing these plans' benefits and drawbacks, I will note that a single silver lining built into this financing is removing the necessity to make monetary decisions with each cycle. Shared-risk plans allow patients to pay once for three or four cycles. The cost of these plans is usually set around the cost of two cycles, with the promise made that most or all of your money will be refunded if you do not have a live birth. Some people purchase these plans not for the financial insurance, but for the relationship insurance—it can be very stressful on a relationship to make decisions about huge sums of money over and over again. You won't know if these plans were a sound financial decision until you're finished with your clinic and know how many cycles it took to either get pregnant or not get pregnant. But if financial issues are causing stress, these plans can help assuage some of that pressure. For more information on these types of plans, as well as on other books covering financing fertility treatments, see the Resources section.

be stopped, and it can zone in on a tiny area. Bombs, on the other hand, are simply dropped . . . and then we wait for the dust to clear to assess the results.

Because its effects are so hard to control, you are more likely to have higher-order multiples (triplets or more) with Clomid than with injectables. This is only one reason why it is important to be monitored by your doctor while taking this medication (see the next section).

Clomid's success rate decreases with each cycle, and its usage is best limited to six ovulatory cycles. Therefore, if you're on your eighth cycle of Clomid, your doctor should be suggesting a next course of action.

Clomid has a tendency to thin the uterine lining (making successful implantation more difficult over time), in addition to drying out cervical mucus. Some Iffers claim to be able to maintain their cervical mucus by drinking decaffeinated green tea. There is no scientific data supporting this notion, but it's widely practiced in the community. See the sidebar "Alternative Fertility Boosters," in this chapter.

no. 0025
THE LAND OF IF VISITORS BUREAU

TIP: Infertility is a consumer industry, which means the choice of where to cycle is often in your hands. It's always good to collect information from friends and family members, as well as online sites and clinic websites. But in the end, everyone should essentially be interviewing a clinic or reproductive endocrinologist during the initial visit. The website for SART (Society for Assisted Reproductive Technology, www.sart.org) lists the success rates of clinics nationwide.

CAREFUL WHAT YOU WISH FOR

With all the talk of multiple births in connection to fertility treatments, it may surprise you if you don't end up carrying twins or triplets. In reality, the chance of having twins via IVF in the United States is about 25 percent. The chance of having twins via Clomid is about 20 percent. There are many things you can do to cut back on your chances of having multiples, though there is little you can do safely to raise your chance of having them. It's just the luck of the draw.

Now I know that there are some people who want multiples (I have to admit, we weren't sad when we found out we were having twins). The politically correct thing to say at this point is that no one should *aim* to carry twins or more. There are risks in a multiples pregnancy—to both the mother and the children. For one, the unusual pressure on the cervix can cause it to open prematurely. Preeclampsia is twice as common in twin pregnancies as it is in singleton pregnancies. Women carrying multiples have a higher rate of gestational diabetes. In order to avoid preterm labor, women carrying multiples almost always require some form of bed rest.

Basically, the higher the number of fetuses, the higher-risk a pregnancy becomes. Still, statistics are on your side. Most people safely and successfully deliver healthy multiples. And they are definitely a reality of fertility treatments. If you are carrying multiples, contact your local NOMOTC chapter (see Resources) because it will be an invaluable resource for information and support.

THE IMPORTANCE OF MONITORING WITH CLOMID

Clomid is often prescribed for unmonitored cycles, and this can be a dangerous practice. First and foremost, you have no idea if you're actually ovulating unless your doctor is using sonograms and blood work to check for ovulation. (Cervical mucus does *not* mean that you are ovulating; it merely means that your body is prime for ovulation whether it occurs or not.) Most doctors begin at the lowest dose—50 mg—and increase it with each cycle if they're not finding strong ovulation. No monitoring means you don't gain this knowledge.

Clomid also can cause cysts to form in the ovaries. When you are having a monitored cycle, your doctor is checking your ovaries via a sonogram on day 3 to make sure your ovaries are cyst-free. It can cause damage to the ovaries to add Clomid to existing cysts.

If your doctor does not traditionally do monitoring with Clomid, you can still request the desired tests (checking for cysts on day 3 and checking for ovulation). If your doctor dismisses your concerns . . . well, that's reason, for me, to get a new doctor.

---

no. 0026

THE LAND OF IF VISITORS BUREAU

TIP: Take your Clomid two hours before bed, and you will probably be able to skip most of the side effects.

Femara

ALSO KNOWN AS: letrozole
ADMINISTRATION: oral
KNOWN SIDE EFFECTS: hot flashes and mood swings (though fewer than Clomid)

Femara is used off-label to inhibit estrogen (see the sidebar "Off-Label Treatment"). For a while, Femara has been in the hot zone, because it is technically approved by the FDA only as a drug to treat

NIXING THE
NYQUIL APPROACH

NyQuil is just one of many medications on the market that treat a whole host of symptoms at the same time. Usually, people don't have every symptom on the list, but they take it anyway, because they have a few symptoms, and it's easier to take one medication that overtreats the problem than to take two medications or more to treat each individual problem. When this "NyQuil approach" is used to treating infertility, it *can* end up saving time, physical pain, and money. But it's a gamble, and your health and success are at stake.

The emotional, physical, and financial stakes associated with fertility treatments start low, with oral medications and suppositories such as Clomid and Prometrium. Then they begin to ramp up—rising higher with injectable medications and procedures like IUI and peaking with procedures such as IVF, PGD, and ICSI. So it makes sense to do the minimum possible to treat the unique problem and to use a methodological approach, ramping up as needed.

If your doctor's level of aggressiveness in treating your infertility is making you uncomfortable in any way, take matters back into your own hands. Remember the Iffer's Bill of Rights (see Chapter 3). Demand that your voice be heard, and find a new doctor if that's what it takes.

breast cancer (and to inhibit estrogen, which can feed breast cancer cells). Since those with breast cancer and those with polycystic ovarian syndrome (PCOS) benefit from the same result—a suppression of estrogen production—the drug has been applied toward fertility treatments, as it tricks the body into releasing FSH correctly. And it has met with great success.

OFF-LABEL TREATMENT

Some drugs are not actually approved by the FDA to be used in treating infertility, even though they are approved for other uses. This can be for many reasons, including a lack of motivation on the part of the manufacturer to seek approval for use of the drug as a treatment for infertility, or because it has not been deemed safe due to conflicting evidence.

But to put things into perspective, off-label usage is common throughout the medical community and in the treatment of many diseases. The FDA will approve a drug for a use, but the doctor is able to utilize it for other reasons when it fits. In fact, you have probably been treated off-label for other conditions or diseases without even realizing it. So if you or your partner just finished popping your third Femara, don't fret. This information is only meant to help you be a careful consumer who is a partner within his or her own treatment. Femara is a widely prescribed drug, and many drugs are actually being used—with great success—off label.

At the same time, issues have been raised about the possibility of birth defects occurring while a woman is on the drug. Of course, the drug is not taken in the second part of the cycle and is metabolized by the body, usually prior to ovulation, so it may not affect the baby at all. But if you are concerned, have a conversation with your doctor about the latest studies on this off-label usage.

Metformin

ALSO KNOWN AS: Glucophage

ADMINISTRATION: oral

KNOWN SIDE EFFECTS: upset stomach, diarrhea, nausea, and gas

Metformin is a diabetes drug that lowers the sometimes elevated blood sugar levels in women with PCOS. The drug helps kick-start ovulation in those who aren't ovulating and regulates menstrual cycles. It is commonly prescribed as a first-line defense for women diagnosed with PCOS.

Make sure your doctor is starting with a low dose and working up to a higher dose, rather than just starting with the normal dose. Metformin has some unlovely side effects associated with it: a package deal of abdominal bloating, gas, and diarrhea, lovingly referred to as "Met gut" by those taking it.

---

no. 0027

THE LAND OF IF VISITORS BUREAU

TIP: To decrease the chance and severity of Met gut, stick to a low-fat, low-carb diet and cut out the refined sugars. I know, it's terrible. You have enough stress with infertility, and now I'm telling you to change your diet, a feat that most find downright impossible when they're already emotional. But . . . . um . . . . raisins are nature's candy. . . . . (I know, you probably wish you could chuck this book at me right about now.)

Progesterone

ALSO KNOWN AS: Prometrium, Crinone, and other forms of progesterone

ADMINISTRATION: oral, vaginal, rectal (rare), or intramuscular (see PIO, below)

KNOWN SIDE EFFECTS: headaches, nausea, drowsiness, mood swings, drippage (for suppositories)

Oral progesterone is the least invasive way to take progesterone, but it's also the least effective. It has to be metabolized by the liver before it gets to where it needs to go, and that makes the delivery system convoluted and inefficient. Still, if there isn't a significant problem with progesterone levels and your doctor has a particular reason for wanting the progesterone taken orally, go for it. Personally, I could never mentally get around the idea that the same thing could go in your mouth *and* inside your hoohaahooterus, but I'm also the type who likes my food neatly separated on the plate.

If you are going the vaginal route, the most important thing to note is cosmetic. Progesterone suppositories and gels are accompanied by leakage and that not-so-fresh feeling that can come only from having yellow peanut oil spilling out onto your pantiliner. But using progesterone vaginally gets the medication directly where it is needed, and quickly. Even when it is working, it will not affect your blood progesterone levels; therefore, you may not get the hardcore proof you need to feel comfortable that all is fine in utero. It's simply a matter of trust. The two most common forms of vaginal progesterone are Prometrium (a yellow capsule) and Crinone (a gel inside a prefilled, disposable applicator).

Here is another fear that often comes up for people who wonder if they truly need progesterone supplements: Can you overdose on progesterone? Let's start by getting to the meat of the

TIP: If using progesterone vaginally, make sure you use a pantiliner at all times and carry a few spare ones with you during the day. No one wants a pair of peanut oil-filled panties. If possible, lie down for a few minutes after insertion to help the progesterone remain up where it is needed.

Progesterone can also make the cervix more sensitive, which can lead to spotting after sex—an important point to keep in mind in case you suddenly see bleeding during the second part of your cycle (which you should, by the way, report to your doctor).

answer: No, you cannot overdose on progesterone, unless you're not following your doctor's orders or you're self-medicating. The placenta is going to create levels of progesterone that are much higher than those of any vaginal suppository. But progesterone (and therefore "too much" progesterone) *can* cause side effects ranging from headaches to nausea—the same side effects that signal pregnancy. Therefore, you'll probably feel "pregnant" even if you're not.

Many doctors prescribe preventive progesterone suppositories—in other words, you may not *need* the extra progesterone, but it certainly can't hurt. Trust your doctor if he or she prescribes progesterone, and know that an extra suppository or two taken over the course of the day if you have borderline progesterone issues is not going to cause damage to an embryo.

While we're on the topic of side effects, I should probably tell you about the side effect known colloquially as "Prometrium rage." Don't be surprised if you find yourself inexplicably weepy or overspilling with anger while taking a form of progesterone. The hormone can wreak havoc on your emotions, though it certainly helps to keep it in perspective if you remember that it's a normal side effect of the medication. This explanation, of course, is not meant to dismiss the emotions, either. They can be a scary and upsetting side effect of treatments. Sleepiness can also be a side effect of all progesterone-based drugs.

Synarel

ADMINISTRATION: nasal

KNOWN SIDE EFFECTS: headaches, headaches, and more headaches

Synarel is a nasal spray that decreases the amount of follicle-stimulating hormone (FSH) and luteinizing hormone (LH) secreted by the pituitary gland. It's used during suppression in an IVF cycle, and it helps the RE override the cycle to better control all hormone levels and to create optimum conditions all the way down the line.

The biggest complaint about Synarel is a complaint applicable to all the suppression drugs—headaches. This side effect comes from hormonal changes, namely estrogen levels. The headaches will go away once the next part of the cycle kicks in and estrogen levels are encouraged to rise.

VIGILANTE
TREATMENTS

There are stories floating around the Internet of women who have self-prescribed Clomid and purchased it online. But you would never do that, right? Because you care about your body, and you care about treating it well and leaving the prescriptions to a doctor, who can see the bigger picture—including the damaging effects of fertility drugs taken without monitoring.

More recent is the self-prescribing of DHEA, a natural-steroid supplement that is used to treat ovulation disorders such as premature ovarian failure (POF), but it is also being self-prescribed by women who read fertility-success stories on the Internet and purchase this over-the-counter medication. However, this drug's effectiveness hasn't been proven, and there isn't enough evidence to warrant the potential risks of taking it. At the same time, many fertility drugs are off-label uses of established medications.

So how should you approach a supplement that sounds like a potential panacea for ovarian dysfunction or loss of ovarian reserves due to age? Especially a medication that serves as a supplement to a hormone your body already produces, simply in declining amounts? You should fall on the same side as your reproductive endocrinologist. I know—not the answer you wanted to hear, and I'm sure it won't be a popular one for those who feel strongly one way or the other about a new medication. But playing with your fertility and basing your decisions on the stories of others, rather than on sound medical studies (and not just any medical studies—those determined to be impeccable in the recording and examination of data), is just one step on the path to regret. You may end up with the child of your dreams, or you may end up with other medical issues. Frankly, it's not worth the risk. And those doctors did have to do a lot of fancy work to get their medical knowledge.

For information on other, less risky approaches to DIY fertility treatments, see the appendix.

Birth Control Pills

ADMINISTRATION: oral

KNOWN SIDE EFFECTS: moodiness, breast tenderness, nausea, dizziness

It may be really surprising to receive a prescription for birth control pills when you're infertile, but they are also commonly used in the suppression phase of IVF. Like Synarel, birth control pills give the RE control over the cycle so he or she can override the body's natural hormone production.

Baby Aspirin and Folic Acid

ADMINISTRATION: oral

Baby aspirin is used to thin out the blood. It also makes the platelets less sticky. Though it is commonly prescribed to people with clotting disorders, doctors have begun prescribing it to those without clotting disorders as well, in order to create better blood flow for implantation.

Though all women should take at least 400 mcg of folic acid if they are trying to conceive, those diagnosed with MTHFR should take an additional folic acid supplement. Folgard is a popular prescription-level folic acid, B_6, and B_{12} supplement.

The Injectables

Injections control the whole cycle, from overriding natural hormones to stimulating follicles to starting ovulation to maintaining progesterone levels. No two cycles are identical, so it's impossible to predict exactly how many injections you'll need for an average IUI or IVF cycle.

The sting factor for injectables will be different for each person, but use this information as a guide. The general rule is that the more the medication stings, the more slowly you should inject it. (Therefore, take your time with Lovenox but feel free to move quickly with Lupron.)

This section is written with the majority of injectees (women) in mind. If you are a man using these medications in order to build your sperm count, I apologize. Also, in the interest of simplifying language, I make the assumption that subcutaneous injections will be self-administered and IM injections will be done by a friend or partner, based on a survey of how the majority of infertility patients administer injections.

Lupron

USE: suppression
TYPE OF INJECTION: subcutaneous
KNOWN SIDE EFFECTS: headaches, moodiness
STING FACTOR: low

Out of all the subcutaneous medications, Lupron has the smallest needle and the strongest side effects. This is an off-label usage for Lupron (see the sidebar "Off-Label Treatment," in this chapter), which is traditionally used to treat endometriosis and fibroids. It suppresses the hormones your body is naturally producing, so your RE can override your body and control the cycle. It is given at the beginning of an IVF cycle, but not during an IUI cycle.

THE LAND OF IF VISITORS BUREAU

TIP: In a report in *Fertility and Sterility* from 2001, researchers found that women who drank coffee saw a boost in their estrogen levels in the early part of their cycle—exactly when an RE wants estrogen production suppressed.[1] But a cup or two of coffee should not make an enormous difference in your estrogen levels, and fellow stirrup queens have reported that coffee, in addition to Tylenol, does seem to help with the Lupron headache.

Ganirelix

USE: suppression
TYPE OF INJECTION: subcutaneous
KNOWN SIDE EFFECTS: burns if it gets on the skin, itchy welts
STING FACTOR: medium to high

Ganirelix is like Lupron in that it suppresses FSH and LH, and it is used for the Antagon or non-Lupron protocol during IVF. In other words, it stops premature ovulation. You wouldn't want those follicles to release their egg before you could get to retrieval!

Follistim

ALSO PRESCRIBED: Gonal-F, Bravelle, or Fertinex

USE: ovarian stimulation

TYPE OF INJECTION: subcutaneous or intramuscular

KNOWN SIDE EFFECTS: bloating, heaviness as stimulation occurs

STING FACTOR: medium (intramuscular Bravelle can burn more over the course of the cycle with each use)

Here's what these drugs can do: They can help a follicle develop and produce a better-quality egg. They are also sometimes used by men to help produce sperm.

Here's what they cannot do: They can't make a woman form follicles if her ovaries are not producing follicles, nor can they help a man produce sperm if his testes aren't already producing sperm.

This means that Follistim and other FSH-based drugs are not miracle workers that can cause a woman who is in menopause to ovulate, much to the chagrin of the media, which would like you to believe otherwise.

Follistim can also be used to produce multiple follicles (and multiple eggs) to make IVF more successful. Follistim and other FSH-based drugs are also given for IUIs, but at a lower dosage. (The goal for an IUI is to produce no more than two or three follicles; the goal for IVF is to produce more than three follicles.)

Sometimes, if the drugs cause you to produce too many follicles or too few follicles, your IUI or IVF will be converted. In other words, an IUI that produces too many follicles may become an IVF cycle, and an IVF cycle that produces too few may become an IUI cycle. Ask your RE about this before the cycle to gauge her protocol when things don't go according to plan; that way, you can foresee the next step.

These drugs come in vials or in a newfangled pen contraption. Your doctor will prescribe one or the other, depending on the dose you are taking. (The vial is used more often in an IUI, because less Follistim is used; the pen is used more often in IVF, because more Follistim is used.)

Follistim and Gonal-F have to be used immediately after mixing if you're mixing your own syringe instead of using the pen. In other words, don't prepare the syringe and leave it sitting around for a few hours. Follistim can be stored at room temperature or in the refrigerator (you want it away from heat and light), but the Follistim AQ cartridges must be kept in the refrigerator. Mixed Gonal-F should be refrigerated.

no. 0031
THE LAND OF IF VISITORS BUREAU

TIP: You can request (though not all clinics will honor it) to do your first injection in the presence of a nurse or doctor. Don't feel bad about asking, and don't be shy. As for me, I'd rather find out that my nervousness is part of a big family joke at the RE's house than sit for hours in my own house, worrying if I'm doing it right. Feh on them—I only hope I'm interesting enough as a patient to make it into dinner table conversation.

Menopur

ALSO PRESCRIBED: Repronex, Pergonal, or Humegon

USE: ovarian stimulation

TYPE OF INJECTION: subcutaneous or intramuscular

KNOWN SIDE EFFECTS: bloating, heaviness as stimulation occurs

STING FACTOR: medium (intramuscular Repronex can burn more over the course of the cycle with each use)

Menopur is a menotropin, meaning that it is a combination of FSH and LH (as opposed to Follistim, which is solely FSH). Like Follistim, it helps the body produce better-quality follicles, and more of them—when the ability to produce follicles is present. Like Follistim, it is also sometimes prescribed for men to help produce more sperm. Lastly, a lot of the information about Follistim applies to these drugs as well.

---

no. 0032

THE LAND OF IF VISITORS BUREAU

TIP: Like Follistim, Menopur has to be used pretty much immediately after mixing it, but some people swear that if you let it sit for a few minutes, it burns less. A few minutes is not going to hurt, so try it out and see if this helps with the sting factor.

Ovidrel

ALSO PRESCRIBED: Novarel, Pregnyl, or Profasi
USE: "trigger shot," meaning it releases the egg during ovulation
TYPE OF INJECTION: subcutaneous or intramuscular
KNOWN SIDE EFFECTS: full, preovulation feeling; pelvic heaviness
STING FACTOR: medium to high

Once ovaries have been stimulated and follicles are produced, it's time to get each follicle to release its egg. This is done with a trigger shot of hCG—yes, the same hormone that your body produces once it is pregnant (the one measured by the beta hCG test, discussed in Chapter 6).

This can be injected either subcutaneously or intramuscularly. Subcutaneous injections of Ovidrel or Novarel are more often prescribed than the intramuscular drugs Pregnyl and Profasi. Some drugs, like Ovidrel, come in a prefilled syringe, while others need to be mixed.

If you pee on a home pregnancy test after taking the trigger shot, you will get to see the elusive two pink lines. Of course, this doesn't mean you're pregnant—it simply means you've injected hCG into your body. It takes several days for the body to metabolize the hCG; therefore, some people will begin peeing on a stick a day after the trigger and keep using home pregnancy tests until the line goes away. If you're the type who likes to test early and often, this is the only way you can be certain that when two lines *do* show ten days postovulation, what you're seeing is a positive pregnancy test, rather than a positive trigger-shot test. The higher the dose, the longer it will take to get the hCG out of your system. Make sure you wait ten days minimum before testing if you haven't been watching the line get fainter each day post trigger.

Progesterone in Oil (PIO)

USE: progesterone support

TYPE OF INJECTION: intramuscular

KNOWN SIDE EFFECTS: knots at the injection site, soreness

STING FACTOR: low, but some pain afterward

Progesterone in oil is usually given with a 22-gauge intramuscular (IM) needle. Just so you know, the lower the number, the bigger the gauge. You can ask your pharmacist for a 25-gauge needle instead. The progesterone will still flow through this needle, and the injection will be less painful than with the thicker needle.

It's not actually the progesterone that is causing the viscosity of the liquid—it's the oil—and you can get PIO in a plethora of oils, including peanut, sesame, and olive. The thinner the oil, the better the medication flows from the needle, leaving fewer knots down the line. Therefore, ask the pharmacist for the thinnest oil (generally agreed upon to be ethyl oleate).

Other advice specific to PIO is to warm the filled syringe inside a heating pad. After filling the syringe, replace the cap, and place it inside a heating pad until it's warm. This will help the medication flow out of the needle, and it's the same thought that suggests using heat after the injection on the site in order to distribute the medication. You can also heat the oil while it's still in the vial. If you're on the road and sneaking a PIO injection in a movie theater bathroom, you can still warm the oil a bit by filling the syringe and putting it somewhere warm—in a sweaty hand or inside a bra—for a bit, or even holding the vial of progesterone before drawing it into the needle in the same warm spaces.

Because PIO is injected into the muscle instead of right below the skin, the oil will sometimes knot inside the muscle, causing a sore lump to form. To keep this from happening (though it's impossible to prevent entirely), immediately after withdrawing the needle, press the site with a sterile gauze pad and begin to massage it vigorously. Keep massaging for a minute or two and then place the heating pad directly against the site for ten to fifteen minutes. This will help the oil—and medication—disperse. You can keep rubbing once the heat is on, too.

Lovenox

ALSO KNOWN AS: low-molecular-weight heparin
USE: clotting factor
TYPE OF INJECTION: subcutaneous
KNOWN SIDE EFFECTS: bruising
STING FACTOR: medium to high

If you've been diagnosed with a clotting disorder or you've had prior failed IVF cycles, your doctor may place you on a low-molecular-weight blood thinner, such as Lovenox. In order to implant, the embryo attaches to the uterine wall, and the cells that will become the placenta

---

no. 0033

THE LAND OF IF VISITORS BUREAU

TIP: Though most subcutaneous injections are given with a dartlike motion, Lovenox causes fewer bruises the *slower* you move (both putting in and removing the needle). In addition, if you have pain afterward, go with ice instead of heat, as some people suggest for other subcutaneous injections.

---

dig down to connect with the woman's blood vessels so the cells can utilize them as a source of oxygen and nutrition. For some women, clots will form at the site, keeping the placenta from tapping into this necessary source. This blood thinner will stop clots from happening at the site and will keep clots from forming in the umbilical cord.

The Stirrup Queen's Guide to Injections

It's hard to cover everything when it comes to writing about giving an injection. First of all, all injectors have their own small variations. And then there are so many variations in protocol (see page 198, later in this chapter) and in the way the medication is packaged. (In my day, we didn't have those newfangled Follistim pens! You mixed it yourself, and you liked it!)

Just adjust accordingly, and always remember that your doctor's instructions take precedence over mine. This is just a guide to give you a heads-up or to help you remember what comes next. It should not be used in place of an injection class or a one-on-one session with a nurse or doctor (see tip, page 181).

It's a good idea to read this section a day or two before your first injection. If you end up realizing that you don't know which needle is for drawing up the medication and which needle is used for the actual injection, you'll have time to call your doctor or the pharmacy and get an answer. It's a good idea to do a dry run, pretending you're going to do an injection and making sure you have everything ready.

Keeping Track

You may want to create a chart for yourself or set an alarm for injections. This isn't a huge issue when you're doing an IUI cycle with a few medications, but it is once you start IVF. Personally, I think a spreadsheet for any monitored cycle is a good idea so you remember what you need to do each day. I've included a simple spreadsheet in the back of the book that you can re-create in Excel or photocopy and reuse each cycle (if you have to have more than one treatment cycle, which I hope you don't).

Choosing Your Weapon

Here's the first rule of needles—the higher the number, the smaller the needle. A 27-gauge needle is thinner and smaller than a 22-gauge needle, and therefore less painful. (Syringes usually come with a big, scary-looking mixing needle attached. But that is not the needle you use for the actual injection.) The other thing to note is that all needles have a beveled edge. When drawing in medications, the beveled edge should be down in the liquid. This helps to avoid drawing in air bubbles.

What You'll Need

If you are not already supplied with them when you pick up your medications, make sure to get the following (the items with an asterisk are for people who are particularly squeamish about injections):

- alcohol wipes
- sterile gauze
- a sharps container
- ice cubes, ice pack, or topical anesthetic, such as EMLA cream*
- hot water bottle (for subcutaneous)*
- heating pad (for IM)
- cleaning solution

You'll need the alcohol wipes to disinfect the tops of vials and to sterilize your stomach or derriere preinjection.

You'll need the sterile gauze on the off chance that you hit a blood vessel (see page 190).

You dispose of your needles and syringes in the sharps container.

You can bring your sharps container back to your doctor's office with you and empty it into their larger bin. Whatever you do, do *not* dispose of needles or syringes directly into your normal garbage can—even if you're the only person who takes care of the garbage in your house.

If you are squeamish about needles (like I am, for instance), you can rub the injection area with an ice cube or ice pack or use a

---

no. 0034
THE LAND OF IF VISITORS BUREAU

TIP: If you order your medications in bulk from a mail order service, or if you pick up all your medications at once from the pharmacy, it can be overwhelming to see all of those needles and vials laid across your kitchen table—kind of like your worst nightmare.

So break it up. Get out some zipping plastic bags and a marker, put the correct syringes in with the correct medication, and label the bag. And then put it away. If the medication needs to be refrigerated, stick it in a paper bag before placing it in the refrigerator so you don't have to see it every time you pull out the orange juice. If the meds don't need refrigeration, put them under your bathroom sink.

When you're ready to do an injection, take out only what you need; that way, you won't get overwhelmed by the sheer number of injections before you.

---

topical agent, such as EMLA cream, to numb your skin before an injection. I prefer ice cubes, because they're cheap and they numb the skin quickly.

You may want a hot water bottle to help with the sting after a subcutaneous injection (again, if you're squeamish like me), and you will definitely need a heating pad for intramuscular injections in order to disperse the medication. Wet heat (using a hot water bottle) works better than dry heat with a subcutaneous injection, and dry heat (using a heating pad) works better than wet heat with an intramuscular injection.

You'll need a cleaning solution to sterilize your injection workspace before and after the injection.

Ice, Ice, Baby: Subcutaneous Injections

"Subcutaneous" means "under the skin," and this information applies to every subcutaneous injection. All injections that come in a vial, or even the sterile water that is used for mixing purposes, are packaged in a vacuum-sealed container. In order to break the vacuum, you draw into the needle the same amount of air as the amount of liquid you will need for your injection and inject it into the vial. In other words, if your intention is to draw 10 cc of medication into the syringe, begin by holding the needle downward and the vial up, and inject 10 cc of air into the vial. Then flip the vial upside down (so the needle is now up), draw the needle toward the bottom of the vial (so you'll catch all of the liquid), and gently guide it out. The plunger will actually move on its own, with a little guidance, and will suck all of that lovely medication straight from the vial.

WHEN MIXING IS REQUIRED

Sometimes you need to mix your own medications with sterilized water. Slow and steady wins the mixing race. Inject the water slowly

GUSHERS: WHEN YOU HIT A BLOOD VESSEL

Do a lot of injections, and at some point, you will probably hit a blood vessel. It happens to everyone, and it isn't a huge problem during subcutaneous injections—either in how it affects your cycle and the intake of the medication, or in how it affects your body. You'll see a small dot, or even a small spurt, of blood as you remove the needle.

Some books and instruction videos warn that you should pull back on the plunger and check for blood before injecting, even with subcutaneous injections. But here's the question books never seem to answer: If you draw back on the plunger and you see some blood, should you throw out that syringe, or is it okay to pull out the syringe and try again with the same needle in a different spot?

Fertility medications are expensive, and the blood in the syringe belongs to the person getting the meds (unless, of course, you are in some strange infertility group that is sharing needles!). Therefore, whenever possible, you should just switch the needle at the end of the syringe and try to inject in another location. When switching to a fresh needle isn't possible, it is still okay to inject. In both cases, bruising is likely.

into the vial; this will create fewer bubbles and make it easier to draw the medication out of the vial afterward. Swirl the vial gently until the medication dissolves. Then, when you're filling a syringe with the reconstituted medication, draw the mixing needle slowly out of the upside-down vial. You need to collect every last drop of the medication without collecting a lot of air. Just make sure you draw out the mixing needle slowly so you catch those last few drops at the bottom.

WHEN IT'S PREMIXED

With premixed medications, or if there is more medication in the vial than you need for a single injection, draw in a little extra (for instance, add 5 cc) and give the syringe a few flicks before pulling it out of the bottle; this helps move any air bubbles to the top. Push the extra ccs of medication back into the bottle and flip the bottle so the needle is pointing down and the vial is right side up. Pull out the needle gently and check for air bubbles.

---

no. 0035
THE LAND OF IF VISITORS BUREAU

TIP: Why do some injections cause bruising? How does one stop it from happening, and will the drugs still work if a bruise forms?

When you slip a needle into your body, it (obviously) creates a microscopic hole in any blood vessels it hits along the way. When you draw out the needle, the tiny hole leaks blood beneath the skin, forming a bruise. It has no impact on the absorption of the medication.

In order to prevent bruising, apply pressure after withdrawing the needle by pressing the sterile gauze against the site and holding it firmly in place for a full minute. It will minimize bruising, if not prevent it altogether. Of course, in the case of reusing a syringe that contains blood drawn out during the first injection attempt, it will also produce a bruise because a pool of blood is beneath the skin.

After you draw the needle out of the vial, pull back on the plunger a little bit more to make sure all of the medication is out of the needle before you switch tops. These medications are seriously expensive, but even if you have money to burn, you still want every last drop in your body—not spilled on the floor or left in the needle.

Put on the new needle—whichever one you've been instructed is for the actual injection, rather than for mixing the medications (again, if you're not sure, call the pharmacy)—and then slowly push the liquid up by depressing the plunger until the medication is in the needle. You want to push slowly until you see one bead of medication at the tip of the needle, so you know it's up at the top and ready to go.

USING INJECTION PENS

Sometimes, you won't be drawing medications from a vial but instead will be using the new injection pens (other times, the injection will come in a preloaded syringe, such as the new Ovidrel trigger shot). The pens are simple to use and come with detailed instructions. One detail to note is that you shouldn't place the needle on the pen until you've dialed up your dosage. If you pass your dosage by accident when dialing up, twist the dial all the way to the end and push it back down.

Unlike with a syringe, you're going to hear clicks as you inject the medication. Each click is a certain amount of the medication, and it's normal to hear it. Also, with any pen, you definitely want to make sure that you count to five when you're finished with the injection before you remove the needle. The medication continues to go in even after the plunger has been depressed, so count to five. Slowly.

THE ACTUAL SUBCUTANEOUS INJECTION

The syringe is mixed, or the pen is dialed correctly, and now we're ready to go with the actual injection. Take a deep breath.

Though you can inject in other places on the body, the stomach area (close to the belly button) is the best place for injections: You can see the site easily by looking down, you're well padded, and the body absorbs the medication best in that spot. Choose a space to the left or right of the belly button or underneath (not above!) where you can pinch the skin easily.

Unless you're not worried about the prick of the needle, use ice or a topical anesthetic to numb the injection site.

Pat your numbed stomach dry with a sterile gauze pad, and rub an alcohol pad across the site to sterilize it. Make sure the alcohol has evaporated before you proceed—the burning sensation associated with many of the injectable medications is made worse by wet alcohol being dragged under the skin when the needle enters.

Pinch the skin with one hand and hold it away from the body. Remove the cap from the needle, and line up the tip of the syringe against the skin. Since all needles contain a beveled edge, the idea is to get the sharpest point of the needle to enter the skin first. Make sure you see that the needle is well placed and ready to go (you've checked for air bubbles one last time, right?), and then pull the needle an inch above the spot so the needle hovers in the air above your stomach.

Close your eyes (if that helps you) and pop in the needle. With the exception of Lovenox (which causes bruising because it's a blood thinner), you want to inject quickly and confidently, with a dartlike motion. Once the needle is in your stomach, look down and check that everything is kosher, and then slowly push down on the plunger. If it is a pen, you will hear a series of clicks as the medication enters the body. If it is a syringe, you'll know the medication is inside as the plunger is depressed and the medication exits the needle.

Count to five before removing the needle. Some people stop pinching before pulling out the needle (figuring that the pinching will squeeze some of the medication back out), but you don't have to in order to have the medication work. Immediately press a piece of sterile gauze against the site for a full minute, applying constant pressure. Finally, to combat the sting, place a warm water bottle against your skin for five minutes or so while you self-congratulate for getting through the shot. (This step is also unnecessary if the medication doesn't sting you.)

You just completed your first subcutaneous injection. Look in the mirror and tell yourself how much you rock!

Some Like It Hot: Intramuscular Injections

Intramuscular (IM) injections are harder to do than subcutaneous ones; therefore, some people ask a partner or friend to perform this one. The needle goes into muscle, so the needle is longer and usually wider, too.

IM injections will cause muscle soreness later on; therefore, make sure you alternate sites, using the left, then right, side of your tushie (or thigh). As far as reducing the pain during the injection goes, people have different positions they swear by as the best position for relaxing muscles. Some recommend standing and transferring all of your weight to the nonutilized leg (as well as leaning against something stationary to help transfer your weight). Others recommend turning the toes inward in order to relax muscles. Still others recommend lying on your stomach with your feet dangling off the bed. The point is to choose a position that feels best for you.

THE ACTUAL IM INJECTION

Follow the subcutaneous instructions on mixing (if needed) and numbing and sterilizing the injection site. But instead of pinching the skin, as you do with a subcutaneous injection, you're going to want it taut. Place your index finger and thumb together against the skin and spread them out, pulling the skin tight. Move quickly and confidently with the injection, as you would when throwing a dart.

Once the needle is in place, draw back a tiny bit to check for blood. If the needle is well-placed, inject the medication slowly into the muscle. You want to make sure you don't press out the medication too quickly, because it is harder for the body to absorb medications injected into muscle. After the plunger is depressed, leave the needle in for a few more seconds to make sure all the medication is out.

TIP: Some people will say you can ask for a one-inch needle for IM injections, instead of a one-and-a-half-inch needle. And it's true . . . if you're very thin. The needle needs to go in the muscle; therefore, it needs to be long enough to reach the muscle. I, for one, have too much padding on my bum to qualify for an inch-long needle, but if you can, ask for the smaller needle.

Put pressure on the site by holding a piece of sterile gauze against the skin, and massage the area to disperse the medication. With some meds, such as Repronex, you may want to ice afterward, and with others, such as PIO, you'll want to put on heat. Experiment and see which works better for you, or skip this step altogether if you find that IM injections do not faze you or cause you knots and welts.

Intrauterine Insemination (IUI)

If no structural issues warranting IVF have been found, most doctors recommend trying three IUI cycles before proceeding with IVF.

IUI has a much lower success rate than IVF, though it's impossible to give an exact number, since so many factors play into success rates, including drug protocol and age. At the same time, IUI may be the only boost a person needs in order to become pregnant, especially in the case of unexplained infertility.

MAKING INJECTIONS A TEAM SPORT

In an online poll I conducted of one hundred stirrup queens in the spring of 2008, 28 percent said they did all of their own injections—subcutaneous and intramuscular; 20 percent said they had someone else do all their injections. And the remaining 52 percent said they did all their own subcutaneous injections but had someone else do their intramuscular injections (no one said they did all their own intramuscular injections but had someone else administer their subcutaneous injections).

If you want to keep your husband or partner involved in the process but you want to do your own injections, consider giving him or her a task to do—mixing the vials or simply handing you materials as you need them. I chose to do my own injections, as I never wanted to associate my husband with pain—even if that pain was for a good cause. To feel connected to the process, my husband remained in the room, but I made him grab a handful of his own stomach fat before I lined up the needle. (I'm not going to be on the receiving end of the needle *and* be the only person in an unattractive pose.)

It is a relatively straightforward procedure, regardless of whether you are using sperm from a spouse or partner, or donor gametes. The medications used (or not used) to create better follicles may vary, but all IUIs follow the same procedure.

The Procedure

Medications may be used at the beginning of the cycle to stimulate the ovaries, or an IUI may be done without medications. If stimulating hormones are used, a trigger shot is given to bring on ovulation, or natural ovulation is noted using blood work and sonograms. Thirty-six hours after the trigger is given (or in the case of natural ovulation, whenever your RE schedules your insemination), the woman will come to the clinic. If the woman is using fresh sperm—from either a partner or a donor—the sample is given two hours before the procedure, so it can be prepared through a process that concentrates a high level of good sperm in a single sample. If the woman is using frozen sperm, the sample is also readied for insemination.

For the actual insemination, a catheter is threaded through the cervix, and the sample is shot into the uterus, close to the fallopian tubes, in order to give the sperm a leg up on getting to the egg. Fertilization takes place within the body. Fourteen days postovulation, blood is drawn to test for hCG levels, which will let the patient know if the IUI cycle was successful.

In Vitro Fertilization

IVF is sometimes referred to as "the big guns" and is certainly considered by some to be "the end of the road" when it comes to attempting conception with your own genetic material (donor eggs and embryos require the use of IVF, though donor insemination does not). However, this "end of the road" is actually an enormous cul-de-sac, with dozens of protocol options.

Understanding Common IVF Protocols

"Protocol" is just a fancy term for summing up the order, dosage, timing, and type of medications used during IVF. There are a few frames that most doctors use, but then treatment is tailored to your personal needs, based on constant blood work and ultrasounds.

Knowing all the protocol possibilities out there can make you a careful consumer and an active participant in your cycle, as well as give you hope that if at first you don't succeed, there are plenty of other paths to try as you try again. Additionally, people rarely consider (and depending on where you live and your financial situation, it may not be an option) that not only can you change protocols and treatments, you can also change clinics and doctors. New clinics mean new protocols and new eyes on an existing problem.

Long Protocol

These are also called "down regulation" protocols, and they involve starting Lupron about seven days prior to your period and then starting a stimulating drug (such as Follistim or Gonal-F) a few days (usually between CD2 and CD6) after your period, with the Lupron reduced as the Follistim is started. This is the most common protocol—though, as you can see, the drugs vary from doctor to doctor, creating many possibilities for future cycles if you don't get a great response on the first try.

Stop Lupron Protocol

If you don't get a great response (read: you don't get many follicles) on your first try—or if there is a reason, such as high day 3 FSH levels, for your doctor to believe that she won't be able to get great stimulation results from a long protocol—she can try a "stop Lupron" protocol. This protocol involves starting the Lupron as you would for a long protocol (usually at a lower dose) and then stopping it completely before starting the follicle-stimulating drugs.

Short (or Flare) Protocol

This is another protocol doctors will try if the standard long protocol doesn't work. It involves starting Lupron *after* you get your period. You usually start the Lupron on CD2, at a very low dose (though sometimes taken more than once a day), and then start the stimulating drugs the day after you start the Lupron. This protocol

ALTERNATIVE FERTILITY BOOSTERS

Spend enough time on the Internet, and you'll find a whole host of things to try, ranging from the well-regarded acupuncture to shoulder–shrug–worthy shot glasses of Robitussin. For every story you read in which the person insists it's the sole reason she is currently holding their three-month-old child, there's another person who laughs, remembering all the things she tried to get pregnant.

Whether to try these alternative means of boosting fertility depends on your comfort level and what you think you will get from it. If it helps you to feel proactive and as if you have a modicum of control, go for it.

A word of caution on fertility herbal supplements: Though they may not be detrimental to your health, that fact hasn't actually been established, since there are no controls when it comes to herbal supplements. Tread with extreme caution.

GREEN TEA: Is it for the antioxidants or for the creation of cervical mucus? People can't seem to agree on *why* they drink green tea to help fertility, but they admit that they do. Make sure you stick with the decaffeinated version.

ROBITUSSIN CHEST CONGESTION FORMULA: This brand name for guaife-nesin is imbibed by some with the hope that it thins cervical mucus. After all, it works to thin mucus causing a cough—why wouldn't it help in the baby-making depart-ment? Some women swear that taking two teaspoons three times daily helped them create better cervical mucus. True or not true, taking guaifenesin cannot hurt.

BABY ASPIRIN: Aspirin has long been used to prevent heart attacks and blood clots, and now it is being used liberally in the fertility community to pro-mote blood flow—especially to the uterine region. If you have a clotting disorder, baby aspirin is often prescribed as part of the regimen. Therefore, it couldn't hurt to take it preventatively. See more information on page 177.

WHEATGRASS: Juice joints serve the dark green liquid in a shot glass, you can purchase frozen cubes of it at your friendly neighborhood health-food shop, and some stores even sell wheatgrass capsules. It is used by both men and women in conjunction with or in place of fertility treatments. Women use it to lower FSH levels, and it's believed that it improves the quality of the sperm cell and increases sperm production in men.

ACUPUNCTURE: Unlike these other alternative methods, the benefits of acupuncture have been well studied and well documented, and even the well-respected journal *Fertility and Sterility* has published studies showing it may increase the success of IVF. If you decide to try this, make sure your acupuncturist has been licensed. Your local Resolve chapter often has recommendations for acupuncturists who work in conjunction with fertility treatments.

tries to take advantage of your body's natural production of FSH and LH at the beginning of the cycle.

ANTAGONIST PROTOCOL

This is a variation of the short, or flare, protocol. Lupron has to be used over many days, whereas some other antagonist drugs work quickly and can be used in its place. The ovaries aren't suppressed prior to stimulation, so women with low ovarian reserves may have better luck with this protocol.

MINI IVF

This is a newer procedure that operates under the idea that some women don't respond well to the follicle-stimulating drugs. It trades hyperstimulation and more eggs for fewer eggs of better quality. With this protocol, Lupron is omitted, and low doses of injectables or Clomid are used for the stimulation phase. Since Clomid can thin uterine lining, sometimes the eggs that are extracted are frozen after embryos are created and used during a different cycle in order to create the best environment for implantation. There are some obvious advantages to this protocol. It's less expensive and slightly less invasive. It creates fewer follicles, but the eggs are of better quality. This may be a protocol to explore if traditional protocols haven't worked, or if you're known as a "poor responder." This protocol also has some obvious disadvantages. Fewer eggs mean there is less of a chance of getting to transfer. Why? Because not every egg will fertilize and make it back to transfer. Therefore, while skipping over most injections sounds like a good thing, it may not be the best starting point for most people.

NATURAL IVF

This is even more "hands off." It uses the surgical side of IVF (retrieval, fertilization, and transfer) but almost none of the drugs follow the natural rhythm of a cycle. Like Mini IVF, it doesn't have the same success rates as traditional IVF, but it's a possibility out there for those who don't respond well to follicle-stimulating drugs or wish to avoid them.

More IVF-Related Procedures

There are plenty of other procedures that go hand in hand with IVF.

Intracytoplasmic sperm injection: ICSI, pronounced "ick-see," is used to circumvent problems with sperm. Sometimes sperm cannot break through the exterior of the egg (called the zona pellucida); therefore, scientists have invented a procedure that pierces the wall of the egg and injects the sperm directly into the egg.

Assisted hatching: With this procedure, used to increase implantation rates, the shell of the embryo is pierced in order to assist the embryo in breaking through the zona pellucida.

Preimplantation genetic diagnosis: PGD takes place after fertilization has occurred. Cells are removed from the embryo and tested

TIP: It's a brave new world of reproductive technologies, and new inventions are popping up all the time. In 2009, the FDA is slated to approve a tube that allows cell division to take place within the body, as opposed to in glass ("in vitro" is Latin for "in glass"). Eggs and sperm will be retrieved from the body, and fertilization will take place outside the body, but the fertilized egg will return to the body immediately for development.

for a wide range of genetic disorders. The idea behind PGD is that only those not carrying the genetic markers for an illness will be transferred back into the uterus. For those trying to screen for certain genetic disorders, this testing is invaluable.

GIFT and ZIFT: No longer widely performed, these two procedures are similar to IVF, except that fertilization takes place entirely within the body. Both procedures do not have the success rates of IVF, but they are allowed by some religions that ban IVF; therefore, they're worth pursuing if IVF is off the table for you due to religious reasons.

In vitro maturation: IVM is a newer procedure that isn't used widely yet. It is similar to IVF, and it specifically benefits those with polycystic ovary syndrome (PCOS). Immature eggs are removed from unstimulated ovaries and are then matured and fertilized outside of the body in a laboratory.

A Sample IVF Cycle

You've already probably gotten a sense of what will happen during my discussion of medications and additional procedures, but it's still good to understand how typical IVF and FET (frozen embryo transfer) cycles work.

Before the cycle begins, most doctors will do what is called a mock transfer. It is used to determine how the catheter will be placed when it comes time for transfer. IVF involves a transfer—not an implantation—of embryos, despite the fact that the media often gets the term wrong when reporting on ART. Doctors cannot implant an embryo—we only wish they could. What they can do is transfer an embryo and create an optimal environment for implantation to occur. A mock transfer is a dry run to make sure your doctor is familiar with your body before transfer day.

The medication varies depending on protocol, but the ovaries are stimulated to produce multiple follicles. Blood work and ultrasound every few days chart the progress of the follicles. Once the follicles reach the right size (typically 18 mm), the doctor will ask you to take a trigger shot; thirty-six hours later, you come to the clinic for retrieval.

Sometimes a cycle is canceled due to either a poor response (too few follicles) or hyperstimulation (too many follicles). Canceled cycles bring with them a lot of frustration, but hopefully also answers that will enable trying another cycle in the future with a different protocol.

Provided the cycle continues, retrieval is the next step. After the sperm sample is collected or the frozen sample prepared, the doctor will use intravenous sedation, and the fluid in each follicle will be aspirated with a needle. The hope is that with the fluid will come the microscopic egg—hence the reason you may have twenty follicles but retrieve only fifteen eggs (not every follicle will produce an egg). When you wake up, you may feel nauseated or bloated. Bring loose-fitting clothing with you, such as sweatpants or pajama bottoms.

THE LAND OF IF VISITORS BUREAU

TIP: Everyone expects the first cycle to work. After all, how many activities in life do you put that much time, energy, physical pain, and money into, and have nothing to show for it in the end? But a failed cycle may happen, because IVF does not have a 100 percent success rate. A failed cycle does not mean that the next cycle will not be successful. Nor does it mean that the next cycle after that will be successful. As with all things associated with infertility, there are no guarantees.

Go home, take it easy, and wait for the fertilization report, which will tell you how many eggs were retrieved and how many were fertilized. You'll receive a second report telling you how many made it to day 3, and, depending on how many eggs were retrieved in the first place, your RE may wait until day 5 to see if the embryos become blastocysts before proceeding to transfer.

There are drawbacks and advantages to a day 3 transfer or a day 5 transfer. If you don't have many eggs retrieved, or if they fail to fertilize, the option to proceed to day 5 may not be available. Day 3 transfers traditionally mean transferring two or three embryos, rather than one, to give people a greater chance of conceiving. On day 3, less is known about each individual embryo.

If you do have many lovely embryos on the third day, your

doctor may choose to wait to see how many are still developing by the fifth day. The danger, of course, is that the embryos could arrest and stop dividing. The general thought is that embryos do better in the body, rather than outside of it, so an embryo that makes it to day 5 is a hearty soul that has a higher chance of implanting and continuing to grow inside the womb. Therefore, you can transfer fewer blastocysts (one or two), and have a lower chance of conceiving multiples.

Embryos are also graded, and each clinic has a different set of criteria for determining whether an embryo receives a grade of 1 (the best) or 4 (excessive fragmentation). Embryologists are looking for even cell division and a lack of cell fragmentation.

We'll get to ovarian hyperstimulation syndrome (OHSS) in a moment, but even in the most textbook retrievals, there will probably be discomfort after retrieval, depending on how many follicles were produced in the cycle. The general rule is, the higher the number of follicles and the higher the E2 levels, the greater the discomfort. Therefore, make sure you clear your schedule, take it easy for a day or two, and drink plenty of liquids, including Gatorade or another sports drink aimed at replenishing electrolytes.

You will usually return to the clinic either three days or five days after retrieval for the embryo transfer. As with an IUI, a speculum opens the vaginal passage, a catheter is threaded through the cervix, and embryos are pushed through the catheter into the uterus. How many are transferred is determined by many factors, including age, past cycles, and quality of the embryo.

Because there is no corpus luteum, which naturally produces progesterone to support the pregnancy before the placenta takes over (traditionally, the follicle becomes the corpus luteum, but since the follicle is disturbed to remove the egg, this doesn't occur), you will need to take some form of progesterone—either suppositories or PIO.

PREGNANT UNTIL PROVEN OTHERWISE

It may be dawning on you that if you do IVF, you are essentially pregnant during the two-week wait. This idea is abbreviated on bulletin boards and blogs as PUPO—"pregnant until proven otherwise." The embryo is created; all you are waiting for is to see whether implantation occurs.

This, of course, leads to many emotions. Unlike an IUI, where the possibility of conception is unknown, IVF produces potential life. Many people who are pro-choice have difficulty wrapping their mind around the apparent contrast between their political ethics and their intense emotional response to a positive or negative IVF cycle. IVF is emotionally messy—it is normal to feel conflicted emotionally and politically. Some people mourn the loss of an embryo as they would any early loss. Others want to move on quickly from the cycle, choosing instead to focus on maintaining a pregnancy rather than mourning the embryos.

Each response is unique, and no one should be judged by their emotional response to a very difficult situation.

Post-transfer, your doctor may recommend bed rest. There are divergent thoughts on the helpfulness of bed rest, but my personal thoughts are that (1) it can't hurt, and (2) it may even help emotionally to have that time to nurture yourself, dream about the future, and pay the physical toll of IVF its due respect.

If there are embryos that were not transferred, they will be cryopreserved—in other words, frozen. Most clinics will ask you to make decisions on these embryos (lovingly called totsicles by fellow Iffers) before they are even created. There are numerous ethical concerns, such as what you will do with these embryos if you choose not to use them in the future, or what would happen to them if you and your partner were to separate. Cryopreservation carries with it an annual or monthly fee. It is important to think through what you would do with these frozen embryos before they're in storage and before you are strapped with cryopreservation payments that forever link you to IVF. A good fertility counselor or a therapist, provided by the clinic, should help you make these decisions. You can also obtain a list of local fertility counselors through Resolve (listed in the Resources section).

Your clinic will schedule blood work somewhere between fourteen and eighteen days after retrieval to run a beta hCG test. This will determine whether the cycle was a success. If it was, you will probably remain with your clinic until a heartbeat is detected (around week six or seven) and then graduate to your regular obstetrician. If the cycle isn't a success, you will either return to your clinic to do another fresh cycle—or a frozen cycle, if you have frozen embryos—or choose to try something else.

Frozen Embryo Transfer (FET)

Fresh and frozen cycles of IVF differ greatly. Frozen cycles have more in common with IUI, in that more attention is paid to creating the perfect environment to receive the thawed embryo.

There are two ways to approach a frozen cycle. Some people will have their natural cycle utilized. In other words, no medications are given beforehand, the transfer is timed with natural ovulation (usually a few days postovulation, depending on the embryo), and the only medication taken is perhaps some progesterone supplementation. Other people will have their cycle suppressed and then take estrogen and progesterone to create the perfect environment for implantation.

In any case, embryos are thawed before transfer. This gives the

OVARIAN HYPERSTIMULATION SYNDROME

Despite the story lines on popular television dramas, the most common problem that occurs with IVF is not mixed-up embryos or octuplets, but ovarian hyperstimulation syndrome (OHSS), a painful and frightening condition that should always be treated and taken seriously.

Ovaries commonly produce fluid, but the more follicles, the more fluid—and this excess of fluid can affect other organs. OHSS symptoms commonly begin after retrieval but can start before retrieval or long after transfer as well. They range from mild to severe and include difficulty breathing, rapid weight gain (more than a pound a day in some cases), abdominal pain and bloating, dehydration, and a lack of urination. If you suspect OHSS, make sure it is treated *immediately* to keep symptoms from worsening with dehydration.

If OHSS is diagnosed prior to retrieval, or if E2 levels are exceedingly high, the cycle may be put on hold—meaning the eggs are retrieved and the embryos are frozen and used later, during a FET cycle, after the body has had time to recover. Sometimes a cycle may be canceled altogether, since the hCG trigger shot can sometimes worsen the severity of symptoms. If OHSS is diagnosed after transfer, you may be treated at home with rest and rehydration. If symptoms become severe and breathing is compromised, you may be admitted into the hospital.

Those diagnosed with PCOS must be extra vigilant about hyperstimulation, because they are more prone to developing OHSS. Make sure your doctor is starting with the lowest dose possible of follicle-stimulating drugs and ramping up to more aggressive treatments.

embryologists a chance to see which embryos make it through the thawing process, and which begin cell division prior to transfer. The transfer is exactly the same as the transfer in a fresh cycle.

Frozen embryo transfers (FET) have a lower success rate than fresh cycles do, but they have a similar success rate in comparison with natural pregnancy achieved by noninfertiles. I know, you'd rather have one of those, lower rates be damned, but since that isn't in the cards, you deal with the ones you're dealt.

Last Thoughts

Fertility treatments are a blessing to many, many people. Of course, no one really *wants* to be assisted with conception: I've yet to meet a person who says she'd rather be impregnated in the stirrups than in the privacy of her own home. No one sane chooses to do IVF unless it's medically necessary (seriously, when was the last time you heard someone at lunch musing, "I really wish there was a situation where I could stick needles into my stomach"?).

On top of the issues of privacy and physical pain, treatments can be financially suffocating and stressful. Each cycle is a bit like a roller coaster—filled with hope in the beginning, and causing a great deal of anger, doubt, and frustration by the end if the ride doesn't end as planned. If you're doing treatments, make sure to review Chapter 2 as needed. At the same time, it's a ride that many will walk away from feeling the dips and loops were worth it because they have the end goal: a child. My hope is that you get the happily ever after.

Chapter 9

ALTHOUGH IT'S NOT a guaranteed one-way ticket back to the mainland, adoption is usually a case of "when" instead of "if." The high level of certainty that comes with adoption is, of course, a very valid reason for choosing this path, but unfortunately, it's also what leads people to ask, "Why don't you just adopt?" (see Chapter 5). That question may be the leading cause of ulcers in the Land of If.

Despite the high level of certainty that comes with adopting, those who take this path will go through the same amount of emotional upheaval as those on other paths. But the upheaval has a different kind of pace. Whereas going through treatments can feel like a roller coaster, with constant dips and twirls, the process of adoption is more like a river-rapids ride, with long stretches of calm interrupted by occasional scary moments and thrills.

FINDING THE RIGHT WORDS

The deeper you get into the adoption process, the more sensitivity you'll see surrounding language, and frankly, that's a good thing. Sensitivity protects the hearts of all adoption triad members, placing none as dominant over the others. Words and phrases that were accepted years ago—as well as words and phrases that were actually never really accepted—are being traded for what is called positive adoption language (PAL). That preferred language is shown here in italics.

The best term for you, in relation to adoption, is *adoptive parent*. The best terms for your son or daughter, in relation to adoption, are *adopted child* or *adoptee*. But prior to the birth, the term *expectant parents* is used in relation to the women and couples who are pregnant and who are creating an adoption plan. After birth, expectant parents become *birth parents* (the person who was the parent at birth) or *first parents,* not "biological parents," which can be seen as reducing them to a biological function. Words such as "real" or "natural" imply that the adoptive parent is imaginary or synthetic. The phrase "own child," used to denote a child who has a biological or genetic link, can also be hurtful, for *all* members of the triad. Verbs such as "relinquish," "surrender," "give away," and "put up for adoption" don't accurately describe the enormous amount of emotion that expectant parents go through when deciding to *create an adoption plan* or to *place a child*. In the same vein, if they change their mind in the process, they do not "choose to keep the baby" (an objectifying phrase), but instead *choose to parent*.

The terms used here are just a guideline, and they may also change over time as people form different opinions, or as new words are introduced into the lexicon. The best way to be sensitive is to ask (when possible) other members of the triad which words they like, to state your own preferences, and then to come to a consensus, disregarding what anyone outside of your triad thinks.

Tough Choices, Great Rewards

The path of adoption is a matter not just of knowing whether the choice is right for you, but also of figuring out which *type* of adoption is right for you. Domestic, international, foster, or familial? Open, semiopen, or closed? A newborn, or an older child, or a child with special needs?

The decision-making process on this path can feel ugly. It can feel small-minded. It can bring out emotions about how you feel about yourself. It can bring guilt and anxiety to the surface, and it can feel as if you are playing a game whose rules you don't know. Rely strongly on your support system and coping mechanisms, and remember: You make decisions every minute of your life, and these decisions do not mean the roads not taken were "lesser" or "not good enough."

And it can also feel beautiful—bringing together long-held beliefs with family-building. Melding two cultures. Opening your world and meeting new people. And, of course, the long-desired goals: parenthood and a child to love.

When going through your decision-making process, I strongly advise you to keep family, friends, and guilt outside of the ring. You can let them whisper their thoughts and judgments once you're already firm in knowing your own opinions (see Chapter 5 on how to prepare for the impolite questions and statements that are bound to come your way), but until then, you're going to consider only the following:

- what is best for you
- what is best for your future child and any existing children
- what you guess is best for other members of the triad (comprising adoptive parents, adoptees, and birth parents)

When you're on firm footing with your choices and they feel right to you, other people tend to follow suit and see all of the joy that you find in the process.

THE PERFECT CHOICE

My husband was not the first person I dated. He was not even the thirtieth or fortieth person I dated. So he certainly wasn't the first choice, the first person I tried. He was, on the other hand, the best choice. We did go through a point early on in our relationship where thinking about first or second or fortieth came up. But now, we have settled comfortably into the knowledge that he chose me and I chose him. However we ended up together, in the end it was the best choice, and I will take best over first any day.

Adoption, for many, may also not be a first choice, but it may be the best choice. Even if other paths were attempted prior to adoption, it does not mean that adoption is second or third; it simply means that it was last and therefore best.

For those who do not take the path of adoption as a conscious first choice, it is important to mourn before moving on so that you enter this path with an open and happy heart. While the point is to come to a place of peace infused with the excitement of this new journey, there is a lot to mourn, including your vision of the future, experiences, and a genetic link. Mourning is not commentary on how you feel about adoption; it is closure with any earlier processes. Some choose to get through this period on their own; others find it helpful to speak with a therapist or write out their feelings. Your local Resolve chapter can connect you with therapists who deal specifically with infertility and adoption.

The Factors at Hand

Below are sections devoted to the number of factors that may come into play during your decision-making process on this path of adoption. Returning to the decision-making tools given to you in Chapter 3, use the factors below to discern your priorities and decide which path works best in your life.

DURATION OF PROCESS

Domestic adoption, for the most part, moves faster than international adoption. Twelve to eighteen months is the norm, although some happen much faster. For international, on the other hand, the waiting time varies from country to country; some waits are comparable to domestic adoption, and others stretch on for three or more years. The general rule is that the more kinds of situations you are willing to consider, the more likely your profile is to be shown to an expectant parent, and therefore, the better your chances of being able to adopt somewhat quickly. That said, remember to keep your other needs, wants, and limits in mind, keeping your eyes on the long-term vision, not the short-sighted goal of being chosen.

SET TIME FRAME

Some people may not need adoption to happen quickly, but they do need to know a predictable time frame for peace of heart. Not every person wants to wake up each morning wondering whether This Will Be The Day.

Domestic adoption does not follow a set time frame. It can be considerably shorter than international adoption, or considerably longer. And you just won't know until you're in the thick of it.

International adoption follows a somewhat set time frame— it may be a long one, but you can predict how long (give or take a few months) the path will be from start to finish. Remember: World politics can affect international adoption, and programs have closed down during a wait. Still, if knowing the "when" is important, put international before domestic.

COST

Here's the thing about cost: Every single person in this country pays money for the privilege of becoming a parent, and they cer-

SINGLE-PARENT ADOPTION

It is a harder adoption road—though not an impossible one—when you are a single parent by choice. Even though you know you are prepared to parent, you will need to jump through an additional hoop that many heterosexual couples do not truly encounter during adoption: You will need to convince those who work in the adoption field (social workers and agency directors) to work with you and listen to your needs.

The same questions and comments that plague single parents by choice who are family-building through treatments are also posed to those adopting: How will you raise a child alone? A child needs two parents! My answer is that you are the only one who needs to live your life, and if you feel up to the task, nothing should stop you from moving forward.

You will need to balance out time (since single-parent adoption tends to take a longer amount of time than two-parent adoption) with your needs and wants.

Make sure you highlight the strength of your home network—the family and friends who are the village, helping to raise the child (as Ms. Clinton would say). Agencies (as well as expectant parents) are going to want to see that you have backup for worst-case scenarios. While everyone will be asked questions about the future during the home study, expect to be asked (and prepare honest answers) about everything from dating to financial stability without the option of an additional salary.

See the Resources section for books and websites specifically about single-parent adoption.

GLBT ADOPTION

While many states do not have actual laws on the books prohibiting same-sex adoption, if you're in a relationship, it may still be a bumpy road for you, considering that only eleven states have laws in place allowing a same-sex *couple* to jointly adopt (in other states, an individual can adopt as a single parent).[1] At the same time, almost every state has laws in place protecting single-parent adoption, which means that oftentimes, that is the way same-sex couples need to adopt, followed by a second-parent adoption after the first partner is established as the legal parent.

The smoothness of your experience reflects the laws and attitudes prevalent within your state. Same-sex couples living in New York and California, where there are antidiscrimination laws, will find adopting easier than those living in the middle of Florida. Like single parents by choice, you may need to balance out three things: the length of time that sits best with you, your needs, and your wants.

This sidebar wouldn't be complete without a mention of the adoption process same-sex couples must utilize, even with treatments. The nonbiological parent usually needs to formally adopt his or her own child in order to ensure legal rights (called second-parent adoption). While this is offensive, it is still recommended as a form of protection, especially in a world that fails to give equal rights to all. Please see the Resources section for GLBT books and websites.

tainly pay a lot once the child arrives. Their cost to become a parent may be minimal—as little as a few copays—but everyone has a bill to pay.

With adoption, obviously, the cost is almost always higher than a few copays. But it's a myth that adoption is outside of the financial capabilities of the average person. Here's why.

On average, domestic adoption costs $10,000 to $25,000 (depending on whether you use a full-service agency, which may provide ease, but will add to the overall cost), and international adoption costs $20,000 to $30,000. However, the federal adoption tax credit may refund up to $10,960 (that amount could change over time, so check for an update). Much less expensive than both of these options are foster-to-adopt programs, which can range anywhere from free to a few thousand dollars. Plus, some employers also offer adoption benefits just as they offer medical insurance.

Listen, I know, it can feel yucky to have to think about how to finance your parenthood. No one wants to make choices on their family's future based on money. But the fact is, we make these kinds of decisions every single day, from choosing housing within our means to limiting the number of children in our families. Making these choices—such as the decision that one of the adoption paths is too expensive for you to consider—means that you are doing an excellent job at preparenting, at living within your means so that you can continuously provide for your family.

ABILITY TO TRAVEL

Although travel can be part of domestic adoption, it is definitely a part of international adoption. This can be a deciding factor for people who cannot travel easily, or who cannot afford the added expense of traveling abroad—especially if they would want to return in the future to the adoptive child's country of origin.

FINDING COMMUNITY

There are numerous volumes on the topic of adoption, and most all of them point toward the complexity of it. It's not a path one should embark upon lightly, and those considering it will bring themselves greater peace if they sign up for a conference on adoption (most agencies offer them throughout the year, and Resolve runs numerous programs) or read some of the books contained in the Resources section to better understand what this path entails from start to finish—from pursuing adoption to parenting and beyond.

In addition to the wealth of written resources, there is a strong, supportive community available for you—not only during the wait, but once a person is parenting, too. Anyone with an Internet connection can tap into bulletin boards and blogging communities focused solely on bringing together adoptive parents to discuss aspects of parenting after adoption, giving support during a wait, or exchanging information. Online sites as well as face-to-face organizations are included in the Resources section at the back of this book.

It is important and necessary to connect with others pursuing adoption, especially to glean advice from others' stories. Adoption, you will find, requires a lot of circumspection, because you are not only navigating your own feelings but also trying to predict the emotions of a future child. If you choose domestic adoption, you may be navigating the feelings of other members of the adoption triad.

CLOSED, OPEN, OR SEMIOPEN ADOPTION

Adoption comes in three forms: closed (or confidential), semiopen, and open. With closed adoption, the birth parents will not have future access to or information about the child, and the child will not have information on the birth parents, beyond whatever limited information is exchanged at the birth. Open adoption (also known as continuing open adoption) is a lifelong process of involving all members of the triad, who share information and even contact. Within the category of open adoption, there is a lot of variety in the level of openness, and that level is decided upon by the members of the triad, to ensure that everyone is comfortable. Semiopen adoption is when information is shared at set intervals, and the child and/or birth parent has a chance to reconnect in the future, if all parties are willing.

In this day and age, domestic adoptions are more often than not open, and international adoptions are more often than not closed. Within domestic adoption, adults make the final decision on the type of adoption based on their needs (in other words, those wishing to have an open adoption will be matched with an expectant parent also seeking an open adoption). With international adoption, the decision will be made either by the program or by circumstances. That's all I can really say: Weighing the pros and cons of the three options is an undertaking too great for this book. And anyway, this is a decision you really need to do a lot of solid research on by yourself. In particular, if you're considering open adoption, make sure to communicate with actual people who have varying degrees of openness in their adoption plan—don't just trust the stories you've heard or the things you've read, as there are a lot of myths surrounding the topic and many good ideas out there on ways to make this relationship work.

ABILITY TO BE FLEXIBLE

Some people don't like surprises. Some people don't react well to uncertainty. Some people simply don't roll well with "seeing what happens." I'm describing myself here: I like to have a sense of what is going to happen next. This personality type may want to consider looking at international adoption, which is usually closed and on a set schedule.

Domestic adoption is typically open adoption, which obviously necessitates more flexibility, because you are navigating not only your own and your children's wants and needs but also the birth parents' wants and needs. And every time you add another person into a relationship, the dance gets a bit more complicated and requires everyone to bend a little more. In addition, domestic adoption can be surprising: You may be going about your daily grocery shopping and receive a call that a child has been born and the birth parent is interested in your profile.

Remember that this factor is about who you *are,* not who you *wish* you were. Avoid forcing yourself to be more flexible than you're really comfortable with. You're going through enough.

BLENDING

It is valid to want your child to visually blend into your family. Even if you are going to be open with your child about the unique way he or she entered the family, you may not want to field questions from strangers about adoption every time you swing by the supermarket to pick up a pack of diapers. Down the road, blending can also be helpful for your child(ren) as they navigate identity issues in adolescence.

At the same time, there are numerous reasons to choose to adopt children who do not resemble you physically—after all, if you're raising them, they will end up resembling you in many other ways. Transracial adoption not only works but thrives in many families. When diversity is already a cornerstone of your life, melding cultures or races within family-building is a natural extension. See the Resources section for websites about transracial adoption.

HAVING INFORMATION

Most international adoptions come with limited information on how the child came to the orphanage and limited knowledge about the child's medical or family history. And while that may not bother you for the short term, or at all, others find it difficult to negotiate down the line, particularly when the adopted child begins asking questions.

Domestic adoption may or may not come with more information, depending on whether the adoption is open or closed, but it certainly offers more of a chance to provide your child with initial information and a story of his or her first family, as well as ongoing information.

AGE OF THE CHILD

Another category to consider is age: whether you are looking to parent a newborn or an older child. Domestic adoption is the only way to have a chance to be there from the very beginning—most international adoptions are for children over four months of age. Not everyone is seeking a newborn, and those who already have a child at home may wish to have their two children closer in age and opt to adopt an older child. The wait is certainly longer for a newborn. Those who wish to adopt domestically but do not want to go through the waiting inherent in adopting a newborn may wish to explore a foster-to-adopt situation with an older child.

SPECIAL NEEDS

Children with special needs may range from those who have an addiction at birth to those who have a condition such as cerebral palsy. In considering this factor, you need to ask yourself whether you are open to *starting* parenthood (or, if you already have children, starting this particular relationship) with the knowledge that the child is not in optimal health—either temporarily or for the long term. I emphasize "starting" because the reality is that good health is never a promise— even in children who had optimal in utero conditions. Even children

I'M OKAY, YOU'RE OKAY

Although all three parts of the triad are equally important, I do want to stress this idea: do what is best for *you*, which includes your partner if you have one, because making choices from a sense of obligation, charity, or guilt can create trouble in the end.

In the long run, choosing what is best for you is also important for your future child and any existing children. Think of it this way: When a plane experiences a loss of oxygen and masks fall from the overhead compartment, a wise parent will quickly affix her own mask, and then her child's. Emotionally, and even instinctively, it might feel unnatural to put on your own mask first. But once you've taken care of yourself, you then have all the resources you need to take care of your child's safety. Likewise, it might feel wrong to think of your personal needs when you're considering adoption (or any of the paths to parenthood, for that matter). But being true to yourself, knowing and respecting your own limits, and ensuring that *you* are happy—all of these things are of utmost importance when it comes to the well-being of your children.

who are diagnosed as healthy at the time of the adoption may, like anyone, develop conditions down the road.

This one is especially tricky, as there are no guarantees—and there is no real way to get details on the level of severity prior to making the decision. These are hard decisions, and you may feel like you need to defend your decisions—even to yourself! The judgments of others certainly don't help the situation, and you need to tune them out and listen only to your own voice (and that of your partner). In the end, only you know whether a special-needs child falls inside your comfort zone.

The Process

Once you've decided that adoption is the right path for you, and you even know which type of adoption you want to pursue, the first thing you need to do is find an agency or a lawyer to work with.

Hiring an Agency or a Lawyer

There are multiple paths you can take on this front, ranging from an independent approach with a lawyer to a full-service agency that will walk you through the adoption process, from home study (that initial visit with a social worker to determine your acceptance into an adoption program) to completion.

You are looking for an agency or lawyer that has great communication skills, and the only way to know is by spending some time with them, as well as by speaking to other people who have used them—both adoptive parents *and* birth parents. (You can do this through established programs at the agency or through bulletin boards on the Internet, which are included in the Resources section.) You want to work with people who are forthcoming, willing to answer any question, and happy to address any concern. If you are having a hard time communicating with the lawyer or agency staff, choose another, even if they come with an excellent reputation. If you're not having a good experience, it's not the right place for you.

The Home Study

Both domestic and international adoption begin with a lot of paperwork, followed by a home study. The home study is conducted by a social worker and gives the agency a chance to look at your home and discuss your vision of adoption. With both domestic and international adoption, the home study is good for one year from the initial home study visit (if it expires, it must be renewed with a new

THE IMPORTANCE
OF BEING ETHICAL

It's safe to say that most adoption agencies and lawyers don't openly advertise that they're breaking laws or coercing people. So how can you tell if you're choosing the right people to help you? There are many thoughts on this, and the topic is always being debated.

With domestic adoption, you are looking for an agency or a lawyer that does not use coercive tactics on expectant parents. Coercive tactics are anything that makes the expectant parent feel obligated to create and finalize an adoption plan—for instance, cutting off an expectant mother from her support system and asking her to make decisions without input, or creating any expectation that the adoption is set until a decision has ultimately been reached. A good adoption agency or lawyer should be working only with placements that are unavoidable—where it was the expectant parents' decision, and in the best interests of the child, to create an adoption plan. Many states keep a list of adoption agencies that meet their ethical standards, and these can be found by searching online for "association of adoption agencies," with your state's name included.

With international adoption, different issues crop up, based on the country, but again, you are looking for a situation free of coercion. There are cases in which the adoption plan is created based on money or pressure, and you do not want to engage with a country that has a poor record of sound adoptions. More problems crop up when there isn't a centralized adoption practice (as opposed to in countries like China, where there is a central agency handling adoptions and making sure they are ethical) and adoption is instead handled by individual orphanages or private facilitators. The United States has laws concerning international adoption, and if this is the route you're planning to take, you should familiarize yourself with those, as well as with the specific adoption practices of

(continued . . .)

your intended country. Please see the Resources section for websites exploring ethical international adoption.

Some people caution against contributing any money used to support the expectant parents prior to the birth, because the exchange of money creates an obligation. It also creates sticky questions later on, when it comes to discussing the adoption with the child, and it can create a sense of finality, of laying claim to a child.

An ethical adoption works best for all members of the triad and looks to long-term (happy, healthy relationships) rather than short-term (becoming parents) goals.

home study). It is normal to have it expire and need to be renewed, since many adoptions take longer than one year.

It can be flustering to have someone come into your home, and it can feel as if you are being judged. But social workers are looking for you to be yourself. They are fully aware that they are conversing with humans and that humans are complex—we all have fears and bad habits and messy emotions. What social workers appreciate is honesty and openness. Glossing over things or lying will raise more red flags than coming clean about things you fear are skeletons in your closet. Many times, the things that have been worrying you the most will turn out to be minuscule in the eyes of the social worker.

As with many other aspects of being in the Land of If, the best way to get comfortable with the idea and the process is to speak to people who have been through the experience. Connect with other adoptive parents through online resources, such as the bulletin boards and blogs listed in the Resources section.

The Parent Profile

Those pursuing domestic adoption will create an adoptive-parent profile (ranging from a letter to a full-blown scrapbooklike book),

CELEBRATING PAPER PREGNANCY

Many people embrace paper pregnancy with the same preparations or celebratory occasions that accompany pregnancy, such as throwing showers or outfitting the child's room and wardrobe. Some relish taking part in celebrations that they miss out on in addition to pregnancy, and others are uncomfortable engaging in any preparations until there is a child. You need to operate within your own comfort level—*and* make your comfort level clear to all around you. If you are feeling stressed out because your mother is pressuring you to set up the room, chanting that "a match could happen *any* minute," remind her that babies don't need a lot of stuff and you could pick everything up within an hour at the local Target.

On the other hand, if you want to celebrate, let people know. If you want to have a shower, tell a friend or sibling that showers are actually becoming more common in the adoption world. No match is a given until the adoption takes place, but that doesn't mean that you shouldn't be hopeful about the future and plan accordingly. If you are emotionally up for a trip to a baby store, register for the items that you think you'll need in the future. The registry will keep on file the things you'd like to have in case a quick match takes you out of town. In your absence, friends and family can use the registry to prepare the room if you don't wish to purchase things before the child arrives.

International adoption, with its more structured timeline, gives people a few weeks' notice before a child arrives. Showers can be held to help the couple pack for the trip, or even to prepare a small scrapbook that can be filled on the trip with pictures and journal entries, detailing the journey with the child. Attendees at the shower can write notes of encouragement and support for the couple to open on the long international flight, and for the couple to "bring a bit of home" with them on their travels.

which gives the expectant parents a sense of who you are. With pictures and words, you will give expectant parents insight into your world, including a description of yourself, details about your home, and information about your family.

The Dossier

With international adoption, there will be multiple steps along the way, depending on the country. After paperwork (called a dossier) is complete and in the hands of the agency and country organizations, there is usually a loosely set wait time until the referral is sent. Travel is arranged to happen during a loosely set wait time after that.

Hurry Up and Wait

Awaiting adoption is sometimes called being "paper pregnant" (see the sidebar in this chapter), and this has its joys and its anxieties. Those going the independent path with domestic adoption need to seek out potential adoption situations, and those utilizing a full-service agency will wait until a suitable situation arises to have their adoptive-parent profile shown to the expectant parent. With international adoption, the wait length until referral will be estimated.

At the very least, to navigate the complex emotions inherent in the wait, consider meeting intermittently or regularly with a counselor. Resolve (see the Resources section) can point you toward resources in your area. Or you can try connecting with others in a similar situation, and vent your feelings. Or start a blog, or read a blog, or join an online community or a face-to-face group.

Last Thoughts

When you see all the things that go into adoption—and this chapter just touches upon some of the most important things—it can become

OF HUMAN
BONDING

It may surprise you to hear this, but you do not need to give birth to breast-feed. The breasts can be stimulated to produce milk through constant pumping, herbs, and sometimes medication. Some people use their time being paper pregnant to prepare their breasts for producing milk, and there are excellent resources listed in the back of the book if you'd like to try this.

At the same time, you should not feel any pressure to breastfeed, even if it is a hot topic right now in adoption circles. It can be difficult to do, particularly with domestic adoption, due to the unstructured timetable. Whatever you do, don't let it become just one more way you feel you missed out on an aspect of parenthood, and don't get sucked into the mantra "breast is best," often chanted without regard to any unique situations (it may be best for immunological health, but it isn't always best for mental health, and one area of the body can't be disregarded for another).

There are numerous other ways to bond with a child, including nonnutritive sucking at the breast. Kangaroo care (cuddling with the child skin-to-skin) provides the same emotional necessity of touch that is gained through breast-feeding. And I don't know about you, but I was bottle-fed formula—and I turned out not only healthy but also brilliant. I am fully supportive of breastfeeding, but I'm also supportive of not breastfeeding, out of either choice or necessity.

The way our family got around the emotions of not being able to breast-feed was to make our own baby food. We steamed vegetables and fruits and never gave our twins food from a jar. Like breastfeeding, it was healthy and nutritious. And frankly, the inconvenience of it made it feel like a loving sacrifice—a pain in the ass, if not the pain of sore nipples.

overwhelming. If this is happening, close the book. Step away. And take a deep breath.

The distance between this island and the mainland can look insurmountable. If it helps to talk to those who have made the journey across, do it. Lean on them and seek any advice they have to make your ride smoother. And again, if talking to them starts to make the mainland feel even farther away, take a break and return to chatting with others still in the Land of If. Either way, take care of yourself. The rest will fall into place.

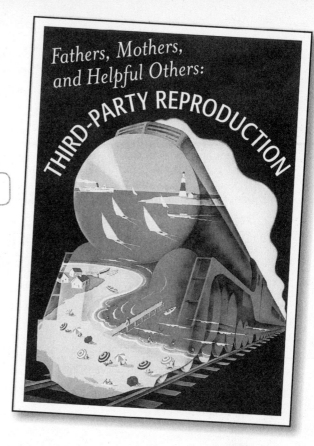

Chapter 10

Fathers, Mothers, and Helpful Others: THIRD-PARTY REPRODUCTION

THIRD-PARTY REPRODUCTION has been around since at least biblical times, yet we're still constantly redefining it as new techniques and new societal structures bring about new permutations on the theme.

There are a plethora of reasons why someone would utilize donor gametes or surrogacy. To begin with, you may not possess viable sperm or eggs, or a viable womb. You may be a single parent wishing to build your family using a means other than adoption. You may be a carrier of genes you don't wish to pass along to a child. You may be a lesbian couple who want to share the creation process by having one mother be the egg donor while the other is the embryo carrier. You may be a gay couple who want to use a surrogate and her egg in order to build your family. And the list goes on.

The Limits of Language

Before we start talking about navigating third-party reproduction, we need to explore some definitions. "Third-party reproduction" is an umbrella term used to talk about donor insemination, donor eggs, donor embryo, and the two forms of surrogacy—gestational and traditional.

- Donor insemination means using donated sperm.
- Donor egg means using a donated egg.
- Donor embryo means using an embryo that is specifically created either from chosen donor sperm and donor eggs or by using an embryo that has already been created and donated.
- Donor gametes is the collective term for donor sperm and/or donor eggs.
- Gestational surrogacy means that the surrogate donates only her womb—the gametes come from the couple or another source.
- Traditional surrogacy means that the surrogate uses her womb and eggs in addition to sperm that is given by either the intended father or another source.

Equally important is defining what constitutes parenthood. A *genetic parent* is one who has provided the gametes for creating the child. A *biological parent* is one who carries the child, since that child will also be exposed to factors in utero. A woman may be both a genetic and a biological parent simultaneously, and this is certainly the case when her eggs are fertilized by either donor sperm or her partner's sperm. A woman becomes solely the biological parent when she utilizes donor eggs or donor embryos. A man can be a genetic parent but not a biological parent because he cannot gestate the child, though if donor sperm are used, he enters into a third category: social parent.

Social parents are those who parent but do not have a biological or genetic tie to the child. Social parents, however, *are* represented in all the other ways we influence the upbringing of our children, including mannerisms and personality. In other words, they are the *parents*— you know, the ones who are going to wake up in the middle of the night to care for a crying baby, or attend a kindergarten graduation.

But what does that make the people who donated the gametes? Are they the genetic parents, regardless of whether they ever parent? Unless the donor is continuously involved in the life of the child (for instance, in a two-mother situation, or if all involved adults agree that the donor will have a parenting role), the term "parent" doesn't really apply. The same goes for surrogates who enter into the arrangement knowing that they will never be making parenting decisions—even at birth—for the child. This is where third-party reproduction differs greatly from adoption.

I've always loved the term originated by psychologist Diane Ehrensaft: *birth other.* The term is immediately accessible, and it sounds like "birth mother," but it doesn't give gamete donors the role of "parent," which they can never fulfill. Still, the term is respectful to the enormous role the gamete donor plays in the child's conception. The term is also perfect for a surrogate who enters into the situation emotionally aware that the child she is carrying is for someone else. When I use the term "birth other" in this book, I am referring solely to anonymous donors or those who will not be parenting the child after the birth.

Even those at peace with utilizing third-party reproduction may have strong feelings about their birth other, from curiosity and gratitude to resentment over the intrusion of always having another person tied to their child's birth story. Some may wish to meet the birth other, and others may be terrified that this person will one day pop up in their life. In the Resources section, I've listed some excellent books on negotiating this birth other relationship.

Hopefully you see that one type of parenting doesn't trump another—"genetic," "biological," and "social" are simply terms used to define roles. They certainly don't speak to the commitment or love of the parent.

Finding a Donor or Surrogate

If you are already ensconced in treatments, your clinic will have suggestions on donor gamete or surrogacy programs they've worked with in the past.

But before we get into details about how one goes about finding a donor or surrogate, we need to talk about two possible kinds of choice: known versus unknown.

Known Donors and Surrogates

A known gamete donor could be an unrelated in-law, a friend, or someone you meet specifically because you are looking for a known donor or surrogate. Sometimes people create arrangements in which someone can be a distant social parent in exchange for gametes or surrogacy. Other times, they want to utilize the same familial genes, albeit from a different family member.

ADVANTAGES

Practically speaking, utilizing a known donor can be less expensive and can speed along the process. Also, when you use a known sperm donor, you can have the choice between either fresh or frozen sperm (more on that later). Using a known person removes the sometimes unsettling mystery that can surround unknown donors. Plus, known donors give you limitless information to pass along to your child, if or when you decide to do so.

With surrogacy, some people want to have someone they know carry their child. They may feel they have more control over the

MORE LANGUAGE LIMITATIONS

This is a good time to also admit that, due to the wide range of situations involving third-party reproduction, there will be times when I make a statement that doesn't apply to your specific situation. Iffish is not a perfect language. As your tour guide, I apologize, I ask you to mentally change the wording to fit your unique situation, and I remind you that *all* are welcome in my tour group.

For example, as you might have realized, in the case of a single parent by choice, the third party in "third-party reproduction" is really the second party, making the term inaccurate. I apologize for using this exclusive term, but for now, there's no other feasible way to refer to this type of assisted conception.

Also, when some people speak about a donor embryo, they use the term "embryo adoption" and classify it as a type of adoption, rather than as a form of third-party reproduction. Since "embryo adoption" is usually a religious term and "embryo donation" is a secular term, for this book, I have gone with the more inclusive and common term "embryo donation." Of course, I encourage you to use whichever phrase feels right for you.

situation if it's someone whom they have an emotional tie to, outside of the conception process. They may like the idea of their child having contact in the future with the person who gestated him or her or gave genetic material.

CALL IN
THE SHERIFF

Perhaps more so than other outposts in the Land of If, third-party reproduction is like the Wild West: Yes, there are a few guidelines in place, but there is also a lot of bending (and breaking) of the rules. Therefore, early on, to dodge as many bullets as possible, you may want to seek out a sheriff, in the form of a therapist trained in fertility issues or a lawyer (or ideally, both).

A therapist will help you work through your feelings about a plethora of issues. If a known donor or surrogate is being utilized, that person should be included in at least some of the sessions.

It is particularly important to cover your legal bases before embarking on the known donor route. There are different laws concerning known donors versus unknown donors in the case of parental rights, especially if a home insemination is done instead of working through a doctor's office. A lawyer—one who specializes in family law and who is knowledgeable about reproductive rights and trends—can help you make informed decisions and save you heartache down the line.

Your local Resolve group (see the Resources section) can put you in touch with therapists and lawyers specifically trained in third-party reproduction issues.

DISADVANTAGES

On the other hand, a known donor can be more anxiety producing: It is one thing to understand that a nameless, faceless gamete provider has a tie to your child, and it is quite another to be continuously in contact with someone who may have an elevated emotional stake in your child—and your child in the donor, as he grows up and starts to assert his own feelings. You may find that you don't make the same parenting decisions, and it can cause friction in your adult relationship to feel that judgment.

Unknown Donors and Surrogates

Third-party reproduction programs—sperm banks, egg donor programs, and surrogacy agencies—exist to provide unknown donors. However, the term "unknown"—especially with surrogacy—is a bit of a misnomer. It merely points to the fact that the person is someone you might not meet face-to-face. This could range from someone who is completely anonymous to someone who is open to child-initiated searches in the future.

As third-party reproduction takes its cues from research conducted in the adoption world, more donor programs are providing information about their clients—both immediately to the parent(s)-to-be and, in the future, to children conceived via donor gametes. Donors also have the right in the United States to be listed as "anonymous" or "open" (other countries, such as those in the United Kingdom, have abolished their anonymous donation programs). Open donors are willing to have contact in the future if the child initiates it after his or her eighteenth birthday. Many parents choose to work with a donor who is open to contact in the future, because it leaves the most doors open for their child. The decision to remain completely anonymous or approachable in the future is made by the gamete donor.

ADVANTAGES

Unknown donors provide distance. You may still worry or daydream about the donor, but not having that immediate access makes his or her hand in your child's conception feel slightly more

REPRODUCTIVE OUTSOURCING

It is becoming increasingly common for U.S. residents to go overseas for treatments, as well as donor gamete or surrogacy programs. In some cases, laws in foreign countries create a more ethical situation than the standards set in the United States. In other cases, people go overseas not only to escape the high cost of healthcare at home, but because these programs have looser laws than the ones in the United States. Whereas some countries ban commercial surrogacy or payment for gametes, others have legalized it, and it has become a form of income within the economy.

If you're going to go this route, it is truly buyer beware. You may have an incredible experience, or you may have a terrible one with no means of making reparations. With little accreditation and no standard regulations, going overseas can be a risk, though sometimes with great rewards. Do your homework thoroughly, making sure you:

- collect recommendations from others who have gone overseas for treatments, gametes, or surrogacy;
- check up on the agency and whether complaints have been filed;
- find out what services exist in the future—for both you and the donor/surrogate—especially down the road, when you're back home.

removed. Unknown donors provide a modicum of privacy from friends and family, as well as create a stronger divide between who is family and who is fictive kin.

While some may relish having information, others may like the distance of having details contained on a slip of paper, rather than being told face-to-face. That way, it is possible to keep "peeking at the gift." And it is always possible to get more information, to set up an account on the Donor Sibling Registry or pass along details to your child. But remember, once you know something, it is impossible to move backward into not knowing.

DISADVANTAGES

The disadvantage, of course, is the lack of information—which means the imagination can run wild. The fantasy may look better than reality, or it may cause undue fear. Not knowing may put you in a perpetual state of anticipation, waiting for information to come. (As much as I hate to wait for beta results, at least they have a finite period of anxiety.)

This disadvantage depends entirely on your personality. If you can close your imagination once you choose the donor or surrogate or look at the situation only with curiosity rather than fear, going with an unknown donor or surrogate may be the perfect solution.

Choosing a Donor or Surrogate

Choosing a donor or surrogate can be a nerve-racking process with long-standing repercussions. But when you step back and think about it, the same can be said of reproducing with your gametes or your partner's. It's all a game of chance, and we have a lot less control than we think over which traits show up in our future child. Therefore, take a deep breath and jump into the process.

For the most part, it is easiest to work with a sperm bank,

egg donor agency, or surrogacy program. They will know the laws and guidelines that are important to follow in the United States. They will also screen donors and surrogates, and in some cases, they will aid in communication. If you are using a U.S. program, you will have more choices to make. With some overseas programs, the donor or surrogate is chosen for the person or couple by the agency. Also in some overseas programs, the person or couple may not have any contact with the donor or surrogate, whereas in the United States, the situation varies depending on whether the person wants a known or unknown donor or surrogate.

If you wish to go with a friend or family member, it's not really so much a matter of choosing as it is a matter of asking—because you probably already have at least one person in mind.

Brother, Could You Spare Some Sperm?

Before you even ask, come to terms with the fact that the answer may be no. It is best to go in with that expectation in mind, as much as it would hurt to hear the answer and to see that door shut. After all, you are asking for the ultimate gift a person can give—part of his or her body, essentially—and a donor should not enter into that contract lightly. You want someone who has thought through this choice carefully, with an eye far into the future.

That said, choosing a quiet space where you can talk, presenting the situation, and giving the person or couple time to think goes a long way. Perhaps begin by admitting that you have something difficult to ask, and that it may take you some time to get out the whole story and request. Explain why you need a donor or surrogate, what the job would entail, and why you are specifically asking this person to help you. End by asking the person not to answer immediately but to spend some time thinking through the decision. You may want to provide timelines, first steps, and other necessary information you think should be factored in when coming to a decision beyond the obvious risks and rewards inherent in the process.

Choosing an Unknown Donor

There are multiple routes you can take when choosing a source for donor gametes. Sometimes you won't have a say in the matter. Other times, you'll get to peruse hundreds of possible donors, and this is when you'll need to decide which criteria weigh heaviest for you in importance. People generally go for a mixture of two criteria: focusing on nonphysical traits, such as education level, profession, or health history, and focusing on looks, such as matching hair color, eye color, or body type.

Your cryobank will provide short profiles on all possible donors. Most provide this information online, and you'll be able to search a website. You can also sometimes do photo matching, where you provide a picture of yourself to the cryobank, and it searches for a donor with similar features. You will then be able to request longer profiles that contain detailed information. Some cryobanks also provide photographs, videos, or audio recordings of the donor in order to get a better sense of the person.

Donor egg programs often have fewer choices inherent in the process, simply because there are fewer egg donors. Harvesting sperm, after all, is a lot easier than harvesting eggs. There are egg donor programs that simply match you with the next available donor based on a small range of criteria. Other egg brokers allow you to consider candidates that they have screened physically and psychologically. Reproductive endocrinologists and your local Resolve group (see the Resources section) have resources pointing you toward donor egg programs.

Many of the embryo donation programs that currently exist are religious in nature, the most famous of these being the Snowflake program. Secular programs exist within clinics themselves, and private donor embryo situations can be negotiated by a lawyer in conjunction with the donating couple.

Using Donor Sperm

Though donor eggs and embryos need to be utilized within a clinic, donor insemination can take place at home or in a doctor's office.

Leaving It to the Pros

Donor sperm can be used in multiple ways within a fertility clinic. If there are no diagnosed female-infertility factors, a person may opt to utilize the less invasive IUI. If there is both male-factor and female-factor infertility, donor sperm can also be used with IVF. The steps for both an IUI and IVF are found in Chapter 8.

If you opt to go to a fertility clinic for the insemination but feel wistful that you're missing out on the intimacy that home brings, consider taking elements of your home with you—music that sets a mood, pictures, a favorite pillow. Don't be shy about making the ex-

TALKING ABOUT THIRD-PARTY REPRODUCTION

Third-party reproduction is still somewhat uncharted territory, and it brings with it questions of openness: Will you tell your child about her conception? Will you give her information on her birth other? Will you tell people about her conception? Will the birth other have an ongoing part in your child's life?

With the exception of surrogacy, third-party reproduction makes it so you don't really *have* to tell anyone. Even if the baby emerges resembling only one parent, people usually assume that the traits they're seeing have come from skipped generations—or they invent similarities.

At the same time, the third-party reproduction community is taking its cue from the adoption community and leans toward openness as the healthier option. In the end, it's up to the parents if they want to reveal the origins of the conception—either to the child or to anyone else.

If you do decide to tell others, make sure to give Chapters 4 and 5 a thorough read.

perience your own. Even if your doctor rolls his eyes, what do you care? Hopefully, you won't have to see him again after you conceive, though you'll always know that you took back some of the control and conceived "your way," even if it had to take into account so many other terms.

Hey, Kids, Let's Try This at Home!

Though it isn't an option for donor eggs or embryos (those pesky laws about not performing surgical procedures in the house!), some people opt to try donor insemination at home. The advantages are clear—you can take back some of the privacy that is lost when you utilize assisted conception, you can create a ceremony around the act, and you will most likely be a bit more relaxed than you would be in an office.

It's Not a Turkey Baster, Friends

There are a multitude of methods to use for home insemination. The "turkey baster" method that everyone jokes about doesn't utilize an actual turkey baster (I'm thinking about the diameter of the turkey baster at my mother's house, and *damn* . . . that would *hurt*) but instead uses a needleless syringe with a plunger. After thawing the sample as per the cryobank's instructions, simply place the tip of the syringe into the sterile cup holding the sperm (and this is where a shallow, wide cup is better than a cup with high sides) and draw back on the plunger, sucking in the sample.

Turn the syringe upside down and tap it a few times, bringing air bubbles to the top, then pushing them out, very, very slowly. You don't want to waste any of the sample, but you want to get out those air bubbles if possible because, with the exception of your lungs, you don't want to draw or inject air into your body. Small ones are fine.

Lie down with your hips up on a pillow (why not help with a little gravity?) and do whatever you need to do to create a warm and meaningful environment. Play some music. Recite a poem. Put on a movie. Light some candles. The point is to take advantage of the fact that you are doing your insemination at home, rather than in an office. If you have a partner, think about letting him or her inject the sample.

Insert the syringe carefully, as you would a tampon. You want

THE LAND OF IF VISITORS BUREAU

TIP: Deciding whether, how, and when to discuss third-party reproduction with the child is something that should definitely take place before the child arrives. The plan may change as new information comes in or new comfort levels are reached, but having a plan in place can make the whole situation less anxiety inducing.

Depending on your comfort level, you can introduce the idea through picture books (books are listed in the Resources section). During the late elementary school years, it may naturally come up in a conversation in which you also explain the way babies are made. Current popular thought is that, like adoption, this conversation about origins works best prior to those already tumultuous middle school years.

The thing you *don't* want is for someone else to tell your child. The only way you can ensure against this is to limit the number of other people who know before your child does.

See the sidebar in Chapter 4 called "Talking to Kids About Infertility" for more advice.

the tip of the syringe to be near the cervix, but not on the cervix (ouch!). The idea is to get the sperm as close to the cervix as possible so they have the shortest distance to swim. Inject the sperm by depressing the plunger slowly.

Avoid inserting anything else into the vaginal canal after you withdraw the syringe, but if you can have an orgasm at this point, some people recommend doing so, as it helps to draw the sperm into the body. Take a half hour to lie still with your hips up. Use positive imagery or watch half of a sitcom—again, the choice is up to you.

The Cap Method

In addition to the syringe method, there is the cap method. This involves using a cervical cap or diaphragm (any cup that fits over the cervix). The cap is filled with the sample, put in place over the cervix, and left inside for a couple of hours. The same ideas as above apply— try to orgasm after the cap is in place, and make the moment special (or, hey, make the moment special by having an orgasm once the cap is in place)—though you can move around after the cap is in place.

Sperm: Fresh or Frozen?

With unknown donors, the sperm are always frozen. With known donors, the sperm may be fresh or frozen. What is the difference? As far as success rates go, the difference is negligible, with a slight advantage given to fresh sperm when using an IUI or IVF. With home inseminations, fresh sperm have a larger advantage, because frozen sperm cannot live inside the body as long, and a lot of their life span is taken up simply swimming toward the egg. At the same time, fresh sperm must be used immediately and kept at body temperature.

In either case, health risks need to be taken into consideration; namely, sexually transmitted diseases. Frozen sperm have been quarantined. The donor is tested for STDs, the sperm are held six months, and he is tested again. This system is not perfect, but it does cut down on the number of STDs (including HIV) that can be transmitted via inseminations.

Frozen samples come in two forms: one for home inseminations (ICI, which stands for intracervical insemination) and one for IUIs. You can use either type of sample for home inseminations (washed sperm for IUIs are more expensive), though you can only use the washed sperm samples in an office. It is something to consider if you are ordering multiple samples for home insemination and don't know if you will move the procedure to an office at some point in the future.

When you order your sample, ask for instructions on the thawing process if you are going to attempt a home insemination. For the most part, samples can by thawed slowly in progressively warmer water (never hot!). You are working to get the sperm sample up to body temperature. Excessive heat can kill the sperm. If you are unskilled in thawing the sperm, you may want to begin by placing the sealed vial under an armpit or between breasts for a while to bring it to body temperature.

If you're aiming for your first child, it may be overwhelming to think far into the future about adding siblings, but that may also be a consideration—whether you'll have access to the same donor down the line, or if that even matters to you.

Using Donor Eggs, Donor Embryos, or Surrogacy

Donor eggs and embryos need to be utilized within a fertility clinic or doctor's office. In both cases, a woman's cycle will be manipulated to create an optimal uterine environment, and after ovulation occurs, the donor egg or embryo will be transferred in the exact same manner as a frozen embryo transfer (FET) cycle (see details on this in Chapter 8) or a fresh cycle after the retrieval. While most embryos will be initially frozen, donor egg cycles are coordinated when possible to match with your donor for a fresh transfer.

Surrogacy—by which I mean gestational surrogacy—is the inverse. The cycle will proceed exactly like a regular fresh IVF cycle (see Chapter 8) but without the second half of transfer. Instead, the embryo will be transferred to the surrogate, with hopes that implantation occurs. The surrogate, on the other hand, experiences and preps her body in the same way any woman would prepare for a donor egg cycle.

In all three cases, the cycle ends, or the pregnancy begins, with the very same beta hCG blood test that comes with every IVF cycle.

Mourning a Loss, Celebrating a Gain

The diversity of reasons why someone would utilize third-party reproduction means that some people will be mourning a loss while others are celebrating a gain. With donor gametes, people who never thought they'd have a chance to experience pregnancy may be excited that options now exist. On the other hand, with surrogacy, one person may get to experience the pregnancy the other has been desiring. Some may feel as if they're getting a second chance for parenthood that they never thought would come, but some who thought they would be able to conceive without assistance may be mourning their inability to pass along their genes or have that genetic tie with their child.

Children entering a family with two parents through third-party reproduction are many times genetically related to one parent and not the other. This can bring about a different kind of mourning for the couple, and sometimes a feeling of imbalance in the relationship.

I'm going to trust that you have celebrating under control, but what do you do if you're mourning a loss? How do you begin to wrap your mind around third-party reproduction and move from mourning to comfort?

THE LAND OF IF VISITORS BUREAU

TIP: Consider writing a letter to the child you won't have—the one with a certain genetic makeup or the one that you won't be able to carry inside of your body. Write all the things you'll miss about that child.

Once you are finished, decide what to do with the note to come to a place of closure. Some prefer to destroy the note after it's written: The process of writing it may be cathartic enough, and the process of burning it or tearing it up provides a release. Other people tuck it away in a box to read far down the line to mark how far they've come from this current point.

Another place you can set it is behind a picture of yourself in a picture frame. Only you will know that it's there or what it means. You can think of it as a symbol of placing that child—that other child—behind you and looking toward your children to come (who will one day be facing that frame and your smiling face).

I think it begins by acknowledging the loss. Instead of sweeping it under the rug or shrugging your shoulders, address it. Set down all of the emotions you've been carrying about the loss and talk it out—with your partner and with a therapist. You are going to a reproductive endocrinologist or a urologist to address the physical side of the problem. You need to go to a therapist to address the emotional side. When you've done that, you've treated your mind as seriously as you've treated your body.

As always, it's important to remember that our best parts—the ones that people remember about us long after they've forgotten our hair or eye color (seriously, think back about all the people you remember fondly from your past and tell me their eye color)—are ones that aren't inherited, but were built by our life experiences and what we learned from our families. And those are things you will pass along to your children, regardless of whether you are genetically related.

Last Thoughts

In a world of sensationalized stories, acidic blogs, and talk-show television, it is easy to get confused on this path. It's an emotionally charged area, and people have strong opinions. If you ever find yourself in information overload, worrying far down the line about how your family will cope when your not-yet child is a teenager or beyond, close the books, snap off the television, and shut down the computer. And stop. And breathe.

This path is marked by huge choices—choices that come sometimes with long-standing effects both on your family and on the child you conceive. It can be overwhelming to consider the whole picture and all the what ifs that it entails all at once. Instead, take it one day at a time. All you can do is your best, and all you can give is your best. The rest is up to chance—and my hope is that chance is always kind to you.

THE PATH LESS TAKEN:

LIVING CHILD-FREE
AFTER INFERTILITY

Chapter 11

EVEN THOUGH IT CAN be exquisitely painful to watch, many inhabitants of the Land of If spend a lot of time down at the docks, watching their former neighbors depart on the trusty, grand S.S. *Parenthood,* bound for the mainland with their tiny bundles or burgeoning bellies.

There is also a second ship that docks at the port—one that gets little attention, even though it, too, takes its passengers straight back to the mainland: the S.S. *Child-Free.* But it definitely doesn't seem as celebratory as the other ship, and the few Iffers who get onboard often seem hesitant and dubious and unsure, and may walk the gangplank several times before taking a seat.

Even if riding this second ship never feels like an option for you, it is still nice to know that it exists. Its mere presence is a reminder that you do not have to live in the Land of If forever. There is a way out—even if that way out seems scary and unpredictable and nothing like you imagined.

It's a Sure Thing

No other path out of the Land of If is less understood, more feared, or harder to step onto than living child-free after infertility. But it is the

no. 0043
THE LAND OF IF VISITORS BUREAU

TIP: You may notice that I specifically added the phrase "after infertility" in the title of this chapter to make a point: There is a thriving child-free movement for those who opt not to pursue parenthood at all. While the result is the same, the intention that brought them to this space is very different from yours. You may experience a very different set of emotions when you see children—you may feel wistful; they may feel grateful. Therefore, if this is a path you're thinking of pursuing, it should be noted that some "child-free forums" may take you to a space for adults who have had a very different path from your own. There are child-free support groups run through Resolve, as well as online sites listed in the Resource sections.

best choice for people who had "Sureness of Resolving IF" at the top of their Chapter 3 priority list, as it is the only way to resolve infertility that is *completely within your power.*

Sit with that thought for a moment, because while this path is the least taken, it is still a valid and important way to get off this island. It is the only path entirely within your control that you can walk on your own terms. You are the only one who will dictate the timing of things. Treatments may work . . . or they may not work. Conditional approval is inherent in the adoption process. Donor gametes or surrogacy simply aren't sure things, since pregnancy itself in even the most fertile of people is never a given.

Ultimately, for living child-free to be a choice, rather than a passive default position, one must take an *active* role in living child-free. Your situation may not change, but your mindset will. This means closing the book on trying to conceive, possibly utilizing birth control, putting away the baby paraphernalia, and redefining your life.

Hey, I said it was within your control and on your terms; I didn't say it was easy.

The Unique Challenges

People say the wrong thing—even your closest friend or partner will say the wrong thing—because we are all addicted to hope. Hope is heady and whispers about the future. And living child-free after infertility or loss is about packing up infertility hope and taking out a very different future. Outsiders sometimes have difficulty allowing you to actively end one phase of your life, even if you are opening up a very exciting and hope-infused new phase.

RESTING IN A HAMMOCK IS NOT LEAVING THE ISLAND

Being on this island can be exhausting, and there may be times when you really just need a breather from jumping through the myriad of hoops on your crazy obstacle path. This is different from actually leaving the island by making a conscious choice to live child-free. When you are taking a break, family-building takes either a dormant or a laissez-faire approach. Either the impulse is simply sleeping and you know it will be back at a later date, or you may be still secretly (or not so secretly) hoping that a pregnancy will happen accidentally on its own. When you choose to live child-free, however, you must take steps to leave the Land of If, and even consciously decide not to get pregnant, in order to take the possibility off the table. Otherwise, you will essentially be living in limbo.

The psychological difficulty of living in limbo is that you're not truly free to move away from the emotionally draining experience of infertility. You are still surrounded by it, considering it, thinking about it, and torturing yourself by staring at possibilities. Which means that you are still affected by it daily. It isn't something that is striking you from time to time—living in it without participating contains all of the rawness of treatments or adoption itself.

If you are having difficulty moving from taking a break to living child-free, consider starting therapy with a counselor specially trained in infertility issues. Resolve (listed in the Resources section) can put you in touch with local therapists who can help with the transition.

no. 0044

THE LAND OF IF VISITORS BUREAU

TIP: For subfertile heterosexuals—couples and sexually active singles—using birth control is one of the first steps to living child-free, as opposed to not trying. But it makes sense to take things slow. Avoid rushing into permanent decisions, such as vasectomies or tubal ligation. Condoms are a good first choice. Even using a fertility-awareness method can be sufficient. Put all those lessons in charting your basal body temperature to use in reverse, avoiding unprotected sex on your fertile days. Without actively avoiding a pregnancy, you can get stuck in a state of still hoping for a miracle.

Oh, the Things People Say!

You are asked to justify your choices on many paths of the Land of If, and living child-free is no exception. Explaining this difficult choice to other people can be a frustrating and emotional task, and you may (or will) be confronted with this task for the rest of your life.

That said, you should never feel as if you owe someone an explanation or a laundry list of reasons for why you chose living child-free over another path. If someone gets a case of oral diarrhea and feels the compulsion to question you, simply go with the brief answer—"It was the choice that worked best for me/us"—and stick to that indefinitely.

Because this is a choice that some people find hard to understand, you may encounter people who want to help you—perhaps by giving you new suggestions or ideas for reaching parenthood—because they think they are giving you hope. Again, stick with your simple answer: "It was the choice that worked best for me/us."

For more on coping with these challenges from other people, see Chapter 5.

When the Feeling's Not Mutual

If you have a partner, you may not be in the same place at the same time about stepping onto the living child-free path. But coming to a consensus is crucial, because living child-free is a very different path from the other three. It is a lifestyle change and requires a reevaluation of your future. And the last thing you want is for the path to be infused with resentment.

Though it may be difficult, talk it out. Exchange a list of questions that you pose to the other person, and have him or her write out answers. Sometimes it can be too difficult to get the words out in the moment, and writing affords additional space and circumspection. When you're ready, exchange your answers and read them together, discussing each point.

Also, seriously consider seeking out a therapist specializing in infertility to help walk you through the first steps of the path.

Remember that you are still a family—a family of two. Make sure to recognize and cherish that. You are a family, for better or worse, and you need to navigate this choice together.

Refocusing Your Life

For a while, your life has been about having a child. You've made choices along the way with the assumption that you'll be a parent. You may have chosen a career that fit your vision of yourself as a parent, or a place to live that's close to family, and now you need to change not

USING YOUR IMAGINATION

Some people are excellent about setting limits and sticking to them: "We will do three IUIs, and then we are finished with trying, and we will be okay with living child-free." But more often than not, deciding to leave the Land of If without children is scarier than ending up there in the first place.

To get a better sense of your readiness for this choice, it helps to employ visual imagery, using your imagination to test the waters to see if making the choice to live child-free feels right. Imagine day-to-day life without children. How does it look? Imagine holidays with nieces or nephews. How does it feel? In other words, imagine being back on the mainland. When you do so, are you itching to get back to the island and keep trying, or do you feel as if you can finally breathe again? What does your future look like without children in your home? What do your relationships look like? Your career? Your retirement years? The great thing about imagining a new future is that you can try out all kinds of new lifestyles.

It's okay if you aren't flooded with peace when you consider a childless future. That emotion may be telling as to where you are with the process, and may reveal that you want to forge on in the Land of If. At the same time, the impulse to become a parent is so strong that it's unlikely that you'll be able to switch gears from trying to living child-free in a matter of minutes.

only how you see yourself right now, but also how you see yourself five years from now, ten years from now, and into your older years.

Changing the way you view your future is not a simple task. Though it's easy to change the superficial elements of ourselves—such as our hair color or style of dress—it is much harder to mess with

TESTING
THE WATERS

One good thing about this island is that there are ins and outs.

Some people stuck in the Land of If decide to try one path, such as treatments, for a certain period of time; then, if they have no luck, they'll try another path, such as third-party reproduction. The path of actively living child-free can also be tried for a certain period of time, though it takes a conscious change in mindset to actually be living child-free, rather than taking an extended break. It may help to try on living child-free for a set period of time before committing to it.

Choosing this path can bring with it a troubling sense of finality. But for some, the good news (if you can call it that) is that you are welcome back to the island anytime, within reason—though obviously, things like age, finances, and stress levels come into play. This can be a relief, making it easier for you to return to the mainland—or it can be detrimental to your ability to emotionally commit to the choice.

Rather than committing to this path forever, set aside three months on the calendar to do a trial period of consciously living child-free. During these three months, you will use birth control to ensure that there is no chance of pregnancy. You will not cycle, pursue treatments, or read adoption blogs. Instead, you'll read about living child-free. At the end of the three months, sit down and list the positive and negative aspects of the experience.

When deciding whether to continue, pay close attention to your reasons for wanting to stay on the island, if any. If they are based on external circumstances (for example, societal or familial pressure) instead of internal ones (your own desire to parent), consider extending this trial period and exploring your feelings again later on down the road.

our ideas about ourselves. How we see our place in the world is part of our hardwiring, and usually dates back to when we were children.

Of course, working with a therapist can help keep the process moving forward. But so can making new friends and finding new hangouts. Even changing your currently child-free spaces can lead to new opportunities and thoughts. For example, switching from one gym to another may open up new opportunities to meet people, or a new daily drive that sparks new ideas and desires. The idea is to create a new life with new goals, rather than live the old life that remains haunted by the unfulfilled old goals.

If you are in an emotional space to do so, consider your reasons for wanting parenthood in the first place. Sometimes we cannot put it into words; it is merely a strong impulse or need driving our actions. At other times, we can put it into simple terms: "I wanted someone to nurture" or "I wanted to continue my family tree."

It will take time to see it, but there may be other ways you can fulfill those desires. If nurturing was your core reason for wanting to parent, you may look into becoming a volunteer in a hospice, channeling your energies into being an aunt or uncle, or baby-sitting. If teaching or passing along lessons was your core reason, you may want to take on a community-leadership position, or change careers, or become a writer. If your reason was to create new branches on the family tree, you may want to become the family's historian—think of yourself as the gardener maintaining that very complex organism— and record genealogy information.

You may need to try on many labels until you find one that fits. You have been mentally calling yourself a parent-to-be for a while now—long before you actually began working toward building your family. Even if you never used that label aloud to describe yourself, it has had a strong influence internally. Now you need to think of yourself with a new label, taking into account the external labels that already define you (teacher, doctor, lawyer, etc.) and adding in new internal ones (community leader, nurturer, best uncle ever).

Change is difficult, but inevitable. After all, there are no constants in life, other than constant change. Look back at all the drastic change that has already taken place, and I'm sure you'll see that time heals all wounds. Even if it takes longer than we would like and sometimes scars still exist. Healing does not imply that the heart will forget what it once wanted.

Last Thoughts

The truth is, if making the choice to live child-free doesn't feel right, it's probably not right. And if it feels peaceful, it probably is. You never have to feel guilty about making a decision that works for you.

I liken the time after making this choice to the time period after the death of a loved one. You will be sad, you will be angry, you will be frustrated. But each day past the initial mourning period should move you toward more and more minutes of peace.

If you feel miserable weeks into living child-free, you may not be actually resolving or moving away from infertility. You may have hit a point where you've stagnated—not actually living child-free, but still in limbo, having simply stopped treatments or trying.

Reevaluate if you find yourself in a place where you are feeling symptoms akin to those of depression. Miserable, of course, is not the same as sad. You will still mourn, but that "wanting to crawl out of your skin" feeling should be gone.

The main thing you have with living child-free is time. You are no longer racing the clock, trying to resolve your infertility with treatments or filling out paperwork for adoption. So take your time, and do this on a schedule that feels healthy for you. One person may resolve quickly, and another slowly—you are simply looking for movement over stagnation, with peace of heart being the ultimate goal.

TIP: Baby paraphernalia—including parenting books or any items you borrowed from friends or purchased, assuming a future child—should be taken from the house rather than packed away. Packing it away implies a future use. Instead of choosing a friend as the recipient—which means you could keep running into the products in the future—choose a donation center, so someone in need will benefit.

Chapter 12

LET ME GUESS: This isn't how you imagined it.

You probably imagined yourself dancing around the living room when your RE's office called and said, "Congratulations, you're pregnant!"—not gaping speechless on a busy street corner. You probably imagined yourself staring down at that positive test with a beatific smile—not poking through the garbage can for that crumpled wrapper to check whether you peed on an expired ovulation-predictor kit by mistake.

If you've learned that you or your partner is pregnant, and you're reading this chapter somewhere beyond those first few giddy minutes, you've probably already started spinning through a whirlwind of emotions. For example, you may be feeling a heaping dose of guilt that it happened for you when it hasn't happened for your fellow Iffers. Or you may be ecstatic, actually—and trying to sweep that whole ugly infertility experience under the carpet as quickly as possible. Or you may be weeping in the grocery store, unable to contain the overwhelming feelings that ride over you without warning. You may even be thinking in a small voice, *Shit. It worked. What have I gotten myself into?* But most of all, even though you are ten kinds of excited and grateful, you're also probably ten kinds of terrified.

And you know what your problem is? You know too damn much.

The Fear Factor

You're probably staring at this page in horror, because you turned here for support—not a round of "Your Worst Fears in Print." But the only way to tackle fear is to consciously address them—and that's what we're going to do in this chapter.

Almost everyone has fears that they'll lose the pregnancy. But there are other layers of fear you may be dealing with, including wondering if you're actually ready for pregnancy or parenthood (yes, even people who have been trying nonstop for years can feel this when they're actually in the moment). If you used donor gametes, you may have a whole host of additional concerns that you thought you were ready to face, such as whom your child will resemble. If you used surrogacy, you may be terrified you won't be able to handle your jealousy of the surrogate.

It would probably be impossible to put together an exhaustive list of all the kinds of fears one may feel during this time. So let's just move on to how to cope with these powerful and influential emotions.

Step 1: Face Your Fears

Fear isn't really one of those things you can talk yourself out of feeling, despite what well-intentioned self-help people would like you to think. The fact is that you have little control over this bumpy

THE MORE,
THE MERRIER!

Chances are, if you did treatments, someone at some point said, "Watch out, you're going to end up with twins!" And of course—whether you secretly desired multiples or not—you can't help but gulp the first time you see two or more gestational sacs on the sonogram screen.

Multiples pregnancies require careful monitoring. You should expect a lot of ultrasounds, especially in the third trimester. Also, visits will become more frequent as the pregnancy progresses, until you are going at least once a week in the third trimester. The doctor will always measure your belly (called checking the fundus) and later in the pregnancy will also conduct a vaginal exam to check for softening (and opening) of the cervix.

Doctors will also be concerned with weight gain—both the woman's weight gain and the babies' weight gain. Multiples tend to have a lower birth weight, which can lead to a host of health problems. Women will also need to gain enough weight, especially before the twenty-fourth week. Make sure you are also taking additional vitamins—especially iron and folic acid, since more are required for a twin pregnancy than for a singleton pregnancy.

Many doctors prescribe bed rest, and there are differing opinions on the usefulness of it. It certainly can't hurt, and intellectually, you can see how circumventing gravity by remaining off your feet can help relieve pressure on the cervix or calm contractions. There are multiple forms of bed rest—some where you simply lie down on your side every few hours, and others where you are completely confined to a reclining position. Make sure you understand your doctor's instructions and ask how often you can get out of bed, use the stairs, or walk around.

Do your best to choose a doctor who has experience with multiples pregnancies. When we were expecting, we called labor and delivery at the hospital and asked the nurse on duty which doctors she saw deliver the most twins. Your local multiples club (see Resources) will also be able to recommend the best doctor in the area to monitor your pregnancy.

ride. You are going to feel fear, so accept it. Write out long lists of your fears, catalog them, and stare at them. Take them out of your head and place them on paper—they will still exist in your head, but looking at them with your eyes, instead of just with your brain, can help reduce feelings of being overwhelmed and will help with the next step.

Step 2: Put Your Fears in Perspective

Fears have a funny way of morphing from "rational" to "irrational."

For instance, it is rational to have a sobering moment every time you get behind the wheel of a car, to consider that accidents happen and to remember that you need drive carefully. But it is irrational to start weeping every time you get behind the wheel (only after checking your last will and testament, of course) and driving ten miles an hour with a large sign taped to your car, begging other motorists to SLOW DOWN, OR WE'LL ALL GET KILLED!

No one wants to have their life stilted by irrational fears, but fears won't go away without hard work and introspection. The way you're going to overcome these temporary fears (yes, temporary—because the longest you could possibly be dealing with these fears is nine months, when they'll be replaced by new fears . . .) is by communicating with your doctor, becoming informed enough to advocate for yourself, and engaging in self-decompression—in the form of therapy, writing, meditation, or enormous containers of ice cream.

Step 3: Embrace Your Fears

Your *rational* fears are a big part of the natural instincts that kick in to prepare you for the task of parenthood. Instead of fighting them, or thinking your fears will make you a terrible parent, consider the idea that what you are doing unconsciously is thinking through all the problems that can arise with new parenthood, and troubleshooting before they get out of hand.

Fear, when faced and put in perspective, is a good thing.

Take the driving example mentioned in step two. Some of the most dangerous drivers on the road are the sixteen-year-olds who've just gotten their license. But it's not just because they are inexperienced. It's because they are fearless and don't believe they could ever be in an accident.

In the same way, a healthy amount of rational fear is key to good parenting. Oftentimes, parents who think they know everything and have the whole situation totally under control are the ones who are messing things up left and right. But the ones who have a solid appreciation for the enormity of the task? Those are the ones who end up doing just fine in the end.

no. 0046

THE LAND OF IF VISITORS BUREAU

TIP: Pregnancies, like a woman's cycle, move in two-week increments. What sucks the most about the two-week wait once you find out you're pregnant? Is it the lack of information on what is happening internally? Or is it the passive nature of the waiting period? After all, it seems the most you can do is sit there and hope everything's okay while obsessively examining in microscopic detail the real and imagined messages from your body.

But obsessing doesn't help a damn thing. What you need are *distractions*. Here is a list of healthy and unhealthy ways to pass the two-week waiting period of early pregnancy.

DO

- take a class
- exercise lightly
- conquer your "to do" list
- volunteer
- hang out with friends
- plan day trips and weekend getaways
- organize your closets
- work your way through every craft project in back issues of *Martha Stewart Living*
- rent or buy TV shows on DVD and watch an episode whenever you start freaking out

DON'T

- attend Google medical school and look up every single symptom
- spend a lot of time reading pregnancy books or looking at baby item catalogs (limit it to under an hour a day)
- watch documentary pregnancy television shows
- rent a Doppler (see the sidebar "The Doppler Effect," in this chapter)

Understanding Prenatal Testing

"Prenatal testing" is an umbrella term for the blood tests and procedures that can give you information on the health of the baby. There are screening tests that look at the possibility of risk, and there are diagnostic tests that give you more concrete information about the baby's health.

The following are the two types of prenatal tests:

Screening Tests

This kind of test includes the quad screen (or multiple-marker test), which measures substances in the blood (including AFP, or alphfetoprotein, a protein secreted by the fetus); the nuchal translucency screen (an ultrasound that looks for fluid collection in the baby's neck, since a large accumulation of fluid can be a sign of a chromosomal abnormality); and routine ultrasounds (or sonograms) to check for fetal development. Screening tests are not particularly invasive and involve either blood work or an ultrasound.

Screening tests cannot tell whether the baby actually *has* that disease or condition; they can only state whether there is a greater risk than average. The problem, of course, is that even if the baby is completely healthy, the doctor may, based on information gained through these tests, declare that there is a greater risk, at which point the parent or parents need to decide whether to move toward more invasive testing, which carries a small risk.

Though the average pregnant woman should receive between two and three sonograms for an uneventful pregnancy, those carrying multiples or experiencing a high-risk pregnancy should receive double or triple that number.

Diagnostic Tests

These often follow a screening test that comes back positive. Unlike screening tests, diagnostic tests are invasive. The most common

A JAR ALMOST
FULL OF SUGAR
HELPS THE MEDICINE GO DOWN

After even a brief stay in the Land of If, you may come to see the world of statistics as The Enemy. After all, the figures have not been in your favor. But you can forget about all that now. Now that you're pregnant, the board has been wiped clean, and there is a whole new set of numbers and chances that things will progress . . . favorably. Yes, I mean it: Statistics really are in your favor.

Still feeling uneasy? Let me help you. From your kitchen, get two measuring cups, two empty jars of equal size, a bag of sugar, and a bag of salt. The sugar is parenthood, the salt is pregnancy loss.

About two-thirds (62 percent) of all pregnancies result in a live birth, meaning one-third (38 percent) do not.[1] (We're going to look just at general data here, not statistics based on specific criteria, such as age or maternal health.) So measure out two-thirds of a cup of sugar and pour it into one jar. Measure out one-third cup of salt and pour it into the other.

Now, here's another general statistic: Of the pregnancy losses, more than half are terminations. While some of these terminations are medical terminations, many more are abortions. Therefore, take half of the salt out of that salt jar. (If you're mathematically challenged like me, that would mean one-sixth of a cup of salt should be left in the jar, because about 15 percent of pregnancies end in miscarriage.)

The point of this is to remind you that you have a much greater chance of carrying this pregnancy to term than you do of experiencing a loss. Label the jars as salt and sugar, and keep them at your desk or somewhere private you can go to when you're feeling scared.

And what do you do with all of that sugar and salt after you bring home your child? You make my grandmother's killer banana cake, of course. (See the appendix for the recipe.)

are *amniocentesis* and *chorionic villus sampling* (or CVS). Amniocentesis is performed between weeks 15 and 18 of the pregnancy and involves having a sample of amniotic fluid removed from the uterus via a thin, hollow needle. CVS is performed slightly earlier, between ten and twelve weeks, and involves removing a sample of the placenta. Unlike screening tests, which determine only a probability, diagnostic tests determine whether or not the child actually has the disease or condition. But diagnostic tests are not perfect—there is room for error—and cannot determine the severity of the condition or disease.

The Pros and Cons of Prenatal Testing

When deciding whether to undergo prenatal testing, people need to ask themselves one important question: *What would I do with the test results?* If the answer is that you would choose to terminate, treat, or otherwise make decisions based on the information, you should go ahead with these tests, because the risks are outweighed by having this information. If you answer that you would do nothing differently, it doesn't make a lot of sense to take the risk (or undergo the discomfort) involved with these tests.

PROS

There are certainly many reasons why people opt to have these tests done. Information gained can either set a mind at ease or help parents prepare for a special-needs child. Some people will opt to terminate the pregnancy if it is determined that their child has certain conditions or diseases. Sometimes, a baby can be treated in utero; therefore, these tests can be lifesaving. Other times, a couple may decide on a method of birth (vaginal versus C-section) based on information gained during these tests.

THE DOPPLER EFFECT

When we were finally pregnant, my husband jokingly asked the doctor when he was going to install that clear panel in my uterus, as drawn in thousands of pregnancy books. And while we all laughed about the idea of walking around with a window into my internal organs, we were all sort of considering how cool it would actually be. Sure, we'd have to contend with seeing a lot of blood and tissue, but I'm willing to bet that we're not the only ones out there who would put up with a little gore in order to have the certainty that all is well with the baby.

It can be tempting to take advantage of any technology that gives insight into the goings-on in that uterus. Even though I'm of the opinion that doctors should give more sonograms, not fewer, I'm not a big fan of the new trend of "sonogram boutiques," which give you a chance to peek at your baby through ultrasound for $150 to more than $500 a pop. Then Tom Cruise took things further and actually purchased a sonogram machine for at-home use. Seeing as few of us can afford the $10,000 price tag for such a machine, chances are you can't afford the cost of being able to see your fetus on a daily basis.

And at some point you're going to realize that you can rent a Doppler and listen for the baby's heartbeat at home. You're going to go online and look into renting one, and you're going to justify the cost for the peace of mind. But somewhere in the back of your head, you'll get this nagging suspicion that it's not as easy as lying on the sofa and blissfully listening to the heartbeat for hours on end. And you'll be right.

Doctors and technicians are trained in using these machines. When others use them, it is difficult to impossible to distinguish technical difficulties from medical difficulties. Say you went to a sonogram boutique and the baby wasn't moving, or rented a Doppler and couldn't find a heartbeat. Imagine the panic you would have to endure while waiting for the doctor to see you. So if you're worried, ask your doctor for another sonogram. And save your money for a really good video camera you can use once the baby is here.

Cons

There are also many reasons why some people opt not to go the route of prenatal testing. Screening tests are a slippery slope. For people who receive results they want to hear, their journey ends with a simple blood test. For others, they are drawn into more invasive diagnostic tests, due to the fact that they fall into a higher-risk category based on their screening test. Their baby may be healthy, but they're put through the emotional wringer—and an invasive test—in order to discover this fact. Some people would rather not go through this stress during the pregnancy.

There are also risks associated with these tests. A small percentage of women will experience a miscarriage because of these procedures. Some women are not willing to take this risk—even though it is below 1 percent—and they should not be pushed to take these tests if they're not comfortable.

There are a few things you can do to actively curb the anxiety that comes from receiving—or not receiving—prenatal tests.

Use the three steps at the beginning of this chapter to tame your fears. Remember, controlling your anxiety is ultimately *your* job—not your doctor's, not your partner's, not your friends' or family's. And accomplishing this will make you feel more empowered.

At the same time, be up-front with your doctor. Talk about your anxiety and what you've gone through to conceive. Your doctor should be on your side. She should not give in to your every whim, but she should be amenable to assuaging your fears—either with an explanation or through a diagnostic action, such as listening to the baby's heartbeat with a Doppler or visualizing the baby with a sonogram. If you find it difficult to speak calmly about your fears, have your partner or a friend or family member do it for you. Remember the Iffer's Bill of Rights (see Chapter 3).

Lastly, be assertive with your doctor. Even if you've stated your fears, you'll still need to be assertive with your treatment. If this is a problem for you, let your partner or friend take on the "bad cop" role. Then you can just roll your eyes with the doctor and say, "Whoa . . . you and I are sane, but let's appease them anyway."

Start Spreading the News . . .

The timing of telling others is a personal decision, and you may decide to tell people in two or more tiers—the first-rounders, who get to know a few hours or days after the first beta, and the second-rounders, who learn the news at three months. You may decide to start spreading the news to everyone a few hours after you see that second line, or you may wait until you're far along before sharing the information with anyone other than your partner. Hell, there are stirrup queens who would like to wait until they're walking out of the hospital with a baby before mentioning the fact that they're knocked up. Like I said, it's a personal decision.

To find your comfort zone, think about what you gain from telling or not telling. Forget the tradition of waiting until you are three months along or following what you imagined you'd do before you ever found yourself in this situation. Go with what you are feeling right now and what would cause you the least amount of stress.

Many people like to tell people face-to-face—after all, this is a hard-won pregnancy, and you've probably had a while to imagine how you'd tell people. But before you start shouting the news, think about whom you're telling and how they'd like to be told. Your parents? They'd probably love to hear the news face-to-face or over the phone— after all, they have an enormous stake in this pregnancy, too.

Fellow Iffers? Give them the news over email or in a letter so they have space to process the news in light of their own situation and can come back to you ready to celebrate.

CELEBRATING
YOUR SUCCESS GRACEFULLY

If, during your stay on the island, you've been supported by fellow Iffers, the time may come when you're having a child-related celebration. You probably want your infertile friends to celebrate with you—after all, they know what you went through to get where you are. But you also know how hard it is to celebrate with mainlanders while still in exile.

Keep this in mind when writing and sending out invitations to child-related events. Send the invitation you always wished you'd received when you were back on the island. When extending an invitation to a lunch where you'll be bringing along your child, give fellow Iffers a heads-up and an easy out. When inviting them to the baptism, make sure you let them know that as much as you want them there, you know they need to put themselves first.

One of the most thoughtful emails I ever received came from a fellow stirrup queen whose treatments were successful. She started off by admitting that I could probably guess the news, and that she knew how hard it was for me. She said she wanted me to take the time I needed to process it before I picked up the phone to call her. I was ready in the three seconds it took to cross the room and grab the phone.

People just want their feelings acknowledged. In just a few words, my friend had made a nod toward my umbrella and empathized with my dreary weather—and with that simple gesture, I was able to quickly and wholeheartedly congratulate her on her sunny blue skies.

Learning to Love the Registry

I know you have your fears and worries, but that doesn't mean you have to hide from the enjoyment of pregnancy and let yourself feel only the hemorrhoids. That's not really fun, now is it? I am of the mindset that you grab happiness when you can.

The three biggest leaps of faith you're going to make during these nine months are:

- buying baby equipment
- having baby showers
- decorating the baby's room

And I'm going to suggest you do all three.

Okay, I know this is easier said than done, believe me. In Judaism, we don't hold baby showers prior to the birth, and it was drilled into my head from long before infertility that you don't decorate a room until the baby arrives. It felt natural when I was panicking over the pregnancy to avoid all of these rituals. I truly believed that having to undo a nursery would be the undoing of me. So if buying a crib is going to bring you more stress than relieve future stress, by all means, leave the shopping until after the baby is born.

On the other hand, if you were looking for permission to stop diving into terrible fears of loss, here is your green light.

You're pregnant—so celebrate! Remember that adage "It's better to have loved and lost than never to have loved at all"? The same goes for loving your pregnancy. Talk to your baby, spend an evening throwing out possible names, and allow yourself to dream—fears be damned. If you spend the whole time trying to protect your heart by sweeping the joy of the pregnancy under the rug, you'll miss out on the whole thing—and you'll have no happy memories to turn to, no matter how things turn out. And if things turn out for the worse, it's not the fact that you have happy memories that will cause you pain; it will be the loss itself.

Tasks for the Pregnancy To Do List

If—despite my encouragement—you're sure that you don't want to shop, decorate, or have showers beforehand, there are a few things to consider as ways to avoid the stress of leaving those tasks until the last minute.

- Keep in mind that most of the necessary items can be picked up on your way home from the hospital, and that the baby can sleep in a Pack 'n Play for many months before you need to consider cribs.
- You can certainly get by in those first few weeks on things you can pick up at your local supermarket, and send visitors to pick up extra clothing or burp cloths.
- Consider storing items purchased in advance at a friend or family member's house—or leaving them on layaway at the store (most stores will allow you to do this for big-ticket items). If you receive gifts at a baby shower, ask a friend or your mother to wash and fold these items so they're ready to use whenever you deliver. She can store them in zippered garment bags at her house and drop them off in your home while you're still in the hospital.
- If you do set up the nursery, keep a folder of instructions and receipts in a drawer. If the worst event were to happen, you would send a friend or family member over to the house to disassemble the room and return any items (unless you think it would be healing to do this yourself). Make sure you set up this plan ahead of time so you don't need to go over these instructions or find your go-to person while you're grieving.
- There's no way to go back in time and say, "I didn't realize it would

STAYING IN TOUCH AFTER YOU LEAVE

This question is always faced by those leaving for the mainland: How do I hold on to the support I found? Too many times, Iffers who reach parenthood admit to feeling lost—to feeling as if they no longer fit in with the islanders, but don't really have enough in common with those who achieved pregnancy easily.

When one friend has resolved infertility and the other has not, it can create an imbalance. It hurts to see your friends leave and move on with their new life. And it hurts to leave friends behind and worry that you may lose their friendship and support, which you've come to depend on.

The truth is that you will not keep all of your infertile friends once you have reached parenthood . . . and chances are, you weren't always there for those who reached parenthood before you. But you will keep more infertile friends by being conscientious and remembering what it was like when you were in the Land of If. Before you speak, before you send an email, before you bring along your child to a meeting with an Iffer, ask yourself what you would have wanted, and act accordingly.

all turn out fine. I'd like a do-over so I can enjoy the pregnancy." So live your life as if you will be bringing home a healthy baby in nine months.

Baby Blues and Darker Hues

According to a study in *Fertility and Sterility*, infertile women are *four times* more likely to experience postpartum depression. The Australian researchers who conducted the study concluded that women who conceive after infertility or loss could benefit greatly from receiving additional support prior to and following the birth.[2]

Many infertile women and men enter into pregnancy already depressed from undergoing treatments or experiencing loss. Those conceiving after infertility or loss should be mindful of the fact that they are more at risk for this form of depression. Putting safety nets in place—such as preventative therapy, anti-depressants for those who have a history of depression, or simple emotional steam valves—can be the difference between success-fully treating the problem and experiencing six months or more of despair.

Even though it's mentioned in most baby books, it feels like few people actually discuss it in real life. Most people I know went through a period of sadness following the birth called the "baby blues." It's not that they weren't grateful to be parents or happy to be with their child. But there were also fits of sadness and crying jags brought about by the lack of sleep, adjustment to a stressful situation, and hormone changes. For both women and men (yes, men—researchers have found that 62 percent of all men experience mild depression in that four-month adjustment period following the birth),[3] it's having your world turned upside down in conjunction with sleeplessness. In both cases, the situation resolves itself over time without intervention, usually by the end of the first two weeks after the birth. It is a matter of adjusting during those first difficult weeks of parenthood.

The darker hue is postpartum depression, experienced by 10 percent of men and 14 percent of women, according to a 2006 article from *Pediatrics* magazine.[4] Not only does it extend well beyond the adjustment period following the birth, but it's also characterized by anxiety and panic attacks. According to the American Academy of Family Physicians, the main signs used to diagnose postpartum depression are:

- loss of interest or pleasure in life
- loss of appetite
- less energy and motivation
- difficulty falling asleep or staying asleep
- sleeping more than usual
- increased crying or tearfulness
- feeling worthless, hopeless, or overly guilty
- feeling restless, irritable, or anxious
- unexplained weight loss or gain
- feeling like life isn't worth living
- having thoughts about hurting yourself
- worrying about hurting your baby

The depression may not begin immediately following the birth and can be delayed by several weeks or months. As with all forms of depression, those experiencing these symptoms should seek medical help that may include therapy and/or medications.

Let's talk more about those emotional steam valves I just mentioned. Infertile men and women often shut off those valves, due to guilt or shame. They feel that complaining, crying, or other ways of venting might seem like plain ingratitude for what they also consider a miracle. Instead, they may internalize the emotions, at which point postpartum depression becomes a very real threat.

Which is why I'm sending you into the world to Take Back the Complaint. If you don't feel comfortable voicing your complaints to someone else, at least start up an anonymous blog and send them out there onto the faceless Internet. Join up with other parenting Iffers and agree to have a bitch session once a week. Prepare all of your friends and family members who have good intentions but may inadvertently make you fall silent by providing them with this disclaimer:

MY EARLY
DELIVERY

Two babies or more usually equal "early delivery"—making this a reality experienced by many Iffers. I'm no exception. At my week 33 appointment, we discovered that our twins were experiencing intrauterine growth restriction (IUGR),
and we were told to go immediately to the hospital. The twins needed to come
out that day.

Amid all the terror I felt driving to the hospital—Would the babies die?
Would they be healthy? How long would they be in the NICU?—was bitterness.
Not only had I not conceived normally, but now I was being cheated out of my
last few weeks of pregnancy, as well as the storybook delivery I had hoped to
have. I had imagined myself delivering the twins and immediately breastfeeding
while my husband and I exchanged a secret smile.

The reality was a lot more sterile and a lot more chaotic. I had my vaginal
delivery in an operating room, and the babies were swept away from me before
I could really see them. It was hours before I was able to get to the NICU, and I
simply felt numb from all of the emotions of the day: angry that nothing had gone
right from start to finish. Frustrated that I couldn't bring my children home like an
average parent. Guilty because I believed it was my fault, yet again, that we were in
this predicament. Sad that I hadn't gotten to experience my version of the beatific
pregnancy and delivery. And yet joy that they were actually here.

If this has happened to you, I want you to know that it will get better. I
promise you. It may never stop hurting entirely, but it will fade to a pain that is
barely noticeable unless the space is irritated. Believe it or not, my difficult feelings
started fading when we left the hospital with the twins to go home. They were still
strapped to heart monitors, but going home with them made me feel like I was
finally a normal mother.

And now, four years later, no other person on the playground knows that
my children's conception and birth were any different from their own. They may
notice that I have the best kids in the entire world, but they don't know that the
secret is all in that special sperm wash they use during treatments.

I'm not complaining because I'm ungrateful or unexcited to become a parent. I'm complaining precisely because this is the most stressful thing I've ever done, and I need a release if I'm going to focus and be a good parent. It is healthy for me to let it all out, to have a long cry, and to release some of my frustrations, so that I can go back to cuddling my newborn.

Last Thoughts

I can't really think of another area in life in which people are more opinionated and believe they have more of a right to infringe on your choices than conception and child rearing. And pregnancy is included in that category.

Before I got pregnant, I walked through the food store completely ignored, and no one commented on what I put in my basket. But after that belly began popping out over my elastic waistband, complete strangers would peer into my cart, making suggestions about changing brands or eating more protein.

Other people (including your mother and mother-in-law) may have had children, but they have not had *your* pregnancy or *your partner's* pregnancy (or, in some cases, your surrogate's pregnancy). You will receive a lot of pressure to do things a certain way. Which is not to say that you should ignore all advice. But even my advice needs to be weighed against your own feelings. No one knows what you need better than you. Listen to the suggestions, weigh them against your own thoughts and feelings, and act only when it feels right to you.

Epilogue

If I am not for myself, who will be for me?
—HILLEL

Be yourself, even within infertility.
—MELISSA FORD

THIS TOUR OF the Land of If has come to an end. Now that you know your way around, it's time to start living here.

It's easy to lose yourself on this island. Draw strength from the rest of the community, draw knowledge from your doctors, and draw a deep breath when things become overwhelming. Take happiness wherever you find it, even if it is for only a few minutes at a time. I know it's not always easy. I have to admit, it took time to get to a place where I could see the joy in an event through the tears.

Hillel's question above is a good one. But you've probably realized by this point that getting through infertility is an act of balancing your own needs and the needs of others. After all, if you're following my sister's advice (doing what you need to do to get through each situation without creating more problems for yourself on the other end), you're probably doing some things that make you happy and other things that make you profoundly unhappy, simply because it's easier to deal with the situation in the moment than to smooth over another person's hurt feelings down the line.

But just because you sometimes choose to put others before yourself doesn't mean that you need to dismiss who you are. It doesn't mean that you can't do infertility your own way. When making any decision related to infertility—from choosing which path you want to take to deciding whether to go to a baby-centered event—remember to account for who you *are,* not who you wish you could be. Own your foibles and your strengths, and use them to live here well. In other words, always be yourself, even within infertility.

May your injections be painless, may your embryos be many, may your waits be short, may your stay be brief, and may your heart be at peace with every decision.

Glossary of Iffish

ADOPTEE: the child who is adopted.

ADOPTIVE PARENT: the parent who adopts the child.

ADVANCED MATERNAL AGE (AMA): a term used to classify women trying to conceive over the age of thirty-five.

AMENORRHEA: a lack of menstruation.

ANDROLOGIST: a doctor who specializes in men's health, specifically reproductive health.

ANEJACULATION: the inability to ejaculate even if an erection can be maintained.

ANOVULATION: a lack of ovulation.

ANTISPERM ANTIBODIES: cells that attack the sperm.

ANTRAL FOLLICLES: small, resting follicles at the beginning of a cycle.

ASHERMAN'S SYNDROME: scarring within the uterine cavity; usually a complication from D&Cs.

ASPERMIA: a lack of semen.

ASSISTED CONCEPTION: any form of reproductive assistance.

ASSISTED HATCHING: when the shell of the embryo is pierced to encourage the embryo to break through the zona pellucida.

ASSISTED REPRODUCTIVE TECHNOLOGIES (ART): treatments in which both the eggs and the sperm are handled; in other words, IVF, ICSI, PGD, and assisted hatching.

ASTHENOSPERMIA: Sperm are in the sample, but the motility is reduced. These sperm do not swim forward.

AZOOSPERMIA: a complete lack of sperm.

BASAL BODY TEMPERATURE: body temperature immediately upon awakening, which can be used to pinpoint ovulation.

BETA: see human chorionic gonadotropin.

BICORNUATE UTERUS: a uterine anomaly in which the uterus has two horns.

BIOLOGICAL INFERTILITY: a lack of ability to reproduce due to problems with either reproductive organs or hormone levels.

BIRTH PARENTS: the people who are the parents at birth (within adoption).

BLASTOCYST: an embryo around the fifth day.

BLIGHTED OVUM: the egg is fertilized and implants in the uterine wall, but no fetus grows in the gestational sac.

CERCLAGE: a stitch that can be made on the cervix during a pregnancy in order to stave off preterm delivery from a weakened cervix.

CHEMICAL PREGNANCY: a very early miscarriage. Often the person receives a positive pregnancy test and then a period begins a few days later. At other times, not enough hCG is made to produce a positive urine pregnancy test, though blood work can confirm a positive.

CONGENITAL ABSENCE OF VAS DEFERENS (CAVD): a condition in which a man is missing one vas deferens. When both vas deferens are missing, the condition is called congenital bilateral absence of vas deferens (CBAVD).

CRYOBANK: a sperm bank.

CYCLE DAY 1: the first day of true menstrual flow. Each day after this is labeled accordingly (cycle day 2, cycle day 3, etc.).

CYCLING: a slang term for trying to conceive. It usually refers to undergoing treatments, but one can also cycle unassisted.

D&C: stands for dilation and curettage; a procedure that cleans out the uterus after a loss.

D&E: stands for dilation and evacuation; a procedure that cleans out the uterus after a loss.

DOMESTIC ADOPTION: adoption completed within your own country.

DONOR EGG: using a donated egg.

DONOR EMBRYO: using a donated embryo or one created out of donor sperm and eggs.

DONOR GAMETES: using the gametes from a person outside the relationship.

DONOR INSEMINATION: using donated sperm.

EARLY MISCARRIAGE: a loss that occurs within the first twelve weeks.

EARLY PREGNANCY LOSS: an alternative and interchangeable term for miscarriage.

ECTOPIC PREGNANCY: the fertilized egg implants within the fallopian tube, rather than the uterus. This type of pregnancy can be life-threatening to the mother and is never viable.

EGG WHITE CERVICAL MUCUS (EWCM): the stretchy, slippery mucus produced by a woman's body prior to ovulation.

EMBRYO: the name for a baby from postfertilization until the eighth week of gestation.

EMBRYOLOGIST: a doctor who works to combine sperm and eggs to create an embryo for IVF.

ENDOMETRIAL BIOPSY: removing a sample of endometrial tissue to check the uterine lining.

ENDOMETRIOSIS: a disorder in which cells from the uterine lining grow outside the uterus.

ESTROGEN: a hormone that aids in thickening the uterine lining (and making it perfect for implantation), among other roles.

FEMALE-FACTOR INFERTILITY: a lack of ability to reproduce, due to problems with the woman's reproductive organs or hormone levels.

FERTILIZATION REPORT: the number of eggs that were retrieved and fertilized during IVF.

FETUS: a baby after the eighth week of gestation.

FIBROID: benign tumors in the uterus.

FOLLICLE-STIMULATING HORMONE (FSH): In men, this hormone controls sperm production. In women, this hormone causes the follicles to mature.

FROZEN EMBRYO TRANSFER (FET): a cycle in which an embryo created and frozen from a prior IVF cycle is thawed and transferred.

GESTATIONAL SURROGACY: the surrogate donates only her womb—the gametes come from the intended parents or another source.

HOME STUDY: the initial visit from a social worker to determine your acceptance into an adoption program.

HUMAN CHORIONIC GONADOTROPIN (HCG): a hormone produced during pregnancy that helps maintain the production of progesterone.

HYDRAMNIOS: too much amniotic fluid.

HYPERSTIMULATIONS: stimulating the ovaries with drugs in order to get them to produce more follicles (and hopefully, by default, also eggs).

HYPOSPADIAS: a condition in which the urethra opening is not in its correct place.

HYSTEROSALPINGOGRAM (HSG): a procedure in which dye is injected into the fallopian tubes to check for blockage.

HYSTEROSCOPY: a surgical procedure aimed at correcting a uterine abnormality.

INCOMPETENT CERVIX: the cervix opens before the baby is ready for delivery.

INFERTILITY: an inability to get pregnant after a year of well-timed intercourse. Included within the definition of infertility are two or more consecutive pregnancy losses.

INTENDED PARENTS: within surrogacy, the people who will parent the child after birth.

INTERNATIONAL ADOPTION: an adoption in which the adoptive parents and adoptee are not living in the same country.

INTRACYTOPLASMIC SPERM INJECTION (ICSI): a procedure used in conjunction with IVF in which a single sperm is injected into the egg.

INTRAMUSCULAR (IM): into the muscle.

INTRAUTERINE GROWTH RESTRICTION (IUGR): when a baby is less than the tenth percentile for his or her gestational age.

INTRAUTERINE INSEMINATION (IUI): a procedure in which semen is placed outside the fallopian tube with the use of a catheter.

IN VITRO FERTILIZATION (IVF): a procedure in which sperm and eggs are fertilized outside the body and the subsequent embryo is transferred back to the body for implantation. "In vitro" means "in glass."

IN VITRO MATURATION (IVM): Immature eggs are removed from the woman's body and matured and fertilized outside the body.

KALLMANN'S SYNDROME: a condition that creates a lack of GnRH, an important hormone related to sperm production.

KLINEFELTER'S SYNDROME: a condition in which the man has an extra X chromosome.

LAPAROSCOPY: a surgical procedure used to treat a plethora of situations, from removing endometriosis to treating an ectopic pregnancy.

LATE MISCARRIAGE: a loss between twelve and twenty weeks.

LUTEAL-PHASE DEFECT: an umbrella term for various problems with the second phase of a woman's cycle.

LUTEINIZING HORMONE (LH): in men, this hormone aids in testosterone production. In women, this hormone triggers ovulation and the release of the egg from the follicle.

MALE-FACTOR INFERTILITY: a lack of ability to reproduce, due to problems with the man's reproductive organs or hormone levels.

MEDICAL TERMINATION: terminating a pregnancy either due to a risk to the mother's life or due to a condition in the fetus.

MICROSURGICAL EPIDIDYMAL SPERM ASPIRATION (MESA): a procedure in which sperm are surgically removed from the epididymis to be used in IVF.

MISCARRIAGE: a loss that occurs prior to the twentieth week.

MISSED MISCARRIAGE: In this type of loss, the fetus dies but isn't expelled, necessitating a D&C. A missed miscarriage is sometimes called an incomplete miscarriage.

MOCK TRANSFER: a practice run at the beginning of an IVF cycle to check the uterus prior to transfer.

MOLAR PREGNANCY: Another name is a hydatidiform mole. This type of pregnancy is very dangerous and can become cancerous. The placenta develops a mass of cysts, and the fetus doesn't form.

MULTIFETAL PREGNANCY REDUCTION: Sometimes called selective reduction, this procedure reduces the number of fetuses in the womb to ensure the health of the remaining fetus(es).

NEONATAL DEATH: a death that occurs anywhere within the first twenty-eight days of life.

OBSTETRICIAN/GYNECOLOGIST (OB-GYN): a doctor or doctors who specialize in female reproductive health. A doctor who combines these two specialties cares for pregnant and nonpregnant patients.

OLIGOHYDRAMNIOS: too little amniotic fluid.

OLIGOMENORRHEA: irregular menstruation.

OLIGOSPERMIA: a reduced number of sperm in the sample.

OVARIAN HYPERSTIMULATION SYNDROME (OHSS): a complication from ovarian hyperstimulation in which having numerous follicles creates too much fluid in the body.

PELVIC INFLAMMATORY DISEASE (PID): an infection of the reproductive organs that can cause scarring and, subsequently, infertility.

PLACENTAL ABRUPTION: when the placenta detaches prior to delivery.

PLACENTA PREVIA: when the placenta lies over the cervix.

POLYCYSTIC OVARIAN SYNDROME (PCOS): a condition characterized by hormonal imbalances and many small ovarian cysts.

POLYP: a benign tumor that grows from a mucus membrane.

POLYPLOIDY: having a set of four chromosomes—an extra copy of the two usual chromosomes.

POSTCOITAL TEST: a test examining the cervical mucus after intercourse to ensure that sperm can survive in the mucus.

POSTEJACULATORY URINALYSIS: a test used to examine ejaculate when retrograde ejaculation is suspected.

PREECLAMPSIA: a serious pregnancy condition characterized by high blood pressure and protein in the urine.

PREMATURE OVARIAN FAILURE (POF): when the ovaries fail to function normally and fail to produce eggs when a woman is under the age of forty.

PREIMPLANTATION GENETIC DIAGNOSIS (PGD): genetic testing on embryos by removing a few cells prior to transfer in IVF.

PRETERM PREMATURE RUPTURE OF MEMBRANES (PPROM): when the amniotic sac ruptures prematurely.

PRIMARY INFERTILITY: the inability to achieve a pregnancy within a year when the person has no living children.

PROGESTERONE: a hormone that aids in supporting a pregnancy.

PROLACTIN: a hormone that aids in the production of breastmilk.

RECURRENT PREGNANCY LOSS: three or more consecutive losses.

REPRODUCTIVE ENDOCRINOLOGIST: an OB-GYN who has completed an additional three-year fellowship in reproductive and hormonal disorders.

RETRIEVAL: the removal of the follicular fluid (and hopefully eggs) during IVF.

RETROGRADE EJACULATION: when semen is drawn back into the body and pools in the bladder postorgasm.

SALINE SONOHYSTEROGRAM (SSH): a procedure in which saline is injected into the uterus to check for polyps, fibroids, and other abnormalities.

SECONDARY INFERTILITY: the inability to achieve a pregnancy when a person has prior pregnancies or children.

SEMEN ANALYSIS: an examination of the semen and sperm.

SEPTUM: a growth that divides the uterus.

SERTOLI-CELL-ONLY SYNDROME: a condition in which there is a lack of germ cells; therefore, no sperm can be produced.

SINGLE PARENT BY CHOICE (SMBC OR SFBC): a person who chooses to approach family-building without a partner.

SITUATIONAL INFERTILITY: a lack of ability to reproduce without assistance, due to situational factors (e.g., GLBT community or single parents by choice).

STERILITY: a complete inability to achieve a pregnancy even with medical assistance.

STILLBIRTH: in utero death after twenty weeks.

SUBCUTANEOUS: under the skin.

TESTICULAR BIOPSY: a procedure in which tissue is surgically removed from the testes to search for sperm.

TESTICULAR SPERM EXTRACTION (TESE): a procedure removing sperm from the tissue sample.

TESTICULAR SPERM ASPIRATION (TESA): using a needle to withdraw fluid (and hopefully sperm) from the testes to be used in IVF.

TESTOSTERONE: the hormone responsible for the development of male sex organs.

THIRD-PARTY REPRODUCTION: family-building using the gametes or uterus of someone outside the relationship.

THROMBOPHILIA: a collective term for blood-clotting disorders.

THYROID-STIMULATING HORMONE (TSH): a hormone that helps regulate the thyroid gland.

TRADITIONAL SURROGACY: when the surrogate lends both her womb and her eggs in order to create and carry the child.

TRANSFER: the placement of the embryo inside the uterus during IVF with the hope that implantation will occur.

TRANSLOCATION: when part of one chromosome is transferred to another chromosome.

TREATMENTS: anything you are actively doing under the care of a doctor to treat infertility, from Clomid to IVF.

TRIAD: the three parties involved in the adoption: the adoptive parents, the adoptee, and the birth parents.

TRIPLOIDY: having three complete sets of the twenty-three chromosomes.

TRISOMY: a third copy of a single chromosome.

UNEXPLAINED INFERTILITY: a lack of ability to reproduce with no known cause (this is usually a case of science not being advanced enough to find the problem).

UNICORNUATE UTERUS: a uterus with a single horn, resembling half of a normal uterus.

UROLOGIST: a doctor who specializes in the urinary tract and in the male reproductive organs.

VARICOCELE: a dilated varicose vein that runs around a testicle.

VARICOCELECTOMY: a surgery used to repair a varicocele and remedy blood flow to the testicle.

VASA PREVIA: when blood vessels are unprotected and over the cervix, as opposed to covered by the umbilical cord.

VASOGRAPHY: a procedure in which dye is injected into the vas deferens to search for a blockage.

VASOVASOSTOMY OR VASOEPIDIDYMOSTOMY: microsurgery to correct a blocked vas deferens.

Using Online Support

SITES SUCH AS Cyclesista (listed in Resources) exist to allow people to find each other and offer support during fertility treatments. The colloquial term for this person is "cycle buddy," though some people may group up with three or more people, all sharing information and cheering each other on and lending a shoulder to cry on when appropriate. Adoption blogs and forums offer the same support as people wait to receive their referral or be chosen from the prospective-parents pool.

Some find blogs helpful because they are searchable and allow you to follow someone's story step-by-step. Others find it cathartic to start their own blog, chronicling their experience with infertility, loss, or adoption. Included in the Resources section is a URL for a blogroll of several thousand blogs, broken down into forty-plus categories to enable you to find a story similar to your own. The blogroll also has its own custom search engine. In addition, bulletin boards offer a space for quick questions and answers, as well as ongoing conversations.

Unlike therapy, or family members who grumble about needing sleep, online support is available twenty-four hours a day. It is support that can travel with you to any place that has an Internet connection. It is also easy to walk away from it all on a day when you feel too raw to speak about your situation: Unlike with family and friends, who may still ask questions, not knowing your current emotional state, you can choose to not turn on your computer and take a much needed mental break from thinking about infertility.

The benefits of online support far outweigh the drawbacks, but the drawbacks do exist, and it helps to address them rather than sweep them under the rug.

When people are "traveling" together, it commonly happens that some people become pregnant or adopt, and some do not—creating a strained dynamic within the group, in which one person feels frustrated and the other person feels guilty. There is no way to ensure that everyone will part without hurt feelings, but you can address this scenario before it happens in order to have people work through what they wish will happen when such a situation takes place.

The benefit of groups such as Cyclesista is that they are not person-specific. The support changes from month to month, depending on who is cycling, and the person who remains behind is still in good company with anyone new who enters for the next cycle. At the same time, online support has an advantage over face-to-face support in terms of the fluidity with which people can seek new support as new situations arise. Unlike face-to-face friendships, which require upkeep and a big investment, online support can shift and be rebuilt with a new group that is now in your current boat.

When you're trying to enter an online community and gather support, it's a good idea to hang back for a bit and simply read along before jumping into the conversation, to make sure you have a good sense of what is going on. This is the same sort of rule that applies to any face-to-face conversation. And when in doubt, pretend the person is in front of you, and act accordingly.

Online Iffish

Each online forum has its own set of shorthand that it uses to define the group and provide a quick way of referring to big ideas. The following list contains the most common abbreviations used on the bulletin boards and blogs, so you can follow the conversation easily.

A few of the abbreviations contain numbers and refer to certain days in the cycle or postprocedure. The first day of a period (the first day of full flow, not light spotting) is referred to as "cycle day 1" and abbreviated as CD1. Therefore, people's inclusion of the number after "CD" allows you to know where they are within their cycle.

Other events that require special numbers are ovulation and transfer. The follicular phase, or first part of the cycle, varies from month to month, but there should be consistency within the luteal phase, or second part of the cycle. Between the follicular phase and the luteal phase is ovulation. Many people will signal how far they are from ovulation with the abbreviation "dpo," which stands for "days postovulation." For instance, "9dpo" would mean that it is nine days after ovulation. Healthy luteal phases are between twelve and fourteen days in length.

Transfer (part of IVF) works in much the same way, with numbers accompanying an abbreviation to let the reader know how far the speaker is from their transfer date—as well as which type of transfer (traditionally a day 3 or a day 5) they used. Therefore, "7dp3dt" means "seven days past a three day transfer."

These are the most common abbreviations you'll find during your travels through the Internet.

2WW: two-week wait (postovulation until beta)

AF: Aunt Flo (your period)

ART: assisted reproductive technologies

BBT: basal body temperature

BCP: birth control pills

BD: baby dancing (having sex—used more commonly on bulletin boards than on blogs)

BFN: big fat negative

BFP: big fat positive

BMOM: biological mother

BP: biological parents

B/W: blood work

CCAA: China Center of Adoption Affairs

CD: cycle day

CM: cervical mucus

D&C: dilation and curettage

D&E: dilation and evacuation

DD: dear daughter

DE: donor egg (sometimes also donor embryo)

DH: dear husband

DI: donor insemination

DIUI: IUI with donor sperm

DIVF: usually IVF with donor eggs, but could be any donor gametes

DOR: date of referral

DOT: date of travel

DP: dear partner

DP3DT: days past three-day transfer

DP5DT: days past five-day transfer

DPO: days past ovulation

DS: dear son

DTC: dossier to China (or DTV, DTE—dossier to . . .)

DW: dear wife

E2: estrogen level

EDD: estimated due date

ENDO: endometriosis

ER: egg retrieval

ET: embryo transfer

EWCM: egg white cervical mucus

FET: frozen embryo transfer

FIL: father-in-law

FRED OR FRER: First Response Early Detection (peestick)

GS: gestational surrogate/surrogacy

HPT: home pregnancy test (also called a peestick)

HS: home study

IF: infertility

IF: intended father (surrogacy)

IM: intended mother (surrogacy)

IM: intramuscular

INS: Immigration and Naturalization Services

IP: intended parents (surrogacy)

LMP: last menstrual period

LP: luteal phase

LPD: luteal-phase defect

M/C: miscarriage

MF: male factor

MIL: mother-in-law

O: ovulate (or O'ing)

OPK: ovulation-predictor kit

P4: progesterone

PAP: potential or prospective adoptive parents

PEESTICK: home pregnancy test

PG: pregnant

PIO: progesterone in oil

POAS: pee on a stick (take a pregnancy test)

PUPO: pregnant until proven otherwise

RPL: recurrent pregnancy loss

SA: semen analysis

S/B: stillbirth

SFBC OR SFC: single father by choice

SIF: secondary infertility

SMBC OR SMC: single mother by choice

SPBC OR SPC: single parent by choice

TEMP: taking BBT

TS: traditional surrogate/surrogacy

TTC: trying to conceive

U/S: ultrasound

Monitoring Your Fertility

THESE PROACTIVE MEASURES may help you pinpoint problems and provide your reproductive endocrinologist with information. Many people use them not only before, but also during, treatments as well to gather more information about their fertility.

Charting Your Basal Body Temperature

One very helpful thing that you can bring to your first fertility-related appointment is a record of your basal body temperature, or BBT. A change in your BBT can signal hormonal changes in the body; therefore, taking your temperature with a special thermometer at the same time every day and keeping a chart of the results can help you pinpoint when it is that you ovulate, in addition to indicating problems such as anovulation and luteal-phase defects.

To do this, begin recording your basal body temperature using an online charting service, such as Fertility Friend (see Resources). The first full-flow day of your period is cycle day one (CD1). For women who spot a few days prior to getting their full period, determining the first day can be a little trickier. What you're looking for is the first day of normal flow.

You can purchase a special BBT thermometer at any drugstore. Set your alarm for the same time every day—including weekends. Pop the thermometer in your mouth before you get up and record the temperature. There are many fine details, such as needing three hours of uninterrupted sleep, and different hours of the morning have different normal ranges, but those types of details can be obtained by reading any of the books or websites provided in the Resources section.

You are looking for a shift in temperatures. Prior to ovulation, your temperatures will be lower. After ovulation occurs, you'll see your temperature rise at least 0.3 degrees and remain consistently in the higher range. If you don't see this pattern, it can indicate a lack of ovulation. Your temperature will remain in this higher range indefinitely if you're pregnant, or will drop to signal the approach of your period.

Ovulation-Predictor Kits and Fertility Monitoring Machines

Another tool you can use to gather information to bring to this first appointment (or to help out with timed intercourse) is an ovulation-predictor kit, or OPK. These tests monitor the luteinizing hormone (LH) in your urine, which shows up immediately before ovulation.

The downside to OPKs is that they apparently do not work for everyone, and they can become expensive very quickly. Even if you require only one box a month and use it carefully, you are still spending close to $20 per cycle, simply to predict ovulation (something you can do for free after investing in a BBT thermometer). In addition, fertility monitoring machines are small handheld computers used to predict your peak fertility days through daily urine tests. While some people swear by them, if you are truly subfertile, a fertility monitor will be redundant in the scheme of all tests being run by the RE.

Decision List Template

JUMP INTO THIS process by filling out the decision list below based on the factors in Chapter 3. Rank each choice using each number once, with 1 being the most important to you and 8 being the least important. If two or more factors are of equal importance, they can each receive the same number.

	NAME	PARTNER
COST		
CERTAINTY OF REACHING PARENTHOOD		
SURENESS OF RESOLVING IF		
POSSIBILITY OF A GENETIC LINK		
POSSIBILITY OF A BIOLOGICAL LINK		
AMOUNT OF CONTROL OVER PRENATAL HEALTH		
SPEED OF RESOLVING IF		
IMPORTANCE OF MATERNAL AGE		
OTHER		

DAY 3 Worksheet

FSH _____ mlU/ml

 (6–9: good; 9–10 fair: 10–13: diminished ovarian reserves;
 13+: hard to stim)

E2 _____ pg/ml

 25–75 pg/ml (lower is better)

LH _____ mlU/ml

 Under 7 (The number should be similar to FSH. A higher
 number than the FSH number can be a sign of PCOS.)

PROLACTIN _____ ng/ml

 Under 24 ng/ml

P4 _____ ng/ml

 Under 1.0 ng/ml

TSH _____ pg/ml

 .4–4 pg/ml (Midrange normal in most labs is about 1.7. A high
 level of TSH combined with a low or normal T4 level generally indicates hypothyroidism.)

T4 _____ ng/dl

 .8–2 ng/dl (A low level may indicate a diseased thyroid gland
 or a nonfunctioning pituitary gland that is not stimulating the
 thyroid to produce T4. If the T4 is low and the TSH is normal,
 that is more likely to indicate a problem with the pituitary.)

Treatment Spreadsheet Template

	Clinic Communication		Medications			Procedures/Tests			
	Results	Other Calls	Oral/Nasal (name/dosage/time)	Injection (name/dosage/time)	Vaginal (name/dosage/time)	Blood Draw or Sonogram (time and tests)	Retrieval	Transfer or IUI	Other
CD 1									
CD 2									
CD 3									
CD 4									
CD 5									
CD 6									
CD 7									
CD 8									
CD 9									
CD 10									
CD 11									
CD 12									
CD 13									
CD 14									
CD 15									
CD 16									
CD 17									
CD 18									
CD 19									
CD 20									
CD 21									
CD 22									
CD 23									
CD 24									
CD 25									
CD 26									
CD 27									
CD 28									
CD 29									
CD 30									

Grandma Sally's
Banana Cake Recipe

1¼ CUPS SUGAR

½ CUP BUTTER, SOFTENED

2 EGGS

4 TBSP. SOUR CREAM

I TSP. VANILLA

2 OR 3 MASHED BANANAS (USE THE OVERRIPE, BROWN/SPOTTY ONES)

1½ CUPS FLOUR

I TSP. BAKING SODA

PINCH OF SALT

CHOCOLATE FROSTING

PREHEAT OVEN TO 350°F.

Cream together the butter and sugar. Add the eggs one at a time, and beat for a minute. Incorporate the sour cream, mashed-up bananas, and vanilla. In a separate bowl, sift together the flour, baking soda, and salt. Mix the wet and dry ingredients together just until combined. Pour into a 9-inch greased, square cake pan and bake for 30 minutes. Once cool, ice with chocolate frosting.

From Me to You

SOMETIMES YOU'RE GOING to choose to attend that baby shower/bris/ baby naming/baptism/christening because you realize that not going will be more trouble than going. Hopefully, you'll bring someone along who knows what you're going through—either a partner or a friend—and you'll stand in the back, perhaps drink from a flask, and try to think happy thoughts.

Women have always utilized emotional safety in numbers (ever notice how we all go to the bathroom in a group?), but men may not realize how nice it is to be with someone who simply gets it.

Of course, you may not have the option sometimes—you may need to go to an event alone. In those cases, bring a figurative friend in your pocket. If you can have a friend write a note to take along, making it specific to you and your friendship, all the better. If you feel shy about asking someone to write you a love note, or if you're a guy and there is no way in hell you are asking Jim in accounting if he'll figuratively come with you to Cousin Amy's baby shower, xerox the one below and fold it up, taking me with you to the party. I am happy to be your pocket best friend.

> *Hey, sweetie, I know it was really hard to come here today, but you're doing great. All you need to do is get through these next few hours, and then you can go home and do something nice for yourself. All that matters is that you make it to the other end of the party still intact. So what if you need to pause and have a cry in the bathroom, or step outside for a few minutes, or even sneak into the liquor cabinet for a drink? If it helps you to get to the other side, it was a success. I hope that one day the party is for your future child, and when it is, I want you to take out this note and take me along there, too, so I can celebrate with you in spirit.*

Books

Adoption

Adopting on Your Own by Lee Varon

Adopting: Sound Choices, Strong Families by Patricia Irwin Johnston

The Ultimate Insider's Guide to Adoption by Elizabeth Swire Falker

Children's Books for Discussing Family-Building

A Mother for Choco by Keiko Kasza (adoption)

And Tango Makes Three by Peter Parnell and Justin Richardson
   (GLBT)

A Tiny Itsy Bitsy Gift of Life by Carmen Martinez Jover (donor egg)

Daddy, Was Mommy's Tummy Big? by Carolina Nadel
   (donor insemination)

Something Happened by Cathy Blanford
   (pregnancy loss, stillbirth, and neonatal death)

Infertility

THE EMOTIONAL POINT:

This one, of course!

THE FINANCIAL POINT:

Budgeting for Infertility by Angie Best-Boss and Evelina Weidman
   Sterling (a new book out there for financing fertility treatments
   and adoption)

THE PHYSICAL POINT:

Resolving Infertility by Diane Aronson (still one of the best books
   around about the physical aspects of infertility)

Living Child-Free
Sweet Grapes by Jean W. Carter and Michael Carter

Loss
Trying Again by Ann Douglas (specifically for trying to conceive
after loss)
Empty Cradle, Broken Heart by Deborah L. Davis

Miscellaneous
Taking Charge of Your Fertility by Toni Weschler

Third-Party Reproduction
Mommies, Daddies, Donors, Surrogates by Diane Ehrensaft
Helping the Stork by Carol Frost Vercollone, Heidi Moss, and Robert Moss

Organizations and Online Support
Adoption
ADOPTIVE FAMILIES MAGAZINE (online site for paper magazine)
http://adoptivefamilies.com

ADOPTION THREADS (a cross-triad bulletin board)
http://adoptionthreads.com

AMERICAN ACADEMY OF ADOPTION ATTORNEYS
www.adoptionattorneys.org

CHILD WELFARE INFORMATION GATEWAY
(a resource based out of the U.S. Department of Health and
Human Services)
www.childwelfare.gov

ETHICA
(an organization dedicated to ethical adoption, with excellent resources)
www.ethicanet.org

FOREVER PARENTS (an adoptive parents bulletin board)
http://forums.foreverparents.com

GLAD
(similar to Lambda Legal in terms of being an excellent legal
resource on same-sex adoption)
www.glad.org

LAMBDA LEGAL
(excellent legal resource on GLBT adoption, in addition to other
GLBT issues)
www.lambdalegal.org

NATIONAL COUNCIL FOR ADOPTION—NCFA
(information about everything concerning adoption)
www.adoptioncouncil.org

NATIONAL COUNCIL FOR SINGLE ADOPTIVE PARENTS
P.O. Box 15084
Chevy Chase, MD 20825

OPEN ADOPTION SUPPORT
(literature and forums on openness in adoption)
www.openadoptionsupport.com

QUEER RESOURCES DIRECTORY
(a general resource that also contains sites for GLBT adoption)
www.qrd.org/qrd

TRANSRACIAL ADOPTION RESOURCES
(a clearinghouse of transracial adoption sites on the Internet)
www.nysccc.org/T-Rarts/T-Rarts.html

Infertility
AMERICAN FERTILITY ASSOCIATION (information and support)
www.theafa.org

AMERICAN SOCIETY FOR REPRODUCTIVE MEDICINE—ASRM
(information and fact sheets)
www.asrm.org

CENTERS FOR DISEASE CONTROL AND PREVENTION
(clinic success rates)
www.cdc.gov/ART

CYCLESISTA (monthly cycle buddies)
www.cyclesista.com

FERTILE HOPE (infertility after cancer organization)
www.fertilehope.org

FERTILITY FRIEND (online charting service and bulletin boards)
www.fertilityfriend.com

IVF CONNECTIONS (bulletin boards for all areas of infertility)
www.ivfconnections.com

IVF SHOOT 'EM UP (online videos of injection, made by other Iffers)
http://ivfshootemup.blogspot.com

RESOLVE (the national infertility association, an invaluable resource
for Iffers seeking information and support)
www.resolve.org

SOCIETY FOR ASSISTED REPRODUCTIVE TECHNOLOGY—SART
(clinic success rates)
www.sart.org

THE INTERNATIONAL COUNCIL ON INFERTILITY INFORMATION
DISSEMINATION, INC.—INCIID (information and support)
www.inciid.org

Living Child-Free
CHILDLESS NOT BY CHOICE (bulletin boards)
www.childlessnotbychoice.com

FERTILE THOUGHTS
(bulletin boards on many topics, including living child free)
www3.fertilethoughts.com

Loss

GLOW IN THE WOODS (an online community for baby loss)
www.glowinthewoods.com

M.I.S.S. FOUNDATION (support for grieving parents)
www.misschildren.org

OUR HOPE PLACE (support after miscarriage)
www.ourhopeplace.com

MARCH OF DIMES
(information about loss, in addition to pregnancy and prematurity)
www.marchofdimes.com

SHARE (pregnancy and infant loss support)
www.nationalshareoffice.com

Miscellaneous

DOMAR CENTER (mind-body connection and emotional support)
www.domarcenter.com

NATIONAL ORGANIZATION OF MOTHERS OF TWINS CLUBS
(the umbrella organization for all local multiples groups)
www.nomotc.org

ONLINE PPD SUPPORT (postpartum depression support for women)
www.ppdsupportpage.com

POSTPARTUM MEN (postpartum depression support for men)
www.postpartummen.com

SIDELINES
(support while on bed rest and during complicated pregnancies)
www.sidelines.org

Third-Party Reproduction

ALL ABOUT SURROGACY (information and online support)
www.allaboutsurrogacy.com

CHOICE MOTHERS (single mothers by choice discussion group)
http://groups.yahoo.com/group/choicemoms

DONOR OFFSPRING HEALTH
www.donoroffspringhealth.com

DONOR SIBLING REGISTRY
www.donorsiblingregistry.com

THE AMERICAN SURROGACY CENTER
(information and online support)
www.surrogacy.com

Blogs

Rather than list examples of a few blogs on the Internet, I give you
my blogroll, which is organized into multiple categories and carefully
maintained and updated daily. Seek out stories similar to your own,
and add your own blog once you start writing.

BLOGGER (free blogging site)
www.blogger.com

STIRRUP QUEEN'S COMPLETELY ANAL LIST OF BLOGS THAT PROVES
THAT SHE REALLY MISSED HER CALLING AS A PERSONAL ORGANIZER
http://stirrup-queens.blogspot.com/2006/06/whole-lot-of-blogging-
brought-to-you.html

WORDPRESS (free blogging site)
http://wordpress.com

Notes

Chapter 1

1. Fertility LifeLines, "State-Mandated Benefits," www.fertilitylifelines .com/paying/insurance/statemandate.jsp (accessed September 2, 2008). "Mandate-to-offer" essentially means that the insurer must offer infertility coverage, but the employer doesn't need to purchase it.

2. Resolve: The National Infertility Association, "Frequently Asked Questions About Infertility," www.resolve.org/site/PageServer?pagename=lrn_wii_faq (accessed August 25, 2008).

3. Ibid.

4. Elizabeth Weil, "Breeder Reaction," *Mother Jones,* July/August 2006, in reference to A. D. Gurmankin, A. L. Caplan, and A. M. Braverman, "Screening practices and beliefs of assisted reproductive technology programs," *Fertility and Sterility* 83, no. 1 (2005): 61–67.

5. M. A. M. Hassan and S. R. Killick, "Effect of male age on fertility: Evidence for the decline in male fertility with increasing age," *Fertility and Sterility* 79, supplement no. 3 (June 2003): S1520–27.

6. Mayo Clinic, *The Mayo Clinic Complete Book of Pregnancy & Baby's First Year* (New York: William Morrow, 1994).

Chapter 2

1. Barbara Collura, "The Costs of Infertility Treatment," Resolve: The National Infertility Association, www.resolve.org/site/PageServer?pagename=lrn_ mta_cost (accessed August 25, 2008).

2. Barbara Collura, "Financing Adoption," Resolve: The National Infertility Association, www.resolve.org/site/PageServer?pagename=lrn_mta_finadopt (accessed August 25, 2008).

3. My husband, Josh, had a great time coming up with some catchphrases of his

own. Here they are, in no specific order: "Mazel tov and good yontiff!" "Well, *that* doesn't suck like a transrectal ultrasound." "We're going to need a bigger boat." "Winner, winner, chicken dinner!" "Goooaaaaallllllll!!!!!!" "I got ninety-nine problems, but your kid ain't one." "It's amazing what they can do with robots these days."

Chapter 5

1. F. M. Hanson and J. Rock, "The Effect of Adoption on Fertility and Other Reproductive Functions," *American Journal of Obstetrics and Gynecology* 59, no. 2 (1950): 311, 314, 316, 317, 319.

Chapter 6

1. American Society for Reproductive Medicine, Patient's Fact Sheet: Diagnostic Testing for Male Factor Infertility, August 2001, www.fertilitytoday.org/factsheets/Testing_Male-Fact.pdf (accessed August 25, 2008).

2. "Boxers or Briefs: Male Infertility," WebMD Live Events transcript of interview with Larry Lipshultz at the Trying to Conceive Cyber Conference on September 25, 2002, www.medicinenet.com/script/main/art.asp?articlekey=54449 (accessed September 1, 2008).

3. All information regarding hormone levels is coming from two sources, which were checked against each other: Diane Aronson, *Resolving Infertility* (New York: Collins Living, 2001) and Rebecca Smith Waddell, "Hormone Levels and Fertility Bloodwork," FertilityPlus, www.fertilityplus.org/faq/hormonelevels.html (last updated September 10, 2001; accessed on September 1, 2008).

4. Ibid.

5. The InterNational Council on Infertility Information Dissemination, Inc., "Polycystic Ovary Syndrome (PCOS) FAQ," www.inciid.org/faq .php?cat=infertility101&id=2 (last updated October 9, 2006; accessed August 29, 2008).

6. Ibid.

7. Roger W. Harms, Mayo Clinic, *Guide to a Healthy Pregnancy* (New York: HarperCollins, 2004).

Chapter 7

1. Evalyn Lee, "Miscarriage Facts," Discovery Health, http://health .discovery.com/centers/pregnancy/americanbaby/miscarriage.html (accessed August 20, 2008).

2. March of Dimes, "Professionals & Researchers Quick Reference and Fact Sheets: Miscarriage," www.marchofdimes.com/printableArticles/14332_1192. asp (accessed September 1, 2008).

3. National Institute of Child Heath and Human Development, "Facts About Down Syndome: The Occurrence of Down Syndrome," www

.nichd.nih.gov/publications/pubs/downsyndrome.cfm#TheOccurrence (last updated August 15, 2008; accessed August 20, 2008); data from E. B. Hook and A. Lindsjö, "Down syndrome in live births by single year maternal age interval in a Swedish study: Comparison with results from a New York State study," *American Journal of Human Genetics* 30 (1978): 19–27.

4. March of Dimes, "Professionals & Researchers Quick Reference and Fact Sheets: Ectopic and Molar Pregnancy," www.marchofdimes.com/professionals/14332_1189.asp (accessed August 20, 2008).

5. Ibid.

6. Ibid.

Chapter 8

1. Jennifer Lucero and others, "Early follicular phase hormone levels in relation to patterns of alcohol, tobacco, and coffee use," *Fertility and Sterility* 76, no. 4 (2001): 723–29.

Chapter 9

1. Human Rights Campaign, "Adoption Laws: State by State," www.hrc.org/issues/parenting/adoptions/2375.htm (accessed September 1, 2008).

Chapter 12

1. National Center for Health Statistics, "U.S. Pregnancy Rate Lowest in Two Decades: New Report Documents Trends in Births, Abortions, and Miscarriages," U.S. Department of Health and Human Services, Centers for Disease Control and Prevention, www.cdc.gov/nchs/pressroom/00facts/trends.htm (released February 11, 2000; accessed September 1, 2008).

2. J. R. W. Fisher, K. Hammarberg, and H. W. Gordon Baker, "Assisted conception is a risk factor for postnatal mood disturbance and early parenting difficulties," *Fertility and Sterility* 84, no. 2 (2005) 426–30.

3. Glenn Collins, "Relationships: Fathers Get Postpartum Blues, Too," *New York Times,* April 6, 1981, http://query.nytimes.com/gst/fullpage.html?sec=health&res=9402E2DE1139F935A35757C0A967948260 (accessed September 1, 2008).

4. J. F. Paulson, S. Dauber, and J. Lieferman, "Individual and Combined Effects of Postpartum Depression in Mothers and Fathers on Parenting Behavior," *Pediatrics* 118, no. 2 (2006): http://pediatrics.aappublications.org/cgi/content/abstract/118/2/659 (accessed September 1, 2008).

Index

Doppler machines: 271

Down syndrome: 143–144, 145

E

early miscarriage: 286

ectopic pregnancy: 132, 151–153, 286

education: from doctors 7–8; of friends/family 100; from personal experience 7; requiring 64; self 104–105

egg white cervical mucus (EWCM): 286

Ehrensaft, Diane: 232–233

email: 100–103

embryos: adopting 235; defined 142, 286; donor 232, 247–248, 286; freezing 207; transferring 205–206

emotions: 29–37; in adoption process 211, 219, 228; and child-free choice 257, 260; delivery day 280; explaining 8; handling public 76; hope: 42–44; of mourning 91, 144, 148, 162; postpartum depression 277–281; upon diagnosis 140

empathy: encouraging 22; unsolicited 96

endometrial biopsy: 133, 286

endometriosis: 132, 138, 286

endometrium: 133

erectile dysfunction: 119

estrogen: in blood work 122, 123; coffee and 179; defined 287; treatments 175

ethics, adoption: 225–226

ethnicity, adoption and: 221

exercise: 24

expectant parents: 212

F

face-to-face discussions: 78

faith, leaps of: 44

family issues: adoption and 213; discussing family building 67–75; for donor/surrogacy pregnancies 240; emotional decision-making 32–34, 39; for families of two 256; pressure 41; selective announcements 77–78

fears, resolving pregnancy: 263–266

female-factor infertility: defined 287; diagnoses 134–140; vs. male 16–19

Femara: 169–171

fertility: compatibility 119; monitoring machines 120; natural decline of 140; treatments. *See* treatments, fertility

Fertility and Sterility: 19, 179, 277

fertilization reports: 287

fetal abnormalities: 153

fetus, defined: 142, 287

fibroids: 127, 132, 138, 145, 287

financial issues. *See* costs

statistics 269; therapeutic
abortion 160

preimplantation genetic
diagnosis (PGD): 202, 290

premature ovarian failure
(POF): 137, 176, 290

prenatal health: 48–49

prenatal testing: 266–273

pressure: of choice 46; dealing
with 39–41; and discussing
infertility 75; by doctors 65; on
pregnancy 281

preterm premature rupture of
membranes (PPROM): 154,
290

primary infertility: 11, 13–14,
290

privacy: 68–69, 71, 77, 239

progesterone: in CD3 blood
work 123; day-21 124; defined
290; follicular production of
137; in IVF cycle 206; in oil
(PIO) 184; treatments 173–175

prolactin: 116, 122, 290

Prometrium rage: 175

Q

quad screen test: 268

R

racial issues: 221

rationing, emotional: 34

recipe, banana cake: 304

regrets: 63

relationships: child-free living

within 256; emotional issues
31; infertility as shared in 94;
mourning loss in 150, 161;
mutual comfort with ART 164;
negating 99; team injections
197; third-party reproduction
in 248; voicing choices in 46

reproductive endocrinologists
(REs): 106, 290

reproductive outsourcing: 54,
238

Resolve: 16, 37, 66

respect: 22, 65

responsibility: 64–65, 75

retrieval: 290

retrograde ejaculation: 116, 291

Rh blood type: 146

Robitussin: 200

S

saline sonohysterogram (SSH):
127, 291

same-sex adoption: 217

sart.org: 28

scarring, in female reproductive
organs: 138–139

secondary infertility: defined
291; insensitive advice for
86–87; vs. primary 11, 13–14;
variables in 17

second-parent adoption: 217

selective reduction: 160

semen analysis: 108–110, 291

semen samples: 108, 110, 111,
198

Acknowledgments

If getting the call from your agent saying that your book is going to be published is the engagement, the "thank you" page is the speech you give at your wedding, when you are overwhelmed by the realization of how many people brought you toward this day.

Writing this book was all about love. And I'm a weepy, emotional, gushy sort by nature.

To start at the end, thank you to the almost 1,500 men and women who contributed their thoughts to create this book. It truly is a literary stone soup, with one person throwing in some information on choosing a sperm donor and another tossing in her feelings about her home study. These people are my bones—they are my support and structure. I could not have written this book without them, and I certainly could not get through the day without them. There are too many to name individually, which breaks my heart, but you can find their names in the comments on my blog. I do need to thank the lovely ladies of the Order of the Plastic Uterus; Lori and Bleu, who both read drafts of chapters; and Lindsay, who provided the water ice and tissues.

Thank you to my editor, Wendy Taylor, who patiently trimmed tens of thousands of words off the manuscript, cheered me on as I crawled toward the finish line, and brought me back to a place of Zen when I was unable to see the big picture.

Thank you to Brooke and Krista and all of the wonderful women at Seal Press. If you weren't holding me to a word count, I would tell everyone the amazing, looping story of crossed emails and fate. I could not have asked for a greater book experience; the women at Seal are fun, daring, creative, and fiercely intelligent. Thank you for taking a chance with me.

Thank you to my agent, Katherine Fausset, who is the agent I always hoped to have—kind, nurturing, and patient beyond belief, despite all of my anxieties. I cannot wait until when we are old and gray and eating steak dinners (because in this daydream, I've apparently given up being a lifelong vegetarian) in fancy New York restaurants and laughing about the first books we published together and how we are now the toast of the literary world. A girl can dream big. In thanking her, I also need to mention Corinne, Jonathan, and Kirsten, the three stones in the river.

Mentioning the stones in the river brings me to thanking Jay Neugeboren, who is my mentor, teacher, idol, and friend. Thank you for answering patiently all of my "what do I do?" emails, as well as providing the spark that lit the match. And from my younger years, thank you to Ron Kuka for setting me on this trajectory.

Thank you to my cousin Lisa, for the harbor on that night. You kept me in Massachusetts. Thank you to Julie, my lady-when-waiting, for the Bueno y Sano when we lived in Massachusetts and the vomit cups during the pregnancy. Thank you to my sister, Wendy, who not only let me borrow her yellow socks (both literally and figuratively), but also talked me through the pre-epidural and then jumped on a plane to see the twins in the morning. I think that sentence lets you know just how amazing my sister is, if you're not lucky enough to have met her.

Thank you to my brother, Randall, who not only sat in the NICU waiting room every single day and ensured our glider was static-free, but has always been the person who steadied me writing-wise when I felt like I was going to fall, nudged me from behind when I needed someone to goad me on, and pointed the way to the finish line when I lost my place. I could not have run this race without him.

Thank you to my mommy and daddy for being such fantastic parents that they made me want to put myself through all of those needles so I could experience parenthood too. This book would not have been possible without them and their toddler-entertainment skills. Thank you for being the most amazing grandparents so your daughter can play writer.

I saved my most enormous thank-yous for last, and at this point, my heart is spilling over. I do not know what I did to get so lucky to bring my husband, Josh, into my life. He is the breath that brought this book to life; he is the giver of the two positions; he is the joy captured in the skip down the aisle. And he is the receptacle of my enormous love. Thank you—for creating the space to do this and for always being awake at 11:00 PM to listen to my feelings. I love you.

To the ChickieNob and Wolvog, you were worth the wait (though I really wish you could have come two and a half years earlier). Every single night when you are asleep, we go in and whisper how wonderful you are into your warm ears. We hope you always hold on to how we see you. We hope you know how much we love you, and if you ever have any doubts, turn to this page. You are why I wrote this book.

© JOSHUA FORD

Melissa Ford received her BA from the University of Wisconsin and her MFA from the University of Massachusetts. She is the author of the infertility website Stirrup Queens (http://stirrup-queens.com) and a contributing editor at BlogHer. She lives with her twins— a boy and a girl born after fertility treatments—and her husband, writer Joshua Ford.

Selected Titles from Seal Press

For more than thirty years, Seal Press has published groundbreaking books. By women. For women. Visit our website at www.sealpress. com. Check out the Seal Press blog at www.sealpress.com/blog.

DELIVER THIS! MAKE THE CHILDBIRTH CHOICE THAT'S RIGHT FOR YOU...NO MATTER WHAT EVERYONE ELSE THINKS, by Marisa Cohen. $14.95, 1-58005-153-7. A smart, informative book that helps expectant mothers explore traditional and alternative birthing choices.

MEN AND FEMINISM: SEAL STUDIES, by Shira Tarrant, PhD. $14.95, 1-58005-258-0. Answering questions about how and why men should get behind feminism, Men and Feminism lays the foundation for a discussion about feminism as a human issue, not simply a women's issue.

THE MATERNAL IS POLITICAL: WOMEN WRITERS AT THE INTER-SECTION OF MOTHERHOOD AND SOCIAL CHANGE, edited by Shari MacDonald Strong. $15.95, 1-58005-243-6. Exploring the vital connection between motherhood and social change, The Maternal Is Political features thirty powerful literary essays by women striving to make the world a better place for children and families—both their own and other women's.

WITHOUT A NET: THE FEMALE EXPERIENCE OF GROWING UP WORKING CLASS, edited by Michelle Tea. $14.95, 1-58005-103-0. A collection of essays "so raw, so fresh, and so riveting, that I read them compulsively, with one hand alternately covering my mouth, my heart, and my stomach, while the other hand turned the page. Without a Net is an important book for any woman who's grown up—or is growing up—in America." —Vendela Vida, And Now You Can Go

CHOOSING YOU: DECIDING TO HAVE A BABY ON MY OWN, by Alexandra Soiseth. $15.95, 1-58005-222-3. The deeply honest memoir of one woman's decision to brave pregnancy and motherhood alone.

A MATTER OF CHOICE: 25 PEOPLE WHO TRANSFORMED THEIR LIVES, edited by Joan Chatfield-Taylor. $14.95, 1-58005-118-9. An inspiring collection of essays by people who made profound changes in their work, personal life, location, or lifestyle, proving that it is indeed never too late to take the road less traveled.